COPING WITH THE
BIOMEDICAL
LITERATURE

COPING WITH THE BIOMEDICAL LITERATURE

A Primer for the Scientist and the Clinician

Edited by

Kenneth S. Warren

PRAEGER

PRAEGER SPECIAL STUDIES • PRAEGER SCIENTIFIC

197938

Library of Congress Cataloging in Publication Data

Main entry under title:

Coping with the biomedical literature.

"Praeger special studies. Praeger scientific."
Bibliography: p.
Includes index.
Contents: The structure of the information systems:
The development and structure of the biomedical
literature/Derek de Solla Price. Selective aspects
of the biomedical literature/Kenneth S. Warren. The
ecology of the biomedical literature and information
retrieval — [etc.]
1. Medical literature. I. Warren, Kenneth S.
[DNLM: 1. Information retrieval systems.
2. Libraries, Medical. 3. Information services.
Z 699.5.M39 C782]
R118.6.C65   025'.0661   81-5149
ISBN 0-03-057036-0   AACR2
ISBN 0-03-057034-4 (pbk.)

Published in 1981 by Praeger Publishers
CBS Educational and Professional Publishing
A Division of CBS, Inc.
521 Fifth Avenue, New York, New York 10175 U.S.A.

©1981 by Praeger Publishers
Figure 4.1, pp. 60-61, copyright ©1980 by William K. Zinsser.
Reprinted by permission of William Zinsser.

3456789 052 98765432

Printed in the United States of America

LIST OF CONTRIBUTORS

William K. Beatty
Professor of Medical Bibliography
Northwestern University Medical School
Chicago, Illinois

Eli Chernin
Department of Tropical Public Health
Harvard School of Public Health
Boston, Massachusetts

Martin M. Cummings
Director, National Library of Medicine
Department of Health and Human Services
Bethesda, Maryland

Eugene Garfield
President, Institute for Scientific Information
University City Science Center
Philadelphia, Pennsylvania

William Goffman
School of Library Science
Case Western Reserve University
Cleveland, Ohio

Edward H. Kass
William Ellery Channing Professor of Medicine, and
Director, Channing Laboratory
Harvard Medical School and Brigham and Women's Hospital
Peter Bent Brigham Hospital
Boston, Massachusetts

Frederick Mosteller
Chairman, Department of Biostatistics
Harvard School of Public Health
Boston, Massachusetts

Derek de Solla Price
History of Science
Yale University
New Haven, Connecticut

Oscar D. Ratnoff
Department of Medicine
Case Western Reserve University
Lakeside Hospital
Cleveland, Ohio

Arnold S. Relman
Editor, *The New England
Journal of Medicine*
Boston, Massachusetts

David L. Sackett
Department of Clinical Epidemiology and Biostatistics
Faculty of Medicine
McMaster University
Hamilton, Ontario
Canada

Kenneth S. Warren
Director for Health Sciences
The Rockefeller Foundation
New York, New York

CONTENTS

INTRODUCTION

Kenneth S. Warren

A primer is usually thought of as an elementary book for teaching children to read. However, it can be any book of elementary principles. We believe that such a book is now necessary for young scientists and clinicians and might even be useful for seasoned individuals who never had an opportunity to explore these principles. In the past, approaches to the literature were taught on an apprenticeship basis, and the student simply went to a library to obtain books and journals from a librarian. With inundation threatening from the exponential growth of the literature and modern technology (that is, computers), information scientists have been thrown into the breach. The complexity of the information systems has increased, therefore, to a point at which a statement of elementary principles governing their efficient use has become necessary. The problem is that the younger people find the literatures so overwhelming that many of them read either exceedingly narrowly or not at all. Seasoned investigators and clinicians rely increasingly on the so-called invisible college—that is, they call a friend or colleague for information. This is an efficient means of information gathering but only for those who know whom to contact and are reasonably sure that their call will be answered.

This book has been written because we are sanguine that the biomedical and clinical literatures can be utilized in an efficient manner. Using new concepts in information science, the development of selective approaches can greatly delimit the amount of information that must be scanned. In addition, it is hoped that this book might serve as the basis for establishing courses at both the graduate and postgraduate levels in using biomedical information.

The editor set out to assemble an outstanding group of experts and is pleased that all those asked have contributed. An unusual aspect of this multiauthor work has been the extent of cooperation among the contributors. Two one-day meetings were held to plan the format and to review the outlines and first drafts. At a final three-day meeting the chapters were integrated into a coherent whole. Nevertheless, the individuality of the members of this outstanding group of authors remained irrepressible. Thus, the reader will enjoy the best of two worlds: a matrix involving both coherence and diversity.

The four sections of the book are concerned with the structure, production, utilization, and sources of biomedical information. In the section on structure, Derek de Solla Price, Professor of the History of Science at Yale University, describes the basic structure and exponential growth of the literature. Kenneth S. Warren, who was both Professor of Medicine and of

Library Science at Case Western Reserve University, shows how the literature clusters both quantitatively and qualitatively and explains how these clusters can be identified and exploited. William Goffman, who was the Dean of the School of Library Sciences at Case Western Reserve University, describes an ecological model of the literatures, showing how the inter-relationships and the feedback among the different phases of the system can be used to maximize information retrieval. This section provides a basic understanding of the information system that will enable producers and users to work more efficiently.

The section on production opens with a delightful series of essays by Eli Chernin, Professor of Tropical Public Health at the Harvard School of Public Health, journal editor, and a teacher of a renowned course in writing for both graduate and medical students. Arnold Relman, Professor of Medicine at Harvard Medical School and Editor of the *New England Journal of Medicine*, provides an overview of journals and how they function. He is one of the new breed of editors who are doing active research on the system. Edward H. Kass, Professor of Medicine at Harvard Medical School and Editor of *Reviews of Infectious Diseases*, discusses reviews and books, those crucial tools for encompassing masses of information in all of their multifarious guises.

The section on utilization begins with a chapter by Oscar Ratnoff, Professor of Medicine at Case Western Reserve University, noted teacher, author, and medical raconteur. His amusing essay on his personal system of information gathering provides the ideal setting for the next two chapters on evaluation. Frederick Mosteller, Professor of Statistics at Harvard and President of the American Association for the Advancement of Science, discusses requirements for scientific proof in an elegant essay on statistics. David L. Sackett, Professor of Epidemiology at McMaster University, and his colleagues provide an exciting excursion into requirements for clinical application.

The section on the sources of biomedical information begins with a description of that great and indispensible institution the National Library of Medicine, by its director, Martin M. Cummings. Eugene Garfield, President of the innovative Institute for Scientific Information, provides a comprehensive description of its services. Finally, William K. Beatty, Professor of Medical Bibliography at Northwestern University, closes with a superb guide to the use of libraries.

Considering the diversity of the authors, it is interesting indeed that the basic tenet for coping with the information system suggested by each of them is the principle of selectivity. In the first three chapters, knowledge of the *structure* of the literature reveals how to approach that relatively small proportion of relevant and useful information. The *production* section begins with the dictum "First, do no harm." This is followed by a description of the journal system, including the importance of peer review in the development of periodicals of quality. Then, the crucial function of review articles in selecting and condensing information is described. The section on *utilization* pragmatically reveals the concept of selectivity as each chapter stresses the principle of identifying and avoiding information of poor quality. The chapters dealing with *sources of information* again emphasize the selectivity inherent in information services. Even the greatest medical information system of them all, the National Library of Medicine, is forced to be selective, as is the Institute for Scientific Information. Finally, selectivity is essential for the optimal use of medical libraries. It is our belief, therefore, that understanding the system and using it judiciously will enable scientists and clinicians not only to cope with biomedical information but to gain more from it and enjoy it as well.

The authors would like to acknowledge the immense help of John T. Bruer, philosopher and Visiting Research Fellow in the Division of Health Sciences at the Rockefeller Foundation. He not only helped in every phase of this complex operation but brought his philosophical expertise to bear on information science and contributed greatly to the ideas brought forth in this project.

PART I
THE STRUCTURE OF THE INFORMATION SYSTEM

1

THE DEVELOPMENT AND STRUCTURE OF THE BIOMEDICAL LITERATURE

Derek de Solla Price

All aspects of human culture depend on our technologies of communication. The evolution of speech, about which we know very little, must have been a major traumatic development of the human animal, and the introduction of the technique of writing, some 5,000 years ago, changed prehistory into history. Almost as soon as people learned to write, manuscript "publication" emerged and slowly and steadily grew. About 500 years ago, scholars had become so numerous that the system became overloaded. Thus, the invention of printing came as a great relief. For a while, communication worked rather well, and then, a century after the coming of printed classics, scholars began complaining that it was necessary for them to read books by people who were still alive. By the 1660s, they again got relief, this time through the new technology of newspapers and the invention of the learned journal, which could publish little units of knowledge without waiting a lifetime for a book.[1,2]

The technique of the scientific paper, though simple and probably accidental in its origin, was revolutionary in its effects. The paper became not just a means of communicating a discovery, but, in quite a strong sense, it was the discovery itself. This resulted from the strange quality that in all scientific endeavor, as distinct from other creative undertakings of humanity, that which we create is entirely exterior to ourselves and our personalities. We act as if the truth is "out there" and is discovered rather that created. We each have our own style, but a scientific truth can only be discovered the one time, and the style, though it may be personally important, is not tied to the discovery in any essential manner.

If Boyle and Marriotte both discover the gas laws (as they did), the credit must go to one or the other. One cannot imagine a Beethoven and Mozart in such a contest, or any pair of painters or novelists, except in cases of ill-intentioned plagiarism. It is not such an easy matter, however, for such contests might well occur with two violinists or orchestras performing the same work, or with two actors playing the same part.

At all events, in order to secure title to the impersonal property of creative scientific discovery, we publish. Quite incidentally, it is to preserve the impersonality that there developed a nineteenth-century fetish of avoiding personal pronouns and using the passive voice of verbs. There really is no salvation in the use of "a tripod was taken" style of language! In a sense, then, we do not know if we have discovered something without such publication, because only through this process does the rest of the world community of our peers have a chance to validate the discovery by acceptance or rejection. Moreover, if it is accepted, they evaluate the discovery by using and incorporating it in all subsequent work. The process is by no means trivial. All research workers have had the experiences of major discoveries that turn out to be technical errors or well-known facts to everybody else in the field and minor discoveries, mentioned only in passing, that unexpectedly have a huge impact on one's peers. It is for such reasons that there is no discovery before validation through acceptance for publication and no evaluation without the embodiment of the discovery in subsequent use by the scientific community. [3-5]

It must be remarked at this point that the true research literature just described (ordinary papers and also rapid publication "letters") is only one part, however important, of the totality of all journal publication and of the biomedical literature. First, it must be noted that all this journal research-front literature packs down after several years of delay into a book literature of texts, reference works, monographic treatments, and encyclopedias that one should (indeed, must) learn to handle in one's student days. If this were not done, the bulk of learning, which increases so rapidly, would long ago have prevented anyone from reaching the current research front. The admirable device for packing down accrued knowledge into a current expertise is called "education," and that it can be at all achieved is something of a miracle.

A special and vital problem of biomedical literature is the existence of a large class of journal publications known as the "clinical research" literature. Some of it, of course, behaves like all scientific research literature in that its purpose is the advancement of a body of knowledge that cumulates. In other words, such papers are to be used as part of the raw material for subsequent papers. This sort of clinical literature can be evaluated by its being cited in subsequent papers, and it can be found and dealt with in the same way as is most of the research literature of the sciences.

However, in addition to this sort of clinical research, there is supposedly another, perhaps even more numerous variety whose function is that it must be read and evaluated by practitioners who are guided and influenced thereby in their clinical practice. Though we have little direct or indirect evidence of this process, one can see that such use, turning knowledge directly into action (an analogue for this literature has also been suggested for technology, in which it is supposed that there may be a "know-how" literature, not cited, but used in engineering practice), must have special library problems. In particular, since the scientific and medical community is not giving rise to further literature in the course of turning clinical research papers into clinical practice, we do not have a process of validating and evaluation such research by its affected community. The heavy responsibility for proper reading and evaluating such clinical literature is a vital technique that must be learned (for this, see Chapters 8 and 9).

There also exist the throwaway magazines and a large literature (some of it of high quality) devoted to professional news and views, current events, and summaries of states of the art.[6,7] In the former, advertisements are also an important source of information. With all these nonresearch journals, the only way of coping is selective reading and browsing in a style formed during the process of professionalization. It is with the vital, cumulating, and learned research literature that the big problems occur.

Thus, with a series of such technological fixes as the invention of printing and of journals, learning grew in quantity and pressed ever more intensely into real time. For more than 300 years, the pace of growth in quantity of all learned literature has been maintained at a compound interest, with an exponential increase of about 6 to 7 percent each year, a doubling in size every ten to 15 years, and a tenfold increase in every generation of 35 to 50 years. (See Figure 1.1.) It is spectacular and unprecedented that year after year such a growth can be steadily maintained. The sustained growth is no sudden explosion or any sort of crisis, but each and every generation has seen its libraries grow by a mighty factor. Moreover, even though individuals and whole nations may slacken or resign, there remain large population masses on the globe yet to develop and take up the race. Therefore, without doubt, this lusty growth will continue for generations yet to come, and they will all complain of the superabundance of riches and the difficulty of coping with so much literature.

The increase has had its recurrent problems. Every few tenfold increases, an organizational hiatus has occurred. When the world count first stood at 300 journals in the eighteenth century, the sheer quantity of knowledge became so monumental that scholars first sought to compress it into books and handbooks and the encyclopedia was born. Then, as the flood kept coming, they compressed it into journals of abstracts and bibliographical indexes. Once more, such a measure worked, and knowledge continued its dizzy pace of exponential growth.

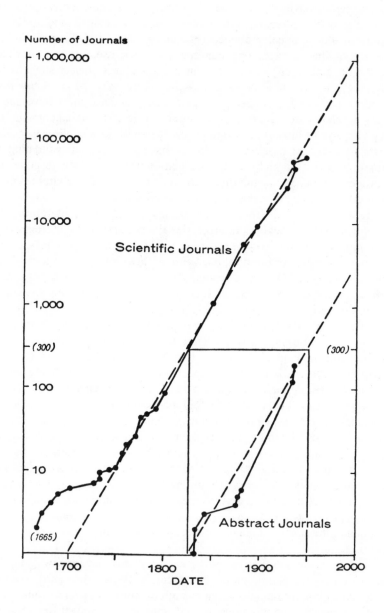

FIGURE 1.1   Number of Journals Founded (*not* surviving) As a Function of Date. The two uppermost points are taken from a slightly differently based list. From Derek de Solla Price, *Science since Babylon*. [New Haven, Conn.: Yale University Press, 1975].

Just a few decades ago, when there were some 300 of these abstract journals alive (yes, it is the same factor of 300) and we all wondered what to do next to manage them, the computer arrived and solved the problem with electronic memories and data banks. Now we have something like 300 (the magic number) such data banks, and movements are underway to manage and unify these by new generations of computerized sophistication.[8-11]

Why has all this happened and how can we learn to cope with it? Basically, the reason, as it now appears, is that each unit contribution to knowledge, as it has succeeded and had effect, has given rise to new opportunities to ask questions and solve problems. If one imagines it as a birthrate phenomenon, the exponential growth rate of 6 to 7 percent per year implies, that about every 15 papers written must give birth to a new paper each year. The cumulation of scholarly papers may also be likened to bricks piled on bricks—a kind of upside-down Tower of Babel. The difficulty is that these bricks seem to breed more bricks at a constant rate. In a sense, science is a sort of conspiracy that makes knowledge run faster than people.

The people of scholarly knowledge, including that special variety in matters biomedical, still read and write for much the same reasons and at essentially the same rate as they did 300 years ago. The trick to coping with the vast increase in the corpus of learning is to realize that knowledge is automatically split into a hierarchy of subdivisions by field and subfield, each containing pieces of knowledge closely related within the unit but not so closely outside. This is due to a built-in balance between researchers' productivity and the rate at which they can scan, monitor, read, and work through all the other material that must be of concern to them. Very roughly speaking, a person who writes and publishes a research communication each year can take in and digest more than one a month but less than one a day. Therefore, with a ratio of between a dozen and a few hundred, it takes a group of about this many individuals, a few hundred, all engaged in the same process to keep each other fully busy. Such was the group size of the early scientific societies, and, as knowledge and numbers of researchers steadily grew, the original single groups split and split again every decade or so, creating new "invisible colleges," each dedicated to concerted researching of a subsection of the original concern of all sciences and technologies.

So far as we can see, the actual amount of work produced by a person active in the research front has not changed in centuries. The productivity and motivation of the individual is reasonably constant. We tend, because life is arranged that way, to measure out our professional activity in plans that run by the year and entail some sort of annual report or set of decisions. Moreover, in many cases, we can only give ourselves permission to take on something new by closing off an old project by reporting on it. Some of the literature is, in effect, produced by this process of giving a fiscal account for time and money invested. If that were all there was to it, such accounts would be of little utility for the knowledge process, and it may be worth stating bluntly that expenditure of time and money gives no right to publication. That must depend on whether the spending and labor has produced something that others in the invisible college want to know and build upon.

Today, these new invisible colleges are concerned with what we denote as a subfield, and they have such names as "Australia antigen," "plate tectonics," "sickle-cell anemia," and so forth. As such a group gets organized, it tends to conventionalize its communication system from a list of names and addresses for offprint/preprint exchange to a newsletter, then to a subsection with its own meeting, and finally to a journal. It is worth making the point that, more often than not, these cognitive fields and subfields do not correspond too well with the organizational and professional structures of specialization. There is always a certain tendency for the professional hierarchy to reflect a sort of fossilized version of the way knowledge used to be structured when the organization was built up. Such structures change more slowly then the living front of knowledge. Those impatient with the lack of correspondence between structure and actuality might remember that old systems do not die out, but their adherents do. In the course of time, as specialization moves on inexorably, the old journals, built to serve a coherent area, also fossilize and become either more and more general or else remain specialized. The field splits by fission, giving birth to new journals of new specialties.

Of course, not all fields and journals survive. Some die along the way, as viewpoints and editors become defeated. Invisible colleges move along to a fresh topic, and publishers decide that 300 authors and a set of libraries of record do not provide a sufficiently profitable distribution list. In much the same way, by no means all those who have been guided to some part of the scientific research front remain active at that front. Indeed, for a large majority of researchers met in one's reading, one will never have heard of them before, *and* one will never hear of them again. Nevertheless, seemingly paradoxically, most of the material one will want to read will turn out to be written by people who are heard from again and again, so that their names become very familiar. With a reading room full of medical journals, most of the titles will only be of passing interest, but most of one's reading, in whatever field of specialization, will be in a core set of very familiar, recurring journals.

This state of affairs with authors, journals, and even individual papers stems from the way chance and probability work in such a situation. Roughly speaking, in all research, success breeds success.[12] Success, in some sense, is a final test of creative contribution. Success is to be taken here, of course, in the sense of doing the research job, rather than receiving monetary rewards, promotions, or grants, though these may also be involved in the process.

Basically, this position, called a principle of cumulative advantage, works because the capability of being creative and finding new knowledge of value is so elusive that one can give no recipe for it. Training, study, and education can all put a student at the research front. Organization can put together publishers and editors and make a journal. All one can do, however, is to "run up the flag and see if anyone salutes." If one starts with researchers who have just published a first article, or with journals that have been perceived to contain a useful or relevant article, or even with papers that have just become available to the scientific community, there follows next a sort of acid test. If the first incident is some sort of success, all signals will indicate "please continue." Without success, no such feedback occurs. When a first paper is only adequate, one might receive a higher degree or even a job, but bells do not ring out over the world or in one's ego. In the somewhat rare event of the world or one's own judgment (better yet, both) smiling, there is an urge to continue, and, at each renewed success, there is amplification and feedback.

To put the arithmetic of the process in simple terms, if the chance of an initial success at first shot is one in two, then, out of 100 starters (journals, people, or papers), we shall have about 50 left standing and 50 with a second success. Next time, however, we start with a select population, and they automatically have a greater chance of another success. If the original rate was one in two, the new success rate is probably about two in three, so that about 33 go on and 17 are left behind. In the next round, there are something like three chances in four of success—about 25 out of the 33 go on. Then we get four chances in five (20 out of the 25), then five chances in six, and so on.

In general, whatever ratio of success one starts with, this pattern of increasing success rates leads exactly to the sort of distributions that have long been known empirically. For example, a law found by George Kingsley Zipf states that the number of authors with n articles published is proportional to $1/n^2$. We know now that the theoretical form should be $1/n(n+1)$ and that the same law also applies to the number of journals containing exactly n articles in a given field. Furthermore, the same distribution leads to the fact that if one starts to collect authors or useful journals, starting with the most prolific, the total cumulated score of successes increases only as the logarithm of the collected authors or journals—a finding much discussed as Bradford's law.

This last is quite a powerful principle. For example, if there existed a million (which equals 2^{20}) medical books in a library or medical authors in the world, and we arrange them in order of merit or usefulness starting from the top, then each power of two will yield 5 percent (100 percent divided by 20) of the total of all successes.* The two top books or people will be 5 percent of the total value. Thus:

Books or People	Value (in percentages)
2	5
4	10
8	15
16	20
64	30
256	40
1,000	50
4,000	60
16,000	70
64,000	80
250,000	90
1,000,000	100

Given this situation, therefore, a small personal or institutional library, *if well selected*, is far more valuable than its proportion to the total literature suggests, and a small institute can be a major part of a large field.

Cumulative advantage works simply because the likelihood of publishing a paper or using a book or journal depends largely on how much has been done already. At all stages of the game, failure is possible. It just becomes less probable with each subsequent success. In essence, quality control is effected by tests of success. Even the empirical finding of exponential growth is contained within this generalization, for it depends quite simply on the fact that success breeds success. Each success of publication, discovery, or use gives rise to progeny that come at a constant birthrate and at the same place, more or less, as their parent successes.

From the principle of cumulative advantage and its consequences just described, one can formulate certain rules of behavior for writers and readers of the literature. Perhaps most importantly, authors must realize that they are not writing for a faceless posterity but for a very real and rather small audience of peers engaged in the conspiracy of making new knowledge in a particular niche of a subfield. The success of the enterprise lies in enabling those peers to build on one's work and take it further. A common error of research writers is to publish as if they wanted to say the last word so that nobody would ever again want to add to or comment on this final and ultimate truth.

---

*This, of course, is only approximate. $2^{10} = 1,024$, but it is convenient to approximate this to 1,000.

By the same token, if reading a paper, one should try to seize on something found in it and develop this further. It may be remarked parenthetically that the straight and direct purpose of the paper as described by authors in the title and abstracts and indexing terms is probably the most barren for seizing upon, because the author and all peers get to this immediately. There is a certain tendency for successful advances to be made because some reader perceives something indirect and incidental, something outside the straight and logical, thereby carrying on the enterprise in a manner unforeseen by the author. When we find a piece of information or a paper really important, half of the time it is because of indirect and serendipitous use of this sort.

Such papers cannot, therefore, be found by mere indexing and keeping in touch with the literature in one's own subfield. For creative contribution, it is also essential to browse with an eagle eye for seeing more into a paper than its authors had in mind. Moreover, in reading and in writing, one must pay close attention to previous successes as well as attempt to cover the whole field. Each time some author or journal or topic is reinforced by success, there is more reason to look there or publish there again, but one must always be on the watch for sources and writers that have not been met before.

The next most important conclusion from the quantitative theory is that, since perfect completeness is impracticable in such a large system as biomedical literature, there must be some trade-off between the degree of completeness and the economics and social limitations of the process of communication. As has been shown, each doubling of size of libraries and groups of authors adds only a few percent to effectiveness, and therefore the basic needs of anyone can be partly met by relatively few, well-chosen peers, books, journals, and reference tools. What one then needs to back this up is a system through which one can reach, at more cost and trouble, some comprehensive network of people, books, and journals, not merely those select ones that provide 95 percent of the use. In other words, one needs a well-selected and highly personal small system of one's own and also the impersonal and unselected giant and universal system provided by the National Library of Medicine and its comprehensive Medical Literature Analysis and Retrieval System (MEDLARS) of bibliographic tools. It is as much a mistake to use the giant system for day-to-day monitoring as to suppose that one's own personalized access can give everything that may be worthwhile.

Quantitative theory tells us much about the workings of the information system, but not all. There is also the matter of its having a structure previously referred to as resembling a sort of modern Tower of Babel. Recent research has had somewhat unexpected success in finding out what the structure actually looks like.[13] This is quite important because it shows that, in principle, computerized techniques will be able to solve quite automatical-

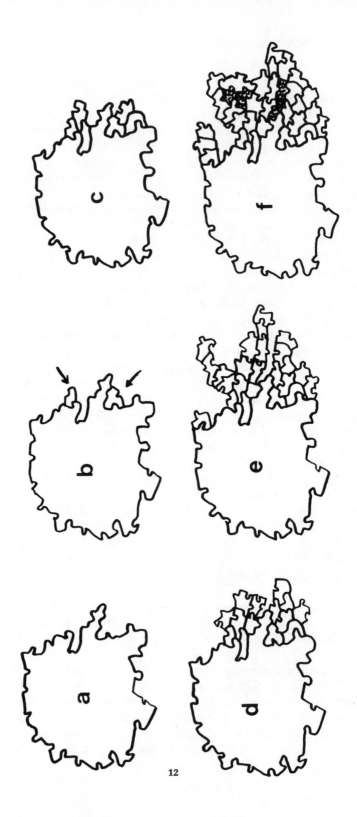

12

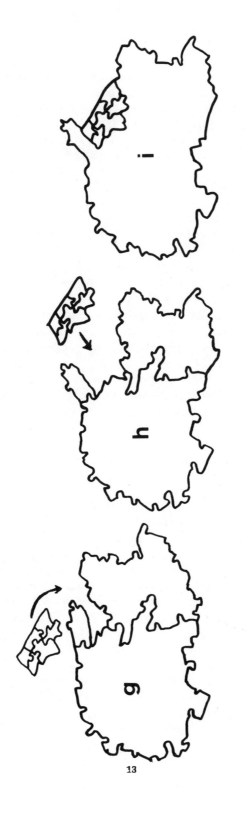

FIGURE 1.2a–i. Jigsaw Puzzle Model of the way the growing corpus of scientific papers fits together. The model shows nine successive stages illustrating the tendency of action to develop where there is action already (**b–d**). It shows the way in which some areas may become contained and fill in rapidly (**e** and **f**) and how islands may develop and require a distortion of the original structure before they can be fitted neatly into place (**g–i**).

13

ly the age-old and previously rather untractable problem of providing a nearly perfect indexing system for a knowledge base.

It turns out that the order that is built into knowledge can be revealed by a technique of citation clustering, and is rather accurately two-dimensional. That is to say, it corresponds to placing items of knowledge like towns on a map rather than in a one-dimensional array like books on a shelf or names in a phone book. The surprise is that the order does not seem to need more dimensions. Two dimensions give so much more flexibility than one that further refinement seems relatively unimportant.

The two-dimensional mapping of knowledge can best be illustrated by a very simple model in which each paper that is published is visualized as a piece of a jigsaw puzzle.

Suppose the puzzle was started some time in the distant past near its center and is now very large with millions of pieces fitted together in an irregular, but roughly circular, disc (Fig 1.2a). The game is to add whatever pieces fit at any place around the perimeter. The rule of the game is that progress is hard to make. One cannot just pick up a piece and set it into place. Some pieces are not yet ready because the puzzle boundaries have not reached that far. Moreover, even for those that fit, one has to see just the right site in the right orientation. Anything that can easily be done by way of fitting pieces together has already been done. One cannot make contributions to science just by being well trained and spending time and money.

The whole situation changes once a new piece is added (Figure 1.2b). At that spot, there are immediately new clues and new opportunities, and it is no longer true that anything that can be done has been done. There is a natural tendency for knowledge to proceed in this chainlike fashion, and that is why the simile of piling bricks upon bricks is so appropriate. It is also likely that the peninsular salients formed in this way, to use yet another image, like the pseudopods put out by an amoeba, correspond to the subspecialty fields staffed by their invisible colleges of researching peers. Sometimes two salients may connect like a pair of pincers to enclose a whole area that can quickly be filled in (Figure 1.2d), and sometimes salients that become overgrown can branch out by fission to form a sort of arboreal process (Figure 1.2e). The jigsaw model also illustrates another sort of process by which islands of knowledge can be formed and later fitted onto the mainland, probably with some pulling and tugging to distort two complex pieces of boundary to fit each other (Figure 1.2g–i).

Going from the model back to the real system of published research papers, each item when published is intimately related to a small group, probably about four or five immediate prodecessors. In actual practice, about half the references in an ordinary research paper provide this sort of linkage, while the other half are scattered around like buckshot fulfilling other functions (such as historical allusion, flattery of the author and author's colleagues, and so forth). Normal indexing descriptors provide a sort of coloration or pattern of the picture printed on the puzzle—the substantive content of the picture—that extends over larger or smaller groups of papers.

The knowledge that this sort of structure exists gives some hope that soon the computer will be able to use routinely this sort of associative, two-dimensional structure together with the cumulative type of memory reinforcement to store and retrieve knowledge in much the same way as does the human brain. It will be a great improvement from the old-style, linear, sequential structure that makes computers think like machines rather than people. In the meantime, a great deal can be achieved if one uses the available mechanized and printed modes of access to the biomedical literature and combines this with the discerning creativity of a human being.

Perhaps, even with perfect aids, the skills of research will remain as they are now, rather closely linked to informal communication that occurs during the act of creation. It is wise for any researcher to learn, above all else, the techniques for tapping knowledgeable peers who act as gatekeepers for the informal exchanges. Better still is to cultivate those skills and knowledgeabilities that will enable one in turn to act as one of the valued gatekeepers in as large a collection of subfields, professional fields, and interdisciplines as can be mustered in a lifetime.

REFERENCES

1. An excellent history of scientific literature containing ample bibliographies is John L. Thornton and R. I. Tully, Scientific Books, Libraries, and Collectors, London, Library Association, 1962.
2. The development of the journal has been definitively treated by David A. Kronick, A History of Scientific and Technical Periodicals, New York, Scarecrow Press, 1962.
3. At stake here is the matter of "norms of science." The ideas were first expounded by Robert K. Merton, Social Theory and Social Structure, New York, Free Press, 1968, pp. 606–15.
4. See also, for a fuller treatment, Norman W. Storer, The Social System of Science, New York, Holt, Rinehart & Winston, 1966, especially chap. 5.
5. An excellent review of the above book is by Norman Kaplan, Science, 7 Oct. 1966, pp. 139–40.
6. Jack Key, Katherine Sholtz, and Charles Roland, The Controlled Circulation Journal in Medicine: R_x or Rogue?, Serials Librarian 41(1), Fall 1979, pp. 15–23.
7. Naomi Bluestone, A Closer Look at the Throw-Aways, Montefiore Medicine 4(2), 1979, pp. 46–52.
8. For a general discussion of exponential growth of scientific literature, see Derek J. de Solla Price, Little Science, Big Science, New York, Columbia University Press, 1963/1965.
9. A whole literature has now grown up concerned with the quantitative analysis of scientific papers, authors, and citations. See Henry W. Menard, Science: Growth and Change, Cambridge, Mass., Harvard University Press, 1971.

10. Francis Narin, Evaluative Bibliometrics, Cherry Hill, N.J., Computer Horizons, 1976.
11. Eugene Garfield, Citation Indexing, New York, John Wiley & Sons, 1979. There is also now a major journal, Scientometrics, published by Elsevier Scientific Publishing Company, and this contains periodical bibliographies dealing with the scholarly literature in this field.
12. The mathematics of this stochastic model are given in Derek de Solla Price, A General Theory of Bibliometric and other Cumulative Advantage Processes, Journal of the American Society for Information Science, 27(5), Sept.–Oct. 1976, pp. 292–306. See also Derek de Solla Price, Cumulative Advantage Urn Games Explained: A Reply to Kantor, Journal of the American Society for Information Science 29(4), July 1978, pp. 204–6.
13. Henry Small and Belver C. Griffith, The Structure of Scientific Literatures I: Identifying and Graphing Specialties, Science Studies 4, 1975, pp. 17–40. See also, Belver C. Griffith, Henry Small, Judith A. Stonehill, and Sandra Dey, The Structure of Scientific Literatures II: Toward a Macro- and Microstructure for Science, Science Studies 4, 1974, pp. 339–65.

2

SELECTIVE ASPECTS OF THE BIOMEDICAL LITERATURE

Kenneth S. Warren

THE INDIVIDUAL

The initial approach of students to information is through textbooks and lectures. On becoming involved in research, they encounter the vast primary literatures, thousands of journals produced weekly, monthly, bimonthly, and quarterly. Keeping up-to-date involves scanning numerous abstracts published at many scientific meetings, and there is the so-called fugitive literature of unpublished mimeographed reports, memos, and so forth. Then students are initiated into the "invisible college" of informal verbal communication, first at the unsophisticated level of their fellow students, then at a more sophisticated level through their teachers, and eventually, on obtaining a position of eminence, through their professional colleagues.

Graduate students in the basic biomedical sciences encounter the primary journal literature relatively early in their careers. As soon as they develop a basic fund of knowledge through textbooks and lectures and begin to approach a thesis subject, they start to read journals. The primary purposes of this reading are to obtain a perspective on the past research done in their chosen field and to be aware of the latest developments for proper preparation and follow-through of their investigations. Reading is supplemented by unpublished information passed through the invisible college. Then, at a variety of encounters, they begin to display their knowledge not only in depth in their particular projects but also in breadth within and even outside of their fields of specialization.

Medical students, who must initially cover a wide variety of subjects in many basic sciences, rely heavily on syllabi, lectures, and textbooks.

Furthermore, they must learn many clinical subjects and skills. Compared to that of graduate students, medical trainees' encounter with the primary literature is delayed (excepting those students who become involved in research projects) until the later clinical years or the period of internship and residency. In this situation, the literature is used for several purposes: to maintain current awareness on diagnosis and treatment of disease, to occasionally survey information for a small-scale research project (often an unusual case report), and to impress colleagues at meetings and ward rounds.

As a consequence of such experiences, young biomedical scientists and physicians develop habits of reading broadly in many journals. These habits are strongly reinforced by their general concept of the scientific literatures. First, it is believed that information of major importance is dispersed throughout a vast array of published and even unpublished literature. It is the responsibility of the investigator to be aware of this material so that his references can be complete. Furthermore, a piece of information in some relatively obscure journal might provide ideas for new and exciting areas of research. The more obscure the source, the less the likelihood that others will be aware of it, and this will constitute a coup in conferences or rounds. The clinician is conscious of the admonition of President Kennedy concerning his recurrent back problems, "I always had the feeling that the surgeons should have read one more book." Second, the keepers of the troves of information, librarians and information scientists, generally appear to believe that the bigger the library the better. This is related historically to the eminence of the fabled library of Alexandria and to the particular prestige accorded to the Library of Congress, the Lenin Library, the National Library of Medicine (NLM), and similar institutions. This respect for the indispensable comprehensive collections, unfortunately, has been extended to all libraries. As the noted information scientist Herman Fussler stated in 1949: "Yet the reverence for size continues. The library that has the most books is likely to be regarded as *ipso facto*, the best." Universities often cite the size of their collections but rarely devote equal time to their quality [1]. As a corollary to the library situation, it is believed that the optimal information system would make all information of any kind freely and instantly available. Thus, both the users and the information specialists who help them tend to equate a successful search of the literature with the number of citations found.

Unfortunately, the effects of such a system on the user are rarely considered. Many users are literally overwhelmed by it and cease to use reading as a major learning device. Others develop a variety of personal and often idiosyncratic defense mechanisms to protect themselves and to cope with the situation. The task is formidable indeed. At the basic level, the individual may receive five to ten or even more journals as a subscriber, as a member of professional or scientific societies, and as "throwaways." These include highly specialized organs, ones of more general interest, and those that cover science or health broadly. For ten of the most widely read journals in internal medicine, this means approximately 200 original articles and 70 editorials each month. The *Journal of Immunology* alone is now publishing almost 80 articles in each issue. Many physicians and scientists also like to visit their institutional libraries to browse among the wide variety of current and past journals to see if they can find articles in related disciplines that might be of interest. Moreover, the abstracts of the big clinical research and scientific research meetings come in each year, with approximately 2,700 in *Clinical Research*, 8,100 in *Federation Proceedings*, plus those of all the other, more specialized societies. *Current Contents* broadly covers the scientific and medical fields, and each week the table of contents of about 200 journals with more than 2,000 titles are presented. The use of other secondary sources, such as *Index Medicus* and *Chemical Abstracts*, provides vast numbers of citations, and then there is the computer. As stated by some of the most advanced thinkers at the NLM, "Paradoxically, the superhuman speed and flexibility of computer searching often overwhelms the searcher with instant bibliographies of hundreds or sometimes thousands of citations, creating a formidable reading burden. Critical perusal may be made difficult by the lack of informative text and data in retrieved records" [2].

The most telegraphic means of entry into the system is the citation. However, reading citations in large numbers is a stultifying task. The information systems available at the present time almost ensure this task because, if one attempts to achieve a high recall that misses almost nothing of relevance, one also retrieves quantities of unwanted material. In order to achieve a high precision in terms of wanted citations, one must also lose significant amounts of relevant information. As Tamas Doskocs, Barbara Rapp, and Harold Schoolman have recently stated, "In practice, precision and recall are inversely related and are rather elusive measures in operational retrieval systems because of the subjectivity of relevance judgements" [2]. Following perusal of the citations, abstracts must be surveyed, and, after further winnowing, the papers themselves must be dealt with. Again, in varying order and to differing degrees, the different parts of the scientific paper—introduction, materials and methods, results, discussion, tables and figures, and references—are perused. (See Chapters 7 and 9.) Thus, no matter what strategy is involved, attempts to deal with the literature in a comprehensive way are time-consuming indeed, perhaps leaving little time for practice and research.

Individuals are often concerned about the consequences of not reading widely in terms of the loss of information of value. Put in another way, the sheer quantity of material available and the lack of effective strategies to deal with it have led to such complaints as "Unless something is done we shall soon reach the position when knowledge is being lost as rapidly as it is gained"[3] and "The mass of professional journals is so indigestible and so little worth digesting that the good papers, though more numerous than ever, are increasingly in danger of being overlooked"[4].

THE INFORMATION EXPLOSION

In order to cope with the vast amount of biomedical information, it is essential that students, scientists, and clinicians have some understanding of the system in both its quantitative and qualitative dimensions. Quantitatively, the information explosion is best likened, not to a terrestrial explosion or even one caused by a hydrogen bomb, but to the primordial "big bang" hypothesized as the origin of an ever-expanding universe. This concept forcefully characterizes the problem faced by the individual scientist and physician. Derek de Solla Price's classic description of the exponential growth of the scientific literature in the last three centuries has clearly posed the problem [5]. In the present century alone, the increase in biomedical serials has been enormous. For example, 70 years ago, there were approximately 1,000; 50 years ago, 1,500; 30 years ago, 4,000; ten years ago, 14,000; and now, more than 20,000 journals. At present, the NLM collects virtually all of these journals, and 3,200 of them from 73 countries are indexed in the computerized Medical Literature Analysis and Retrieval System (MEDLARS). Approximately 250,000 articles from these journals are indexed annually in MEDLARS Online (MEDLINE), all intensively from the full text. The MEDLINE files going back to 1966 contain more than 3 million citations [2]. In 1976 Donald King estimated the total number of scientific and technological journals as 49,440 worldwide, with 8,460 in the United States [6]. There have been comparable increases in other sources of biomedical information, including books and indexes.

In spite of this seemingly impossible, inchoate mass of information, it is of immense importance to realize that a clustering process occurs in the literature and that a selective system is constantly operating. In 1946 Samuel Bradford claimed that 500 to 1,000 journals are required to obtain 95 percent of the significant literature in any given field [7], and Eugene Garfield has pointed out that there are major overlaps among the various scientific fields [8]. Studies of specific literatures have revealed the following statistics. The entire literature on schistosomiasis over a period of 110 years (10,286 citations) was dispersed among 1,738 different periodicals, but only 19 journals contained almost one-third of the literature and about 50 journals contained 50 percent [9]. The mast-cell literature over a period of 86 years consisted of 2,978 articles in 587 journals. Of this literature, 25 percent was contained in 20 journals and 50 percent in 78 journals [10]. The transplant immunology literature in *Index Medicus* for a four-year period was found in

272 journals, with 50 percent of the 1,120 articles contained in 15 journals [11]. When all of these figures are transmuted into simple equations, they follow the laws so well described in Chapter 1.

There is also a marked clustering in journals demanded by users. Thus, in a large medical library serving both the academic and practicing communities, only 371 of 3,000 journals (12.4 percent) were circulated 876 times in a one-month period, and half the circulation was accounted for by only 76 journals (2.5 percent) [11]. Of the small number of journals circulating, 50 percent did so only once during this time period.

Another aspect of this problem is the relatively small body of literature that is likely to stand or has stood "the test of time." John Ziman has claimed that "science is public knowledge" in that "its facts and theories must survive a period of critical study and testing by other competent and disinterested individuals, and must have been found so persuasive that they are almost universally accepted" [12]. In this sense, therefore, it is startling to encounter Garfield's statement that 25 to 50 percent of the scientific papers published are never cited even once [8]. Since the *Science Citation Index* is relatively new, as is citation analysis, it is interesting to note the results of an examination of a major medical literature for a period of 110 years. In this case, papers of importance were selected in an open-ended manner by a board of 47 experts. Of the 10,268 citations, 70 percent were not selected even once, and only 15 percent were selected two or more times [9]. As to the journals (rather than the papers), all of the articles selected one or more times were found in 691 journals, or 40 percent of those containing the total literature. Those selected two or more times were found in only 350 journals [8]. Garfield has developed a journal citation index in which the journals are ranked by the number of times cited and also by an impact factor, which is the times cited divided by the number of articles published in a given time period [8]. These systems provide a reasonably objective aid in establishing Bradford's core group of 500 to 1,000 journals.

The practical implications of these statistics are well illustrated in the information-transfer project of the NLM—"an easily and immediately accessible information system that will provide practitioners with information needed to deal with their day to day real world patient problems" [13]. (See Chapter 10.) This project began with a synthesis of current knowledge on viral hepatitis. A baseline search was made, not of the 20,000 NLM journals, but only of the English-language serials in the MEDLINE file of 3,000 journals. For a period of ten years, there were 16,000 citations. Since the one individual involved in the synthesis process could not encompass this literature in a reasonable period of time, an information base consisting of 575 articles was constructed from 40 recent reviews on the subject. A body of ten experts was then organized to update the base, but they balked when confronted with the 5,700 articles in English on hepatitis generated within the previous 2.5 years. On going back to the reviews initially consulted, it was found that 47 percent of the 575 articles cited were found in five journals and 80 percent in 18 journals. By looking only at these 18 journals, therefore, the citations for updating were reduced from 5,700 to 620, a number that, when divided among the ten experts, was found reasonable.

SELECTIVE INFORMATION SYSTEMS

Thus, it becomes clear that the undifferentiated information available in virtually every area of biomedical and clinical science is too much for the individual to encompass. Awareness of the different types of information available in journals or stored in computers can enable the scientist/clinician to greatly circumscribe the size of the information base perused. This can be on the basis of defining the function of the information (that is, separating that which is intended for current awareness from that intended to add to our permanent fund of knowledge), delimiting the subject matter (in Ziman's words, "this traditional process of evolution by speciation" [14]), and, most importantly, determining the quality of the information source.

With respect to the information type, Sir Theodore Fox, editor of the *Lancet*, in his *Crisis in Communication* has divided journals into two types, many of which have overlapping functions.

> The first, for want of a better name, I shall call the medical recorder [often called archival]. This is a journal which records new observations and experiments and techniques. As one of the principle means of communication between investigators, it is at present necessary for the advance of medical knowledge. The second is the medical newspaper [often called current awareness]. Its function is to inform, interpret, criticize and stimulate. It is necessary for the advance of medical practice [15].

In effect, many of the major medical journals subsume both the archival and current-awareness functions, and often do so in almost equal proportions. Why, then, do many major information systems record all of the contents of the medical and scientific journals that they select for indexing? The current-awareness function is essentially an ephemeral one, reporting the latest approach to a problem (this includes many reviews and case reports), and its maintenance for decades or forever in a data bank, to be reproduced with archival literature in every search even when it is not wanted, will only serve to clutter up the information system. It is worth thinking of flagging such items within computers so that they would self-destruct after a reasonable period of time, or at least providing the searcher with the ability to delete current-awareness citations.

Another delimiting factor in science and the literature of science is the phenomena of specialization and subspecialization. General practitioners become internists who become cardiologists or gastroenterologists. Surgeons become abdominal surgeons who become proctologists. Immunologists become cellular immunologists and immunochemists and immunopharmacologists. Each of these disciplines and subdisciplines spawns societies and, most importantly in this context, subdivision of journals and formation of new journals. Ziman has observed that this "may be a natural consequence of scientific progress...one response of the system [being] further differentiation and subspecialization of journals" [14]. For example, the *Journal of Immunology* is now divided into seven sections and *Gastroenterology* into 12. In addition to *Immunology* and the *Journal of Immunology*, we now have *Immunochemistry*, *Cellular Immunology*, *Immunogenetics*, the *Journal of Immunogenetics*, *Immunopharmacology*, the *Journal of Immunopharmacology*, the *Journal of Reproductive Immunology*, and *Parasite Immunology*. Thus, as Byron Waksman has recently written, "One library may serve immunochemists and immunogeneticists well while providing inadequately for immunobiologists, immunopharmacologists and clinical immunologists; another may do the reverse" [16].

Perhaps the most important potential factor in circumscribing the amount of literature perused is the obvious fact that a large proportion of the literature is inadequate in terms of originality, design, methodology, interpretation, or reference. Before going on to a discussion of the qualitative aspects of the information system, however, it would be well to suggest that, in practice, this involves quite a gross system of estimation. Since, in the previous essay, Price chose to emphasize the unique characteristics of Beethoven and Mozart, it should be pointed out that our qualitative criteria would include at least 10 percent of all of the composers working in that period. We do not confine ourselves merely to the Nobel laureates—the Eliots, the Bellows, the Cricks—but are concerned with about a tenth of the poets, novelists, and scientists practicing their respective arts.

Quality of information has been studied in relation to authors, journals, and individual papers. With respect to authors, Price's essay "Galton Revisited" described the nineteenth-century geneticist's pioneering studies on the quality of scientists. Price reexamined this problem and demonstrated "a reasonably good correlation between eminence of a scientist and his productivity of papers" [5]. The analysis of a complete literature, both quantitatively and qualitatively (by William Goffman and Kenneth Warren [10]), supports this belief in that, as the quality of work increased (as determined by the frequency of selection by a group of 47 experts), so did the number of papers per author. As Price has observed, good publication experience will encourage productivity. Furthermore, the number of authors per paper rose with the quality of the work. Thus, the lowest-quality group of all was comprised of single papers with single authors. This literature had only one international network of authors who were linked by collaborative work, as compared with many national networks. The proportion of authors in the international network was directly related to the frequency with which their papers were chosen by the experts. Goffman has recently established a synthesis factor in which removing an author from the collaborative network of investigators reveals the degree to which that author contributes to the cohesiveness of the network [10]. Henry Small has also analyzed the role of synthetic authors who provide a major stimulus to a field through collaborative research using cluster analysis [17].

The quality of journals has clearly been delineated by Garfield's journal citation index and impact factors, and it has also been shown that quality authors tend to publish in quality journals. On a gross level, many journals can be quickly and easily assessed with little more than a cursory glance. One of the most traumatic moments this author has faced occurred on first attending a meeting of the MEDLARS literature-selection consultants, the group that decides the 3,200 of 20,000 biomedical journals that should enter the computerized data banks of NLM. That day the committee was to examine the middle European journals, and there seemed to be literally hundreds of journals in such languages as Lithuanian and Polish. In spite of the language barrier for the committee (the journals had already been gone over by staff language experts), reaching a consensus on good and bad journals was surprisingly easy. The key characteristics of the bad journals were few or no tables or figures containing data and few or no references. In terms of deciding which journals to include in the *Science Citation Index*, Garfield has described the following factors: the reputation of the journal's publishers; regularity of its publication; geographic representation of its editorial board; and its format and bibliographic standards as reflected in articles, titles, references, authors' addresses, and abstracts [8].

When dealing with the individual articles, it is again obvious that all papers are not equal. The gross factors described above clearly apply to papers as well as journals. Philosophically, as John Bruer has pointed out, the work of scientists begins with the design component, an egalitarian stage when they "should be given maximal freedom and privacy to pursue their interests" [18]. This is only prudent, given our relative ignorance of from where and from whom the most useful ideas might come. Later, a filtration component acts "to discover true or reliable theories about the world. Filtration occurs in the scientific community when researchers' views are substantiated, criticized, or refuted by their peers" [18]. These judgments are made on the basis of many factors—from the initiating hypotheses to experimental design, methodology, data statistical analysis, interpretation, and citations—and can lead to an overall judgment as to whether a paper is relatively good or bad. Optimally, these judgments can be made a priori (at the time the paper appears in print), although some of them can only be determined a posteriori.

In terms of hypothesis, it must initially be stated that there is a school of investigation that essentially does not believe in starting a research project with an idea or hypothesis, the so-called inductive school. An inductivist would examine a large number of patients using many clinical and laboratory tests to see if any startling findings or patterns occur. Bad ideas are likely to be either illogical or ignorantly (as opposed to deliberately) antithetical to known facts or can simply turn out to be wrong. An excellent example of a brilliant hypothesis that eventuated (a posteriori) as a bad idea was described by Francis Crick, who in 1956 was searching for the nucleic acid code of DNA. "Aha!" he said, "The nice thing about the comma-free code is that it was a very beautiful idea and it was wrong—and it's always nice to have one or two examples of that, just as a cautionary tale" [19].

The importance of good experimental design is particularly evident in the area of clinical trials for new drugs and other forms of treatment. Frederick Mosteller, in a recent preliminary survey of such papers, has revealed that all of them suffered from basic errors in design [20]. Of seven crucial items—survival curves, blindness, explanation of randomization, quality of life, informed consent, statistical devices, and the power of the experiment as based on the sample sizes and tests to be used—only 0 to 45 percent of these items were reported with a median of 25 percent. Louis Branscomb described an analysis of 30 independent reports on helium ionization cross section in which only 10 percent of the papers had even rudimentary evidence concerning essential questions, such as the prevention of secondary emission from the electron beam collector or the definition of the path-length of the electrons in the ionizing region [21].

Bad methodology may either be due to failure to use the best methods or instruments for performing certain experiments or to a flaw in the state of the art at the time the experiments were performed (a posteriori). Branscomb noted the lack of proper criteria for determining positive ion and electron recombination [22].

The problem of bad data is well illustrated by the fact that the vast smallpox eradication campaign was initiated on the basis of strikingly false information (a posteriori). Donald Henderson has stated, "In the light of nine years' experience we now believe that when the program began not more than one percent of all cases were actively being reported" [23].

Good statistical analysis, as well as experimental design, is essential for the proper evaluation of data. Often the design of the experiment does not include enough people, animals, or test tubes for proper analysis. The statistical method chosen may be inappropriate. Even more glaring are such statements as "The data were not statistically significant, but a clear trend was perceived" or "The results support this contention though the differences were not significant."

The need for good interpretation suggests that, even though all of the systems may be in order, important implications of a major finding may be either under- or overemphasized. As noted in *The Eighth Day of Creation*, Elliot Volkin and Lazarus Astrachan had essentially discovered RNA in an elegant series of experiments, but it took several years of added experiments and interpretations by others before it was realized that a fundamental discovery had been made (a posteriori) [19].

Finally, the list of references at the end of the paper is of great importance in establishing the place of the work being reported in the jigsaw puzzle created by many investigators. A small and insular bibliography usually indicates failure by the authors to perceive the larger picture. Interestingly enough, an overinflated, thoughtlessly compiled bibliography is also revelatory of failure to visualize the picture clearly.

To summarize the situation with respect to the qualitative state of the literatures, in an address to the graduating class of the School of Library Science at Case Western Reserve University several years ago, the author stated that we could look upon the scientific literatures from the classic viewpoint of the Western movies—in terms of the good guys and the bad guys. The good guys, who add to our state of knowledge, make up only a small proportion of the total literature. In the relatively clean area of physical phenomena, it has been noted that, over a period of 40 years, a constant percentage of authors—only 10 to 14 percent—wrote up their work in such a way as could be said on subsequent inspection to contain useful information [21]. There is a vast middle area that includes the nondescript cowpokes and the horses, and then come the villains at the end.

Inadvertently, the villains produce wrong information or strongly advocate a false position, which essentially requires a major effort and the development of a significant literature to eventually disprove their contention. The analysis of data on the efficacy of vitamin C in the treatment of the common cold led that great scientist Linus Pauling to a position of strong advocacy in 1970 [24]. This position, which was vehemently challenged at the time, led to an extensive research effort over a period of almost ten years. In the five-year period up to and including 1970, a MEDLARS printout reveals that there was a total of ten papers (an average of two per year), while the numbers in the next five years totaled 77 (15.4 per year), with another 32 papers appearing over the subsequent four years. The present consensus appears to be that vitamin C does not significantly affect the course of the common cold [24]. (Note the discussion of a controlled trial of vitamin C for cancer therapy in Chapter 8.) Poorly controlled primary studies advocating new forms of therapy, pharmacological (anesthetics) or surgical, require enormous subsequent efforts to validate their claims. Unfortunately, in more than half of the instances, the treatment is shown to have been of little or no value [25].

The necessity of evaluating the quality of information has been expressed pungently by Branscomb.

> Food and energy challenge because they are in short supply in major areas of the world. In both cases the challenge seems to be, how do you manage shortage? Information is quite different. It is in quantitative surplus.... Indeed there seems to be more information around—good and bad—than anyone can use. I have heard it said we are living in a world of information junk...." [22].

SOLUTIONS

Suggestions for solving the problem of information overload have also never been in short supply. Many of these either do away with the traditional, written system of scientific communication or attempt to ignore it. A more frightening situation is the use of modern technology to provide vast amounts of information, and even multiply it by extensive cross-indexing. Although each of these approaches, if utilized properly, could contribute eventually to alleviating the situation, their blind use may either have a negative effect or exacerbate the problem. The basis of this belief is Ziman's statement that "the invention of a mechanism for the systematic publication of fragments of scientific work may well have been the key event in the history of modern science" [26].

Nevertheless, J. D. Bernal, in his *Social Function of Science*, suggested doing away with the traditional scientific journal by sending papers to a central source that would distribute abstracts to interested individuals who could then request the full text. He actually stated that "all schemes have in common the remodeling, and to a large extent the abolition of all existing scientific periodicals, at any rate those which contain, for the most part, separate scientific papers or monographs" [3]. Interestingly enough, Fox (one of the great editors of the *Lancet*) supported this approach to the recorder literature but believed that newspaper journals should still be published in traditional ways [15]. In 1980, Byron Waksman also advocated this adoption of an abstract mode of publication with the articles on demand in a central repository. Furthermore, he suggested eliminating refereeing and "eliminating financing of unnecessary publications" [16]. David Durack, perhaps with tongue in cheek, suggested that we "limit the number of publications by each author to five a year, with a step wise reduction in NIH support as an automatic penalty for each paper published above five.... Alternatively, the total number of publications allowed to an author in his lifetime could perhaps be limited to 50 papers or books" [27].

Price's idea of the invisible college [5] was elaborated further by Diana Crane [28]. This approach was claimed to solve the "communication crisis by reducing a large group to a small select one of the maximum size that can be handled by interpersonal relationships" [5]. It is interesting to note that the more advanced the scientist or scientific administrator, the greater his reliance on this system and the greater its effectiveness. But not everyone can ring Lew Thomas or Josh Lederberg to get a quick summary of an issue. Another factor that must be taken into consideration is that most scientists at the bench are deeply enthusiastic about their own work in progress and that of their younger colleagues. Many an incipient breakthrough is tempered by the sober process of writing an introduction, materials and methods, results, and discussion. Just think of the chaos engendered by a word-of-mouth system that could not be carefully and objectively examined. Crane has clearly posed this problem as follows: "The informal communication system is concerned with disseminating new information. The formal communication system of journals, books, and review articles first evaluates knowledge and, second, disseminates it" [28].

Handling quantities of information has been enormously facilitated by the computer, and the future described by Branscomb is mind boggling [22]. Several years ago, the computer at NLM was handling the citations from 2,200 journals, and the online printout system of MEDLINE provided those from 1,100. With improvements in both hardware and software, the citations from 3,200 journals then became available (both off-line and on-line), complete with abstracts and indexed in-depth from full text. As Fox noted, this form of indexing will enable the average article to appear under eight to ten headings instead of two, thereby multiplying citations four- to fivefold [15]. The future promises vast computer capacity (now increasing at an average of 35 percent per year) maintained in relatively minute space through superconductance. Inputting systems by voice and by reading through pattern recognition will be exceedingly swift, and a new science, called human-factor research in the United States and ergonomics internationally, is planning to make us as comfortable with the computer as the heroes of *Star Wars* were with those delightful robots C3PO and R2D2.

What could be profitably added to these systems is more extensive filtration at either the input or output level. This is the selective strategy that we believe is a reasonable solution to the problem at the present time. It would not destroy the ecology of a complex and effective information system that we are only beginning to understand. It will be synergistic with the invisible college, and it will enable us to use computer technology intelligently. The old cliché "garbage in, garbage out" cannot be argued with. It seems, however, that, if the computers have the capacity, the speed of input, small size, and low cost, the greatest effort should be placed, not on what is input, but on how it is identified and on different strata of output. Branscomb has observed, "It is just as absurd for the user to tap the total collection of new material for his data as it would be for the jeweler to order six tons of gold-bearing ore when he wants to make a cufflink" [21]. Thus, it would not be inconceivable in the near future to enter the contents of all 20,000 journals received at NLM and then to address various subsets of information—articles and journals with various levels of impact factor, articles only in English, articles with different levels of citation indexing, articles by scientists with high-citation indexes, and all sorts of different groupings (such as the 110 clinical journals in the *Abridged Index Medicus*). The input mechanism would be consonant, therefore, with Bruer's philosophical concepts of literatures' egalitarianism [18], and various methods of filtration could be applied to the output, thereby adapting the information system to the needs and capacities of each scientist and physician.

REFERENCES

1. Fussler, HH. Characteristics of the research literature used by chemists and physicists in the United States. Library Quarterly: 19:19–35, 119–43, 1949.
2. Doszkocs, TE; Rapp, BA; and Schoolman, HN. Automated information retrieval in science and technology. Science 208:25–30, 1980.
3. Bernal, JD. The Social Function of Science. Routledge and Kegan, London, 1939.
4. Quine, WV. Paradoxes of plenty. Daedalus 103:38–40, 1974.
5. de Solla Price, DJ. Little Science, Big Science. Columbia University Press, New York, 1963.
6. King, DW. Statistical indicators of scientific and technical communication (1960–1981). Vol. 2. National Technical Information Service, Springfield, Va., 1976.
7. Bradford, SC. Complete Documentation. Report of the Royal Society Empire Conference. London, pp. 729–48, 1946.
8. Garfield, E. The Science Citation Index As a Quality Information Filter. In Coping with the Biomedical Information Explosion: A Qualitative Approach, edited by KS Warren and W Goffman. Rockefeller Foundation, New York, 1978, pp. 68–77.
9. Warren, KS, and Goffman, W. Coping with the Biomedical Literature Explosion: A Qualitative Approach. Rockefeller Foundation, New York, 1978.
10. Goffman, W, and Warren, KS. Scientific Information Systems and the Concept of Selectivity. Praeger, New York, 1980.
11. Goffman, W, and Morris, TG. Bradford's law and library acquisitions. Nature 226:922–23, 1970.
12. Ziman, JM. Public Knowledge: The Social Dimension of Science. Cambridge University Press, Cambridge, 1968.
13. Bernstein, L. The Hepatitis Knowledge Base. In Research on Selective Information Systems, edited by W Goffman, JT Bruer, and KS Warren. Rockefeller Foundation, New York, 1980, pp. 72–105.
14. Ziman, JM. The proliferation of scientific literature: A natural process. Science 208:369–71, 1980.

15. Fox, T. Crisis in Communication: The Functions and Future of Medical Journals. Athlone Press, University of London, London, 1965.
16. Waksman, BH. Information overload in immunology: Possible solutions to the problem of excessive publication. Journal of Immunology 124:1009–15, 1980.
17. Small, H. Quality filtering using citation data and the structure of paradigms. In Research on Selective Information Systems, edited by W Goffman, JT Bruer, and KS Warren. Rockefeller Foundation, New York, 1980, pp. 17–45.
18. Bruer, JT. Selectivity and the Values of Science. In Research on Selective Information Systems, edited by W. Goffman, JT Bruer, and KS Warren. Rockefeller Foundation, New York, 1980, pp. 117–35.
19. Judson, HF. The Eighth Day of Creation: The Makers of the Revolution in Biology. Simon and Schuster, New York, 1979.
20. Mosteller, F; Gilbert, JP; and McPeck, B. Reporting standards and research strategies for controlled trials: Agenda for the editor. Controlled Clinical Trials 1:37–58, 1980.
21. Branscomb, LM. Misinformation explosion: Is the literature worth reviewing? Scientific Research 3:49–56, 1968.
22. Branscomb, LM. Information: The ultimate frontier. Science 203:143–47, 1979.
23. Henderson, DA. Eradication of smallpox. Scientific American 235:25–34, 1976.
24. Coulehan, JL. Ascorbic acid and the common cold: Reviewing the evidence. Postgraduate Medicine 66:153–60, 1979.
25. Gilbert, JP; McPeck, B; and Mosteller, F. Progress in Surgery and Anesthesia: Benefits and Risks of Innovative Therapy. In Costs, Risks, and Benefits of Surgery, edited by JP Bunker, BA Barnes, and F Mosteller. Oxford University Press, New York, 1977, pp. 124–69.
26. Ziman, JM. Information, communication, knowledge. Nature 224:318–24, 1969.
27. Durack, DT. The weight of medical knowledge. New England Journal of Medicine 298:773–75, 1978.
28. Crane, D. Invisible Colleges. University of Chicago Press, Chicago, 1972.

3

THE ECOLOGY OF THE BIOMEDICAL LITERATURE AND INFORMATION RETRIEVAL

William Goffman

The basic unit of the formal scientific information system that has evolved over the past 300 years is the scientific paper. A paper comes into being by the following process. An author or team of authors produce a manuscript reporting observations or research results that they then submit to a journal. The journal may either reject or accept the manuscript. If it is rejected, the authors will probably send it to other journals until it is accepted or withdrawn. Once a manuscript is accepted, it will, after some revision and editing, be published by the journal and will thereby be disseminated to the community of readers. Not every subscriber to the journal will read the paper, but, from among those that do, some will find it of sufficient relevance and quality to incorporate its results in their own work, which will become manifest by its appearance as a reference at the end of their own manuscripts. In some cases, the paper may initiate an idea that culminates in the production of a manuscript by the reader. As this cycle repeats itself over time, a literature dealing with a given topic or set of topics is generated.

The gross dynamics of this process has been modeled as an epidemic process with an intermediate host in which authors actively publishing in a given field represent infectives; readers not publishing in the field, susceptibles of the definitive host population; journals actively publishing in the field infectives; and journals not publishing in the field, susceptibles of the intermediate host population.[1] As the literature of a given field develops over time, the field is said to be in an epidemic state if the change in the number of active contributors (authors and journals) is increasing. In general, the literature of a given field will behave like a recurring epidemic process entering an epidemic state, reaching a peak point, and then receding only to repeat the cycle.[2] Each cycle might be thought of as representing the current paradigm of the given field.

Describing the growth of the scientific literature in terms of a disease model, however, adds support to the pejorative view of the literature that has prevailed among elements of every generation of scientists, namely, that the formal system of scientific communication is in a mess and something ought to be done about it. (See Chapter 2.)

On the other hand, J. M. Ziman has pointed out that proliferation of the literature may not necessarily be a sign of ill health in science but may be the consequence of scientific progress.[3] In fact, it has been shown that the growth of the literature is more or less parallel to the growth of the scientific community.[1,2,4] Thus, the continuously increasing crop of scientific papers is produced by a continuously increasing crop of scientists.

If we accept this view and think of the growth of the scientific and biomedical literature as a natural consequence of scientific progress, rather than an abnormal phenomenon, a complete change in attitude toward the growth of the literature will occur. It will be removed from the purview of plague and pestilence and inserted into the fields of biology and ecology. A change in thinking from epidemiology to ecology would be accompanied by a desire to understand and preserve—rather than to stamp out, cure, and prevent—because we realize that, in a cyclical, intertwined system that involves all sorts of feedback mechanisms, a drastic change in any part of the cycle will have a major effect on all parts of it and may even result in its destruction.

THE ECOSYSTEM OF SCIENTIFIC COMMUNICATION

The system of scientific communication that has served the scientific community so well for so long is describable as an ecosystem. (See Figure 3.1.) The major elements of this system are funding agencies, authors, readers, journals, libraries (that is, all types of information-retrieval systems), and professional societies. The interaction among these basic components constitutes the ecosystem of scientific communication.

Of this system, Eli Chernin has said:

Drastic tampering with the scientific ecosystem invites unknown hazards. We don't know how the whole enterprise either creates change or adapts to it. If we are to improve an evolving man-made ecosystem that is beset with uncertainty, we would well be advised to strengthen what we can and take

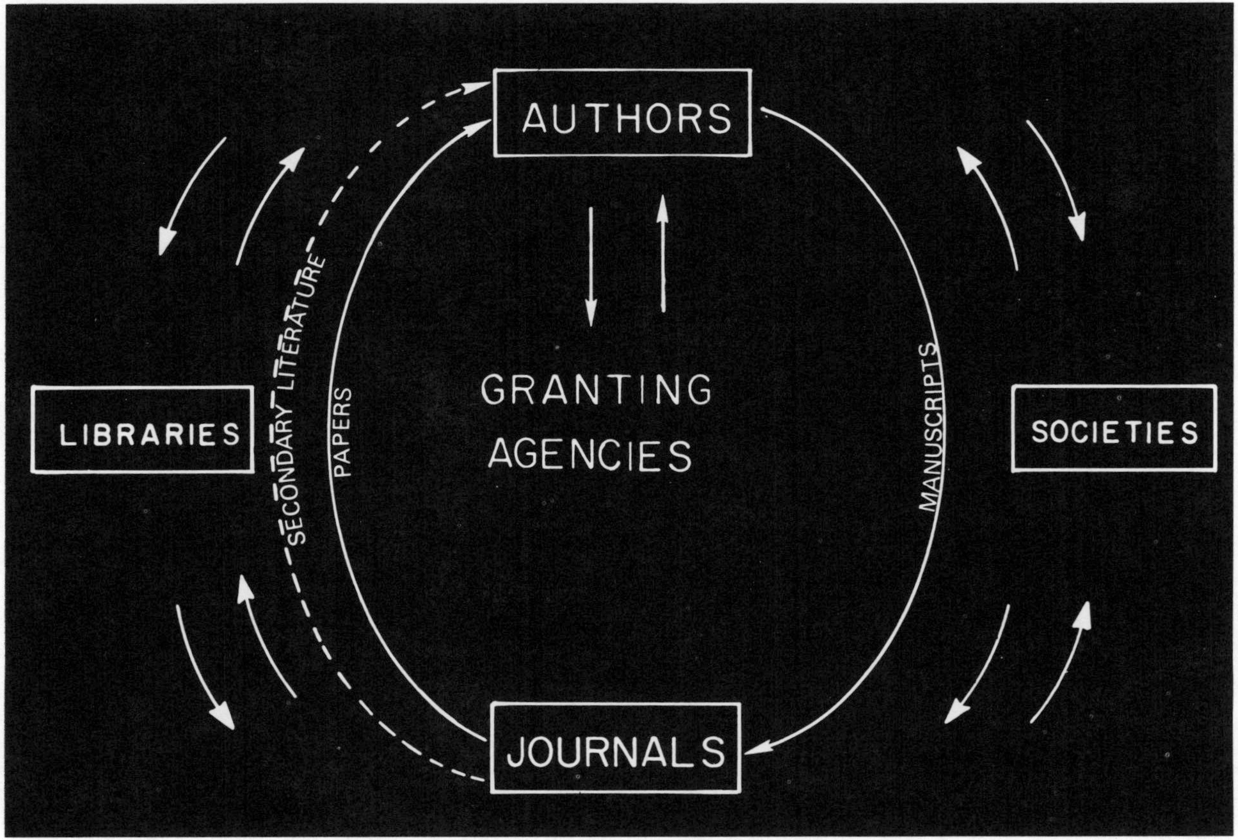

FIGURE 3.1 The Ecosystem of Scientific Communication

pains not to destroy the food chain of journals that has nourished science for three centuries. On the other hand, some of the stuff that flows through journals represent unprocessed sewage that clogs the mind it is meant to enrich; eutrophication can smother scientists just as it does aquatic life.[5]

How to eliminate the sewage without drastically altering the ecology constitutes a major problem. Drastic changes in the environment could affect the communication system in several ways. First, reduction in training funds for a given field could lead to a significant reduction of potential contributors to the field and so upset the balance needed to maintain the recurring up-surges of interest that characterize scientific activity. Second, reduction of research funds for a given field could result in a substantial decrease in active contributors to that field that could lead to eradication of activity. Because the system is cyclic (see Figure 3.1), reduction of journals in significant numbers could lead to similar results. Third, changes in library policies, publication policies, editorial policies, and so forth, could also disrupt the entire system. On the other hand, changes at various points in the ecosystem could be beneficial.

Note from Figure 3.1 that embedded in the communication cycle are a series of information-retrieval processes. The most prominent ones are

Between funding agencies and researchers (who eventually become authors and readers), through which the funding agency must select from among the file of submitted proposals those of sufficient relevance and quality to warrant support

Between authors and journals, through which the journal editor must select from among all submitted manuscripts those of sufficient relevance and quality to warrant publication

Between readers (many of whom are also authors) and journals, through which the reader must select from among the vast number of journals those of sufficient relevance and quality to peruse

Between readers and papers, through which the reader must select from among the published articles those of sufficient relevance and quality to read

Between libraries (information-retrieval systems) and journals, through which the library must select from among periodicals those of sufficient relevance and quality to warrant subscription

One might thus describe the ecosystem of scientific communication as a collection of interacting information-retrieval processes. It is these informa-tion-retrieval processes that constitute the strategic points in the cycle. Consequently, a primary resource for dealing with the expanding scientific and biomedical literature (thereby helping to preserve the ecosystem) is effective and efficient information retrieval.

INFORMATION RETRIEVAL

A major research and development effort to achieve the goal of efficient information retrieval was launched over a quarter of a century ago. The origin of this effort in the United States is generally credited to Vannever Bush, science advisor to the president, who warned of a coming crisis in scientific communication in a 1945 *Atlantic Monthly* article.[6] Since that time, there has been a great deal of activity aimed at producing large-scale, mechanized information-retrieval systems, which, it was believed, would solve the problem of managing the vast amounts of scientific and biomedical literature.

Due to the rapid advances in computer and communications technology in the last decade or so, large-scale, mechanized information-retrieval systems have been developed at a remarkable rate. It has been estimated that there are, as of early 1980, over 500 publicly available bibliographic data bases, containing more than 70 million citations, spanning almost every scientific subject area, the majority of which can be searched on-line.[7]

In the biomedical field, the most notable among these are the Medical Literature Analysis and Retrieval System (MEDLARS) of the National Library of Medicine, which stores the contents of over 3,000 biomedical journals, and the *Science Citation Index* (*SCI*) produced by the Institute of Scientific Information, which lists all references to papers published in a selected set of about 2,500 scientific journals, including about 1,000 of the most prominent biomedical periodicals.

Technology has thus been successfully applied to gathering vast amounts of bibliographic material into computerized information-retrieval systems. The question is, however, have these remarkable technological achievements led to the hoped for solution to the problem of managing the ever-increasing scientific and biomedical literature? Although conclusive evidence pro or con is unavailable, judging from the continued disaffection with the literature by many prominent scientists, the answer would seem to be negative. For example, writing in 1978, Lewis Thomas was of the opinion that the literature is too vast to comprehend, so that communication among scientists, as well as between scientists and the public, has become a serious problem.[8] A team of National Library of Medicine researchers in April of 1980 expressed the view that, despite the speed and flexibility of automated retrieval systems, their impact on the scientific community has been lessened by, among other things, the uneven utility of the product, namely the system's output.[7]

Why has a major research and development effort in the information-retrieval field resulted in systems whose utility has been seriously questioned? This seems to be due to two fundamental problems of information retrieval that have not yet been operationally solved but upon which the utility of the output depends. These are the relevance problem and the quality problem.

UTILITY

The fundamental importance of utility in the process of acquiring knowledge was well stated almost a century ago by the renowned fictional detective Sherlock Holmes. In responding to Watson's astonishment that Holmes knew nothing of the solar system, Holmes said:

> "I consider that a man's brain originally is like a little empty attic, and you have to stock it with such furniture as you choose. A fool takes in all the lumber of every sort that he comes across, so that the knowledge which might be useful to him gets crowded out, or at best is jumbled up with a lot of other things, so that he has difficulty in laying his hands on it. Now the skillful workman is very careful indeed as to what he takes into his brain-attic. He will have nothing but the tools which may help him in doing his work, but of these he has a large assortment, and all in the most perfect working order. It is a mistake to think that that little room has elastic walls and can distend to any extent. Depend upon it there comes a time when for every addition of knowledge you forget something that you knew before. It is of the highest importance, therefore, not to have useless facts elbowing out useful ones."
>
> "But the Solar System!" I [Watson] protested.
>
> "What the deuce is it to me?" he [Holmes] interrupted impatiently: "You say that we go around the sun. If we went around the moon it would not make a pennyworth of difference to me or to my work" (A. Conan Doyle, *A Study in Scarlet*, 1893).

The notion of utility, however, implies two even more fundamental notions, namely relevance and quality; that is, the utility of a piece of information depends upon it being of sufficient relevance and of sufficient quality to render it useful to its recipient. Thus, relevant information of low quality would not be too useful, nor would irrelevant knowledge, regardless of its quality.

However, both relevance and quality are vague concepts that cannot be precisely defined. Thus, to program a computing machine to separate contributions of quality that are relevant to the user's inquiry from the vast and continually expanding universe of scientific literature is a formidable task that operating systems have not yet been able to effectively manage.

The Relevance Problem

In most operating retrieval systems, such as MEDLARS, relevance is established in terms of a semantic relationship between articles in the system's file and the user's query. Specifically, the informational content of each article is represented by a set of index terms or descriptors as is each query directed to the file. Relevant articles are identified by matching the index terms of the query with those assigned to each article in the file. Those items for which there is a match are retrieved as relevant to the query. This generally is done by means of the so-called Boolean search strategy.

The Boolean strategy derives its name from the fact that queries are represented by logical statements of descriptors and answers by sets of articles. Both the algebra of statements and the algebra of sets are special cases of a more general algebra called a Boolean algebra.[9] Because the algebra of statements and the algebra of sets have similar structures, to every unique query there corresponds a unique set of articles, its answer. This works in the following way. In the algebra of statements, new statements can be formed from other statements by means of three basic connectives: conjunction, disjunction, or negation. Given two statements A and B, then the statement "A conjunction B" is roughly a logical translation of the English statement "A and B"; the statement "A disjunction B" is roughly a logical translation of the English statement "A or B"; and the statement "negation A" is roughly a logical translation of the English statement "not A." Similarly, in the algebra of sets, new sets can be formed from other sets by means of three basic operations: intersection, union, and complement. Given two sets X and Y, the set "X intersection Y" is the set containing all elements that belong to both set X and set Y; the set "X union Y" is the set of all elements that belong either to the set X or to the set Y; and the complement of X is the set of all elements not belonging to the set X.

In terms of information retrieval, if a query is represented by a conjunction of two descriptors, then the answer will be the set of all articles in the file to which both descriptors have been assigned. This set is identical with the set of articles formed by taking the intersection of the set of articles to which one of descriptors has been assigned with the set of articles to which the other descriptor has been assigned. If a query is represented by the disjunction of two descriptors, then the answer will be the set of all articles in the file to which either of the two descriptors has been assigned. This set is identical to the set of articles formed by taking the union of the set of articles to which one of the descriptors has been assigned with the set of articles to which the other descriptor has been assigned. If the query is represented by the negation of a descriptor, then the answer will consist of all articles in the file to which that descriptor was not assigned, in other words, the complement of the set of articles to which the descriptor was assigned.

Clearly, queries can be represented by very complex combinations of conjunctions, disjunctions, and negations. In all cases, however, there will exist a unique subset of articles in the file corresponding to the query. This set is formed by taking intersections of sets of articles corresponding to the conjuncts of the query; unions of sets corresponding to the disjuncts in the query; and complements of sets corresponding to the negations in the query. Thus, an article must contain the same logical configuration of descriptors as the query to be judged relevant. This argument is based on the assumption that, if an article exhibits semantic characteristics similar to those of the query, the article is therefore relevant to the query.

John Bruer has suggested that relevance established in this way might more aptly be called semantic relevance and that, furthermore, the relationship between semantic relevance and relevance is not known. There are several, quite evident defects in the semantic approach to information retrieval. First, since indexing is generally done by humans, descriptors tend to be inconsistently assigned. Second, descriptors assigned to a given article are generally given equal weight of importance. This is also true of descriptors in the query. Third, the richness of natural language results in the use of a variety of different terms to describe the same concept. This is the so-called synonym problem. As a consequence of the above, spurious material is often retrieved, whereas relevant material may be overlooked.

There are, furthermore, serious deficiencies in the Boolean strategy itself that are independent of the semantic relationship between the query and the articles in the file.

In the first place, the Boolean strategy is very strict, demanding that each relevant article contain all terms of the query in the same logical configuration. This is a severe demand, for the addition or deletion of a single term to the query could lead to a substantial change in the output. If the query, for example, is expressed as a conjunction of n terms, then adding an $n+1$ term can result in a sizable reduction in the output if the set of articles to which all of the $n+1$ terms have been assigned is very small compared to the set of articles to which only the first n terms have been assigned. On the other hand, deleting a term from the query may considerably increase the size of the output. This will occur if the remaining $n-1$ terms have been assigned to a large number of articles to which the deleted term has not been assigned. If the query is expressed as a disjunction of n terms, then the addition or deletion of a single term could lead to the reverse effect. The addition of an $n+1$ term to the query could lead to a sizable increase in the output, namely, by the addition of all articles having the $n+1$ term but none of the others. The deletion of the term could result in a substantial decrease in the output, namely, the loss of all articles to which the deleted term was assigned but none of the others. Thus, a slight alteration in the input could result in a considerable change in the output.

Here we are faced with one of the fundamental principles of information retrieval, namely, that recall (ratio of relevant items retrieved to relevant items in the file) is inversely related to precision (ratio of relevant items retrieved to the number of items retrieved). Consequently, an alteration in the query aimed at increasing the recall (broadening the search) will lead to the retrieval of more spurious material, whereas narrowing the search so as to increase the precision will result in the loss of relevant material. Because of the nature of the Boolean search strategy, such changes are likely to be substantial.

Second, the Boolean search strategy treats the relevance of each article in the file to a given query as being totally independent of the other articles in the file. In other words, relevance judgments are made strictly on the basis of the relationship between each individual article and the query. Experience, however, tells us that the relevance of a given article may clearly depend upon other articles. For example, an article might appear to be not relevant to a query when judged against the query but might become highly relevant in concert with other relevant articles. On the other hand, an article may appear to be relevant when judged against the query but become irrelevant in conjunction with other relevant material. In other words, the notion that relevance depends on what is known by the inquirer is ignored in the Boolean search strategy.

Although most operating information-retrieval systems are based on semantic relevance judgments, there is one outstanding exception, namely, the *SCI*. In the simplest case, the user enters the system with a known article, and the output will be all articles in the file that have cited the given article. This output constitutes the set of known articles relevant to the query as represented by the input article. The argument here is that, if an article M cites an article N, the author of M has judged the material in N to be relevant to the work he is reporting in M. This argument for relevance would appear to be much stronger than the semantic one, since the act of citation is strong evidence in support of the utility of the cited paper to the author of the citing article. Bruer has therefore suggested that this relation be called pragmatic relevance. As in the case of semantic relevance, the relationship between pragmatic relevance and relevance is unknown—as is, moreover, the relationship between pragmatic and semantic relevance.

Complex queries can be formulated in the pragmatic case by constructing Boolean functions of articles instead of descriptors, as is done in the semantic systems. For example, if a query is expressed as a conjunction of two articles, then the output would be the set of all articles in the file that have cited both articles. On the other hand, if the query is expressed as a disjunction of two articles, the output will contain all articles that have cited either of the articles in the input statement.

Although the pragmatic relevance relation has much to support it, there are clearly some problems with this approach. To begin with, since the query must be formulated in terms or articles, one cannot readily search on a subject or concept as in the semantic case. Because articles generally deal with a variety of concepts, a search, in some cases, may tend to be too broad, thus drawing in much irrelevant material. In other cases, a search may be too narrow, since it is demanded that relevant articles cite the input articles, which may have been missed by a number of relevant papers for a variety of reasons. Consequently, much relevant material may be lost. Moreover, if the query is in the form of a conjunction, one can only retrieve articles more recent than the most recent article in the input statement. If the query is in the form of a disjunction, one can only retrieve articles more recent than the least recent paper in the input statement. Finally, one is still committed to the Boolean search strategy with all of its inherent defects.

The Quality Problem

The physical problems of coping with the literature are so vast that attention has been focused on the quantitative aspects of information retrieval rather than on the qualitative aspects. Almost all large-scale retrieval systems are quantity based in that they treat all of the literature stored in their vast files as equal in quality. Thus, they seem to be more concerned with the input side of the system than with the output. By storing large quantities of material, they want to be sure that all useful material is captured in their files. On the other hand, there has been little attempt to select from among these files the material that is of the highest quality at the output stage in response to users' queries.

However, it seems clear from Chapters 1 and 2 that, although the size of the literature continues to increase, only a small portion of it appears to be of significant value. The question arises as to whether the scientific and biomedical literature has been evolving in the direction of the dinosaur, becoming ever larger in size but smaller in brain. Is the rapid growth of the literature leading to its own extinction? This is rendered the more likely since the growth of the literature has been likened to the spread of an infectious disease. This pejorative conceptualization of the literature has led to the natural attempt to apply curative and preventive medicine. In his book *Crisis in Communication*, Sir Theodore Fox, former editor of the *Lancet*, speaks to this point.

> Anyone with a proper sense of medical priorities will turn first to prevention. If we blindly pin our faith on more journals, better indexes, and cleverer librarians, are we not encouraging authors to produce more papers? When other forms of reproduction are excessive, we prefer if possible to stop them at the source—by some form of contraception. But how can we stop the production of scientific literature?[10]

THE QUANTITY-QUALITY DILEMMA

Herein lies the quantity-quality dilemma. Is it not possible that, if we cure the infectives (authors), prevent the susceptibles (potential authors) from being infected, and eliminate large numbers of intermediate hosts (journals), we may in the process significantly reduce the amount of literature of quality? Or might we decrease the opportunity of the brilliant individual in an unusual locality to communicate or smother the brilliant idea that is not accepted in its time? If we say that only those papers of the highest quality should be published, then how will the selection be made and by whom? No one is yet endowed with the insight to select a priori only those papers that will prove to have lasting value. Is there a way out of this dilemma?

QUALITY FILTERS

A reasonable approach to the quantity-quality dilemma may be the introduction of "quality filters" at various strategic points in the ecosystem.[11] These filters would act as qualitative points of entry into the literature by a posteriori selection of authors, journals, and papers of quality. At the same time, no tampering with the overall system is advocated, so that the user would have access to the entire literature if desired.

Clearly, the information-retrieval processes embedded in the ecosystem of scientific communication constitute the strategic points in the cycle at which quality-filtering mechanisms should be placed. It may be argued, however, that such filters already exist, for example, the review process of funding agencies, the refereeing process of journals, and the acquisition policies of libraries. Judging from the continual criticism of these mechanisms, it would seem that they have not been too effective. For example, J. H. Comroe and R. D. Dripps reported in 1976 on a project aimed at demonstrating that "objective scientific techniques instead of the present anecdotal approach can be used to design and to justify a national biomedical policy."[12] They proposed that data from objective studies be applied to all aspects of scientific research for the purpose of establishing funding policy on a systematic basis.

The effectiveness of the conventional refereeing system employed by most reputable journals, which determines when and where an author may publish, has been constantly under attack (see Chapter 5), and library acquisition policies do not seem to have been too effective, if utility is taken as a criterion for effectiveness (see Chapter 2). Library acquisition policies, like funding policies, tend to be more anecdotal than systematic. It is therefore essential that the present quality-filtering mechanisms be strengthened by basing them on data, rather than instinct, as is often the case at the present time.

It is also essential that new filters be introduced, particularly in the output phase of the information-retrieval process. In the input phase, filtering already takes place. For example, the National Library of Medicine employs a panel of user-experts that meets periodically to decide which journals should be included in the Medical Literature Analysis and Retrieval System (MEDLARS). As a result, the total biomedical population of 20,000 journals is reduced to about 3,000. Nevertheless, the size of the remaining literature is overwhelming. For example, for the six tropical diseases designated by the World Health Organization as among the most important health problems facing humanity (filariasis, leishmaniasis, leprosy, malaria, schistosomiasis, and trypanosomiasis), there were more than 13,000 citations listed in MEDLARS for the ten-year period 1966–75. Since these are diseases that have been relatively neglected, the numbers for less neglected diseases are considerably more impressive. For example, a MEDLARS search over the last ten years revealed 16,000 citations on viral hepatitis in the English language.[13] (See Chapter 2.) These data suggest that further filtering is needed, particularly in the output phase.

In the case of MEDLARS, an additional filter would be provided by an evaluation of the MEDLARS files by a panel of experts. That such an exercise would yield a significant reduction in the size of the literature is supported by two major studies in which this method was employed.

Kenneth Warren published a bibliography of the world's literature on schistosomiasis covering the period 1852–62 that consisted of close to 10,000 journal articles.[14] This bibliography was evaluated for quality by a panel of 47 experts chosen by the World Health Organization.[15] (See Chapter 2.) The results of the evaluation revealed that only about 3,200 articles, or about one-third of the total, were selected by at least one expert and that only 50 percent of these were selected at least twice. Thus, only 15 percent of the total literature was selected for quality by at least two experts. Warren subsequently published an updated bibliography covering the period 1963–75 that consisted of about 4,000 citations,[16] as well as a selected literature for that period chosen by a panel of 25 experts in 37 research areas.[17] The resulting collection of selected literature contained about 10 percent of the total.

Comroe and Dripps, in analyzing how and why lifesaving advances came about for cardiovascular and pulmonary diseases, filtered an initial collection of 4,000 articles to 529, or about 13 percent of the total, that they and a panel of 140 experts considered essential.[12]

However, there are obvious drawbacks to filtering the literature by panels of experts that would seem to render this approach impractical. First, the procedure takes a great deal of time to carry out. For example, the Comroe–Dripps study took nearly ten years to complete. Second, it is very difficult to get the extremely busy experts to devote the necessary time to perform the task. Third, and most importantly, the size of the literature makes the task almost physically impossible. Assessing the hundreds of thousands of articles in the MEDLARS files is of an entirely different order of magnitude than selecting 3,000 journals from among the 20,000 published. Fortunately, there exist two characteristics of the biomedical literature that allow for an *implicit* assessment by user-experts. These are the listing of references at the end of each article and the periodic publication of review articles on the state of the art.

Eugene Garfield has stated:

> Authors refer to previous material to support, illustrate, or elaborate on a particular point, so that the act of citing is, in general, an expression of the "importance" of the material cited. It appears that the number of times a given journal has been cited is an objective indicator of the quality of the journal. Thus, a useful tool to aid in journal selection and evaluation is a statistical report on the frequency of citation.[18]

This argument might equally apply to authors and papers. If we accept it, then the act of citation is not only an indicator of relevance but also an indicator of quality. When we consider that an estimated 25 to 50 percent of scientific papers published are never cited even once,[19] citation analysis can constitute a substantial filter of the scientific and biomedical literature. However, citation analysis of an entire field would require the collection of the entire literature of that field, from which the citation frequencies would then have to be computed. In the case of the six tropical diseases mentioned above, this means that over 13,000 articles would have to be analyzed just for 1966–75, and this only includes articles published in the 3,000 journals in the MEDLARS data base. Moreover, although citation frequency may imply a user consensus of the importance of an article, it does not necessarily imply an expert consensus, since every citation is treated as equal. In other words, citation by a poor paper or mediocre investigator counts as much as citation by a good paper or a Nobel laureate.

The use of review articles as an intermediary filter would seem to be a reasonable approach to this problem. Since reviews are produced by experts in a given field, by analyzing the citations in all reviews for a fixed period of time, one should, in principle, arrive at a quality assessment of the literature of that field as viewed at that period of time in the selection process. Moreover, computing the frequency of citation by review articles of a given field would require the analysis of many fewer articles than would computing the frequency of citation from the literature at large. For the six tropical diseases, for example, only 134 review articles were listed in the bibliography of reviews of the *Index Medicus* from 1966–75. Consequently, 134 rather than 13,000 articles would have to be analyzed. In fact, there were approximately 4,000 unique articles published from 1966–75 that were cited by the 134 review articles or about 30 percent of the total number of citations listed in MEDLARS for the same time period. Of these 4,000 articles, about one-third, or 10 percent of the total listed in MEDLARS, were cited by at least two review articles.

It should be noted that review articles themselves, however, are of unequal quality. The review article worth reading, according to David Sackett, is one that sets down rules of evidence before it summarizes and synthesizes an area of knowledge. Moreover, expertise in a subject area carries no guarantee of competency in methodology or in critical assessment of evidence. Thus, review articles constitute another existing quality filter that is in need of strengthening and systematizing.

Since review articles are an integral part of the communication system for the biomedical sciences (both MEDLARS and *SCI* identify review articles in their data banks), they constitute a relatively simple, though flawed, device for identifying authors, journals, and papers of quality for any given field. It would thus be possible to develop quality-based subsystems for rapid access to the quality literature and insert them at the strategic points in the ecosystem of scientific communication. Such systems could be easily kept current, would become more reliable as the quality of the review articles improved, and, most importantly, would depend on the existence of the presently used, more comprehensive systems, such as MEDLARS and *SCI*, from which they would evolve. In all likelihood, the quality-filtered author files would be of most interest to the funding agencies; the quality-filtered journal files, to conventional libraries; and the quality-filtered paper files, to operators of large, mechanized information-retrieval systems. These files could be searched in the conventional way on any topic or subtopic in order to identify either authors, journals, or papers of quality.

Here, however, we are again faced with the deficiencies of the Boolean search strategy and the semantic–pragmatic relevance problem. As to the latter, a reasonable approach may be to use both. For example, one might initially search for semantic relevance for the purpose of identifying a relevant article or set of articles. Once this is achieved, one could carry out a pragmatic search to identify those articles that have cited or are cited by the initial relevant set. One could then repeat this process by using semantic relevance to filter out spurious material from the newly obtained set of citations, identify the articles citing or cited by the remaining relevant ones, and so forth. In this way, one should arrive at a highly selected set of quality articles that are both semantically and pragmatically relevant to the user's inquiry. Moreover, methods have been developed that generalize the Boolean strategy into one in which its major defects are corrected. However, although these methods appear in the literature, they have not yet been operationally applied.[20]

Recently, the National Library of Medicine has developed the newest form of automated information retrieval, which they call a knowledge base. A prototype of this system is the hepatitis knowledge base, in which knowledge pertaining to viral hepatitis is synthesized from review articles by experts in the field. The library is also experimenting with an English-language inter-face to its various data bases.[7] This points to systems of the future in which queries are posed in the natural language and answers are, not bibliographic citations, but facts or data drawn from the literature.

Meanwhile, what do scientists do while waiting for these new systems to emerge? They heed the words of Sherlock Holmes by not overcrowding their "brain-attics" with useless information and by identifying a small set of journals selected for relevance and quality and regularly perusing them. This may be the best way for a scientist to maintain a reasonable level of current awareness in a rapidly developing field of research. At the same time, if necessary, the scientist can always fan out through review articles and other secondary sources and eventually through the great archival data banks to encompass more of the literature. Thus, quality filters act only as a qualitative point of entry to the literature. Access to the total literature would be preserved through the large archival systems, such as the National Library of Medicine. In this way, effectiveness and efficiency of information retrieval would be enhanced without interfering with the ecosystem of scientific communication that has so greatly contributed to the advancement of science.

To call for quality filtering of the literature, it should be noted, is, not to advocate a new, revolutionary, or unconventional notion, but to simply ask that an already existing process be carried further and that this be done in a systematic way.

In conclusion, it must be pointed out that effective communication ultimately depends on how closely the interpretation of information by its receiver compares with the meaning intended by its sender.[21] It is therefore critically important that authors write their manuscripts so that they can be understood by their potential readers and that readers know how to read a scientific paper. These topics will be discussed in detail elsewhere in this volume.

REFERENCES

1. Warren, K. S., and Goffman, W. 1972. The ecology of medical literature. Am. J. Med. Sci. 263(4):267–73.
2. Goffman, W. 1966. Mathematical approach to the spread of scientific ideas. Nature 212:449–52.
3. Ziman, J. M. 1980. The proliferation of scientific literature: A natural process. Science 208:369–371.
4. Goffman, W., and Warren, K. S. 1980. Scientific Information Systems and the Principle of Selectivity. New York: Praeger.
5. Chernin, E. 1975. A worm's-eye view of biomedical journals. Proc. Fed. Am. Soc. Exp. Biol. 34(2):124–30.
6. Bush, V. 1945. As we may think. Atlantic Monthly 176(1):101–8.
7. Doszkocs, T. E.; Rapp, B. A.; and Schoolman, H. M. 1980. Automated information retrieval in science and technology. Science 208:25–30.

8. Thomas, L. 1978. Hubris in science? Science 200:1459–62.
9. Dwinger, P. 1961. Introduction to Boolean Algebras. Wurzburg: Physica-Verlag.
10. Fox, T. 1965. Crisis in Communication: The Functions and Future of Medical Journals. London: Athlone Press.
11. Ezioni, A. 1971. The need for quality filters in information systems. Science. 171:133.
12. Comroe, J. H., and Dripps, R. D. 1976. Scientific basis for support of biomedical science. Science 192:105–11.
13. Bernstein, L. M. 1980. The hepatitis knowledge base. In Research in Biomedical Communications: The Problem of Selectivity. New York: Rockefeller Foundation.
14. Warren, K. S., and Newill, V. A. 1967. Schistosomiasis:Bibliography of the World's Literature from 1852 to 1962. Cleveland, Ohio: Western Reserve University.
15. Warren, K. S. 1973. Schistosomiasis: The Evolution of a Medical Literature, Selected Abstracts and Citations, 1852–1962. Cambridge, Mass.: M.I.T. Press.
16. Warren, K. S., and Hoffman, D. B. 1976. Schistosomiasis III: Abstracts of the Complete Literature, 1963–1974. Washington, D.C.: Hemisphere.
17. Hoffman, D. B., and Warren, K. S. 1978. Schistosomiasis IV: Condensations of the Selected Literature, 1963–1975. Washington, D.C.: Hemisphere.
18. Garfield, E. 1972. Citation analysis as a tool in journal evaluation. Science 178:471–79.
19. Garfield, E. 1978. The science citation index as a quality information filter. In Coping with the Biomedical Literature Explosion: A Qualitative Approach, edited by K. S. Warren and W. Goffman. New York: Rockefeller Foundation.
20. Goffman, W. 1969. An indirect method for information retrieval. Information Storage and Retrieval 4:361–79.
21. Weaver, W. 1963. Recent contributions to the mathematical theory of communication. In The Mathematical Theory of Communication, edited by C. E. Shannon and W. Weaver. Urbana, Ill.: University of Illinois Press.

PART II
PRODUCING BIOMEDICAL INFORMATION

4

FIRST, DO NO HARM

Eli Chernin

In starting this chapter on biomedical writing, I have already sinned: the title tells neither people nor computers what to expect. This is a serious matter, for an uninformative title deters or misleads the reader. Furthermore, "A good title," according to Samuel Butler, "should aim at making what follows as far as possible superfluous to those who know anything of the subject." Alas, had I obeyed Butler's dictum, this piece just begun would now be ending.

Well, what does that odd title connote? The ancient aphorism *Primum non nocere* enjoins physicians from harming their patients. So much for that. But what of physicians and scientists who harm by writing unintelligible papers laced with literary soporifics and barbarisms? For these writers (who are legion), "First, do no harm" is honored only in the breach. Indeed, most of them overlook another worthy aphorism: "He who relieves pain is blessed, but he that causes none is doubly so."

Editors are notoriously prone to pain, and they claim that the only effective analgesics are good articles. And what, pray, is a good article? Stephen Lock, editor of the *British Medical Journal*, says that such an article has a "definite structure, makes its point, and then shuts up."[1] Exactly so. Now try it.

Good writing reflects good biomedical work, and the writer's capacity to think logically is the sine qua non of the writing process. Bad writing, of course, casts its own uncomplimentary shadow upon the author. Lest you

This work was supported, in part, by a Research Career Award from the National Institutes of Health. I thank my colleagues for fruitful discussions.

think that only editors attach importance to clear writing, a recent series of videotaped interviews, entitled "Leaders in American Medicine," has revealed how often notable physicians emphasize good technical writing and insist that their junior colleagues master the craft.

Impoverished thinking and pedantry plague biomedical writing. Since I am not optimistic that presenting another discourse on "how to write a paper" will prove original, reform any sinners, or suffice to instruct beginners, I will not remap that territory. Surely, enough rules have been published to satisfy anyone's writing needs.[2-9]

Rather than describe the mechanics of writing a paper, therefore, I will proffer brief comments on common problems, big and small, of writing and publication. I do not apologize for being opinionated because, after all, editors and teachers are paid to have opinions. Moreover, if some of my opinions seem familiar, I make no excuses either, for, as an eminent physician-teacher once told me, the essence of good medical pedagogy is to say something familiar. These half-serious disclaimers aside, one cannot escape feeling diffident about discussing something as personal and sensitive as writing. My more cynical colleagues caution that trying to improve people's writing is probably naive and about as futile as trying to nail jelly to a wall.

WHY BOTHER?

What are the purposes of publication? Making money is not one of them, but staying employed is.

Socrates once said of the market, "How many things there are here that I do not want," a remark that applies equally well to the printed offerings of biomedicine. In the first scientific journal, the *Philosophical Transactions* of the Royal Society (1665), the founding editorial offered these comments (which most would endorse today): that nothing is more necessary for improving philosophical matters than communication and that it is therefore fit to employ the press so that those "addicted to and conversant in such matters, may be invited and encouraged to...find out new things, [and] impart their knowledge to one another...."

Those "addicted and conversant" have employed the press so liberally as to choke printed communication. In desperation, one journal editor (the story goes) changed the final question on the reviewer's form sheet from "Is there any reason why this paper should not be published?" to "Is there any reason why this paper *should* be published?" The number of recommendations for acceptance plummeted. There are other ways to dissuade excessive publication. But overpublication can hardly be remedied when the academic community encourages the worst excesses.

Now living in a world hardly envisaged by the founders of *Transactions*, we are still fumbling with the concept of "communication" and with our new printing and electronic toys. But do we still abide by the precept that scientific work is incomplete until published? And is it all worth "communicating"? Aye, there is the rub. I say no, and therefore must note some of the issues that maintain tension among medical scientists, their journals, and the need or urge to publish. For example, authors may achieve fame by papers that establish the "priority" on which reputations are built. Yet more: the same publications and reputations are parlayed into promotions, tenure, professional offices, awards, symposia, and, of course, more and bigger grants, the very stuff of empire. Need I add how gratifying it is to see one's name and work in print? As lovingly as Midas do we add each new reference to our publication list, the tail that wags the curriculum vitae. Checking on your own citation frequency can also be an instructive pastime, especially if you suspect your competitors of peeking too. Finally, somewhat like the medieval seigneur, whose prerogative it was to spend the marriage night with each new bride in his domain, many department heads or chiefs of service feel entitled to add their names to all papers from their fiefdom, whether deserved or not.

Despite the pressures, or because of them, some working scientists publish little or nothing, perhaps from sloth, phobia, or revulsion to writing. The thought of finding their names irrevocably before the public, the goal sought by most others, seems to frighten some scientists, much as the sick frighten some physicians. Perhaps we should be grateful that they do not clutter the literature, but are they scientists? Still other special circumstances abound. For instance, in the developing countries, the publish-perish syndrome may have the same rationale as elsewhere, but those who publish consistently may also be digging escape tunnels to Geneva or Boston. Westerners are just as culpable. Which of us can resist preparing an invited paper for a symposium in Tokyo or London, all travel expenses paid, or preparing a chapter in a book (*this* book) in which one participates with distinguished colleagues?

So we publish for many reasons, some admirable. More papers, however, do not necessarily make for better or critical science. And, as I have said, it is worrisome when irrelevancies, such as speed of publication, are cherished beyond sound or effective scholarship.[10]

THISTLES IN THE UNDERBRUSH

I plan to touch on several general, but rarely discussed, aspects of biomedical writing as a prelude to other problems of exposition.

J. M. Ziman argues brilliantly that the scientific paper is fragmentary, derivative, and edited or censored into "a cunningly contrived piece of rhetoric... [which] must persuade the reader of the veracity of the observer, his disinterestedness, his logical infallibility, and the complete necessity of his conclusions."[11] A paper is, in fact, "an idealized report of an idealized sequence of events and ideas that were chosen afterward out of the mishmash of the reality of the experiment and theory."[12] Ziman is a tough-minded, but accurate, analyst. Papers are indeed more idealized, stereotyped, and inaccurate than most physicians and scientists realize or would care to admit publicly.

Does any of this reflect on the psychological problems many encounter in writing papers? Can the compulsive scientist who conducts scrupulous experiments find himself irresolute or intellectually impotent when faced with the different mode in which he must describe them? Does that dichotomy of style and mode lie near the aching tooth of some "writing problems"? In experimental work, furthermore, the results are unknown until the experiments end, but, when writing a technical paper, you know the end before you start. That should ease the writing, one would think, but it may occasionally engender the opposite effect, and not just in novices.

I also wonder how much of the inner difficulty of writing springs from needing to conform to the peculiar demands of the conventional format and the editor while trying to "write well." This may be an irreconcilable conflict, since parts of the typical paper are perforce rigid, such as Materials and Methods, while others are more flexible, such as the Introduction or Discussion. The problem of accommodating the requisite difference in writing styles is little appreciated. In my experience, furthermore, the greater the permissible latitude of the piece, the more likely will the average writer encounter difficulty or quit in frustration. Comfortably circumscribed entities, such as the conventional scientific paper, are easier to write and less threatening than are searching book reviews or open-ended essays. Only the best thinkers should be given—or should take—enough rope.

Ziman's ideas are echoed by Joshua Lederberg. "One of the major trends of scientific writing for the past century," he says, "is the systematic falsification of the actual technique and method of discovery...." Further,

   ...in our own...scientific reports, we do not make anecdotal statements; we do not make historically correct statements; we generally do not report the experiments that didn't work. We are content in our publications...[to present] recipes for replication of the results....[T]his model of representation of scientific discovery as the neat packages in which [the reports]... are finally published... [has] a highly pernicious effect in the selection against creativity in the...granting system.[13]

To borrow from an ancient confessional, we have "sinned the sin" of falsifying our reports—historically, if not literally—and of using them to win grants and fame.

In writing grant proposals, I might add, as in writing papers, two issues override: having something to say and saying it clearly. A tediously written or confused grant application will suffer the same fate as a bad manuscript sent for publication. But then, if there are enough bad grant applications, there may be fewer bad papers.

IN SHORT

Sermons on brevity and chastity are about equally effective. Verbal promiscuity flows from poverty of language and obesity of thought, and from an unseemly haste to reach print—a premature ejaculation, as it were. A trenchant comment, made 300 years ago, epitomizes this tale. Pascal wrote to a friend apologizing for a long letter and explaining that he had not the time to write a short one.

Any scientist wishing to see his papers rejected by the best journals should submit two or three times more pages than his important new data and their interpretations require. I find it remarkable how often a 15-page manuscript, returned to the authors for condensation, soon reappears cut to five pages or even to a 500-word letter. Cutting a "final" manuscript is painful work, akin to tearing one's own flesh. Yet it is hard to sympathize with the agonies of postsubmission amputation when reasonable thought beforehand could have produced a paper of suitable length. However, better late than never. The original 15-page paper doubtless featured flatus aplenty, pumped in by authors exhibiting their diligence and wares ad infinitum. Authors may not initially grasp their failure to write to scale, but editors and reviewers spot the miscreants easily. Joseph Garland, the late editor of the *New England Journal of Medicine*, once remarked that "...what is worth setting down at all can be done twice as well in half the number of words, only it takes twice as long to do it."[14]

The nearly universal unwillingness or inability to season and shorten a paper, to rework it three or four times or more, is part of the headlong rush for publication. Publication pressure is real, no doubt, but it is not a recent phenomenon. Juvenal, in the first century, wrote in his *Satires* that "The itch for writing and making a name holds you fast as with a noose." Your Dean, who never read Juvenal, knows all about this.

Authors should take their time in writing and learn to be coldly deliberate in distinguishing the important from the junk in preparing papers.

Furthermore, long "scholarly" papers are not necessarily "worth more" than are briefer communications. Inflated manuscripts are commonly submitted out of ignorance or sloth or on the gamble that they may get past the editors. The paper, goes the reasoning, can always be cut if bounced. What a waste! If the point of writing and publishing is to diffuse information, do authors appreciate that the short paper is more likely to be read than is its loquacious cousin?

LAMBS AND ELEPHANTS

Many authors neither know nor care about their readers, except perhaps for the few working in their own narrow specialties. This disregard creates obstacles to comprehension.

A paper is already half done if you know for whom you are writing. The author who knows his intended journal and audience also knows what and how much to describe. Terms that are used often in papers published in specialized Journal X may be incomprehensible to the reader of general Journal Y. The editor of Y knows this and, if he finds a paper basically acceptable, will insist that specific matter be simplified, explained, or deleted. At all events, the author is now stuck with making the changes demanded by the editor, changes he can undertake only after the mandatory week of sulking and resentment. Then he does what he should have done months earlier. He drafts the paper for a specific audience by consciously placing himself in the position of the reader and writes to please them, not himself. As one editor advised, go sit in the chair where you read the papers of others before you write your own. And remember as you do that a journal's editors and reviewers—red in tooth and claw—will not gladly suffer a paper unsuited to their journal's audience. Some authors persist in trying to peddle papers that will serve any journal, but that is foolish, for, as it is truly writ, one cannot expect to provide water in which lambs may walk and elephants may swim.

New technical terms, borrowings, and jargon have helped create nearly unbridgeable chasms between adjacent biomedical fields. One may simply decry and avoid this Babel or even assert, with George Pickering, that its method is deception and, ultimately, self-deception.[15] (George Orwell, a master of prose, expressed precisely the same idea 15 years earlier in his classic essay "Politics and the English Language": "...bad prose...is a conscious attempt to deceive.")[16] Whatever opinion the writer adopts, an accommodation to the reader must be achieved even at the cost of "hard" writing. For his part, the writer wants to know—but cannot—whether anyone out there is listening.

EENIE, MEENIE...

Although nearly all biomedical "repository" journals are good for insomnia, they differ otherwise. Even at the risk of repetition, I think it important to expand upon some points to which I have already alluded. Thus, the journal you choose for your paper affects how you write, and it defines the audience. Since journals usually protect their own subject-turf from encroachment by "foreign" matter, you must choose wisely lest the manuscript antagonize reviewers and editors and make work for everyone, especially for the author who must revise the rejected paper to seduce another journal.[17] A rejection letter that reads, "This paper is needlessly long, and its subject does not meet the interests of this journal's readership," would probably cover 75 percent of all rejections. One frustrated author prepared a rejection slip addressed to editors, as follows: "Your rejection does not meet the requirements of the author...." Severe criticism does not sit well with some people. According to legend, the composer Max Reger sent this peevish note to a reviewer: "Dear Herr _____, I am sitting in the smallest room of my house. I have your review before me. In a moment it will be behind me."

Most journals publish a statement of purpose and scope, but these guidelines are usually uninformative. You are better off reading the journal itself to absorb its subject matter, style, and level of sophistication. Sooner or later, the journal's "personality" will emerge, reflecting the editor's talents or quirks and the journal's apparent place in the biomedical pecking order.

A journal's real or imagined prestige may loom large to an author. However, given the large pool of submissions, prestigious journals will select only a few manuscripts, rejecting 85 percent or more. Publishing the best further enhances eminence, thus providing yet another example of the proverbial "Matthew effect" ("For unto every one that hath shall be given..." [Matt. 25:29]). Poor journals weep because not enough bad papers filter down to fill the next issue, and good journals weep because too few superb papers materialize often enough. Ah, to be a "rich" journal and in need!

The author must decide whether his paper is narrowly focused and belongs in a specialty journal or whether it is interesting enough to gain acceptance in a general journal such as *Science* or *Lancet*. This choice carries some important overtones. The general journal will tend to be better known; its circulation will be large; its publication time will be comparatively short; and it is likely to appear weekly or biweekly, rather than monthly, bimonthly, or quarterly. Some scientists and physicians place a high premium on rapid, widely circulated publication in the few first-rate journals. But since most papers prove to be ephemeral, some observers—including me—look askance at this rush for publication.

RIGHT WRITING

Nearly everyone who writes for the biomedical "literature" agrees that most of the writing is bad, especially the other fellow's. Saul Radovsky explains some of this by pointing out that we write less often than in former days.[18] We dictate letters and memorandums (and papers?) and, except for making notes in charts or lab books, rarely write. In short, if we had any native gifts, or if we absorbed the slim offerings of the schools, our skills have lapsed through disuse.

The modes of prevention or rehabilitation are evident. I once wrote down the names of the best writers in my own field, quitting after the first eight because I ran low on ideas and because the list startled me. Five of the eight names belonged to physicians or scientists of the Rockefeller Foundation. You may suggest bias or point to small sample size or contend that the men had been hired only because they could write. Maybe, but the more proximate explanation for their exemplary prose is that each man was required to keep a journal. What better exercise than to write every day for an entire career! You would learn to write out of self-preservation, if nothing else, and the daily experience would soon produce the brevity and crisp style shared by my favorites. Whether any of them owned a book on writing is debatable.

I wonder whether books about writing are read when someone sits down to confront the blank pages on which a paper is to materialize. At the "blank-page" stage, I would guess, it is probably too late for books, except for a dictionary and a thesaurus. If I had to recommend one book for pleasant reading and instruction in writing and thinking, I would unhesitatingly nominate William Zinsser's *On Writing Well: An Informal Guide to Writing Nonfiction*.[9] Zinsser's purpose "is not to teach good nonfiction, or good journalism, but to teach good English that can be put to those uses." Zinsser says nothing about biomedical writing, but his book is superb for anyone striving for literary excellence.

Many have urged, and I concur, that we should encourage young physicians and scientists to start reading good *non*-professional literature, of any vintage, to help change their prose. Surely, when students, physicians, and scientists read nothing but the biomedical literature they will write as they read. In order to find pleasure in the form and precision of words, one must read widely, and this provides a long-term route to better writing. There are no short routes.

But why do all the books, articles, and short courses about writing fail to exorcise bad writing? Little of lasting consequence seems to be retained by the "targets." In teaching biomedical writing, I give few or no lectures, require no outside readings about writing, and build the work instead around the students' writing and editing their own manuscripts—in brief, a workshop. No magisterial or bookish dicta approach the value derived from workshop criticism of manuscripts.

In the best of all possible worlds, scientists would know to ask only nontrivial questions in the laboratory, seek incisive answers, write readable reports, and expect quick publication in good journals. Most of us, however, stumble at one turn or the other, and so our modest contributions swell the archival journals. The nub of the matter is that writers must have something worthwhile to say. Indeed, Plato commented that "wise men [write] because they have something to say; fools because they have to say something."

But even if you have something worth saying, a decent respect for your fellow scientists demands that you not publish the same research twice. Multiple publication or undue fragmentation of findings has been painfully common, and their cost and stultifying effects are immeasurable. "Self-plagiarism," as some call it, may swell bibliographies, but it breaks the integrity of a publication process that is overburdened already. The best journals will have no part of duplicate publication or those who perpetuate the artifice. If you do have something to say, say it well and say it once. Interestingly, outright plagiarism, just like outright fabrication of data, is rare, despite ample temptation to do otherwise. Reviewers, for example, whether evaluating grant applications or papers submitted for publication, are nearly all highly professional and scrupulously honest. It is only the uncommon breach of trust or honesty that attracts undue attention. I have been privy only to three such affairs in 30 years, a total hardly worth mentioning. We do have problems, of course, such as the unattributed quotation passed off as one's own; or the common practice of citing some well-known papers but not others that are equally good or better; or the ignorance or high-handed avoidance of copyright laws, permission to republish, and the like; or the ethics surrounding preparing or publishing of unethically conducted studies, even supposedly "valuable" ones.

EDITING AND WRITING

Although I have long taught a workshop called "Biomedical Writing," only recently have I realized that the title is inaccurate. I don't "teach writing". The students do improve their skills by writing but mainly by editing, and experience persuades me that learning to edit the work of others, and one's own, represents the most constructive way of sensitizing the writer's mind to the nuances of language and logic.

Physician-scientists who are convinced they cannot write owing to massive mental embolism can take courage from a changed perspective. If they cannot "learn to write," they can learn to edit. I would stress that, except for the rare literary talents in our midst, most of us write by repeatedly editing badly written drafts. The typical motion picture, to invoke a related example, is made by *editing* 40 or more hours of film down to about two hours and by switching and deleting sequences endlessly. The process takes six to nine months and great cost, effort, and talent. But even though the first draft of a scientific paper rightly belongs to the wastebasket, this grotesque newborn is frequently dropped—warm and quivering—into the nearest mailbox, and soon after dies.

The writing-cum-editing course, it turns out, is not a wholly novel concept, considering Garland's remark that "if editors have any function it is that of persuading authors that there is no good writing, only good re-writing.... Original writing, like tapping a maple tree, is tedious business, but the really slow work, and the hard sugar, come in the boiling down of the sap."[14] Garland's "re-writing" can be learned more readily, rapidly, and effectively than can "writing." Indeed, editing as a mode of teaching is abroad in the land. Zinsser, who taught a course at Yale in writing nonfiction, referred to it as a course in "pruning"; Nadine Gordimer, the eminent South African novelist, is convinced that one cannot teach writing but that one can teach people to edit what they write; and Theodore Morrison, former director of Bread Loaf Writers School, says flatly "that writing cannot be taught, although as a skill it can be learned."

Figure 4.1 shows part of the final manuscript of Zinsser's book *On Writing Well*. While the revisions suggest that it is a first draft, it is really about the fifth draft. The text and the editing are equally instructive, and the process exemplifies the point I have tried to make.

Authors should also think of more mundane matters in selecting a journal. For example, some journals reproduce photographs beautifully, while others do not, an important consideration for, say, a microscopist. Also, while some specialty journals limit papers to three or four pages, others are less restrictive. Also, an author may be asked to pay page charges upon publication. Some journals allow a few pages free and then charge $40 to $100 per extra page, while others charge for all pages.

If it comforts anyone, the *Index Medicus* lists about 3,000 journals. Many are less than illustrious, but at least there are plenty from which to choose. You can hardly miss.

SHORTCUTS TO NOWHERE

What would the biomedical literature be like without its frenzy of ad hoc abbreviations and acronyms (AA)? Better off!

A recent lexicon of AA, comprising some 255 double-column pages, opens with the remark that "there has been ... criticism of the increasing use of [AA] ... in medicine and the allied health professions .... We in no way condone the use of cryptic notation. However ... such shortcuts ... appear to be rapidly proliferatting. In our opinion this is merely a manifestation of the increasingly complex nature of the health professions."[19] Can it be that AA add to the complexity rather than "merely" arise from it?

AA were once so conventional as to be instantly and unmistakably identifiable, and some recent ones have also achieved that status (for example, RNA and DNA). Now we use some phrase in a paper, find we have repeated it twice more in the text, and proudly generate an unneeded abbreviation. The abbreviation is usually an evanescent creature and not a coinage others will likely adopt. But still more phrases appear to cry for abbreviation, their cries are answered, and papers become impenetrable blizzards of AA. The AA are hard to manage even when they are defined in a box at the paper's start, as in some journals, let alone when defined elusively somewhere in the text, as in most.

Why the growing craze for AA? Well, they are thought to "look scientific," everybody does it (at least in the United States), and they save space. Nonsense. Science and scientific writing are supposed to enlighten, not obfuscate, and any peculiarity that makes the reader's life tough does a disservice. Authors should know that whatever provokes the reader's yawns or annoyance may signal the paper's end. Any paper that must be broken with a code book is not one I will read gladly.

I do not think that AA save much space. I have not measured AA versus words, but I have looked hard at them and convinced myself that any supposed space saving must be vanishingly small and, in any case, insufficient to compensate for their stilted opaqueness. If you think they are space savers, I would point to the increasing number of journals that have switched from abbreviating to spelling out journal names in full in their reference lists. Abbreviated journal names, it turns out, save only a few pages per volume, and the errors and confusion they create can be monumental.[20]

AA are confusingly familiar but eminently forgettable. (Do you still remember what AA means?) To illustrate the point, I quote the following AA: VIP, rather than connoting someone famous, means variable incentive pay, vasoactive intestinal polypeptide, and venous impedance plethysmography, as the case may be; AS may refer to acetylstrophanthidin, androsterone sulfate, ankylosing spondylitis, aortic stenosis, aqueous suspension, arteriosclerosis, ascending aorta, atherosclerosis, atrial septectomy, and sickle-cell trait; and MR can stand for medical rehabilitation, medial rectus, menstrual regulation, mentally retarded, metabolic rate, methemoglobin reductase, methyl red, mitral regurgitation, modulation rate, and multicentric reticulohistocytosis.[19]

There are lots more—14,000—where those AA came from, but I still prefer to use words, not their brief symbols (BS). Any disbelievers are welcome to translate "U.S.S.S.L.L.L.A.L.A. Syndrome."[21] The author of

5 --

is too dumb or too lazy to keep pace with the ~~writer's~~ train of thought. My sympathies are ~~entirely~~ with him. ~~He's not so dumb.~~ If the reader is lost, it is generally because the writer ~~of the article~~ has not been careful enough to keep him on the ~~proper~~ path.

This carelessness can take any number of ~~different~~ forms. Perhaps a sentence is so excessively ~~long and~~ cluttered that the reader, hacking his way through ~~all~~ the verbiage, simply doesn't know what it ~~the writer~~ means. Perhaps a sentence has been so shoddily constructed that the reader could read it in any of several ~~two or three different~~ ways. ~~He thinks he knows what the writer is trying to say, but he's not sure.~~ Perhaps the writer has switched pronouns in mid-sentence, or ~~perhaps he~~ has switched tenses, so the reader loses track of who is talking ~~to whom~~ or ~~exactly~~ when the action took place. Perhaps Sentence B is not a logical sequel to Sentence A -- the writer, in whose head the connection is ~~perfectly~~ clear, has not bothered to provide ~~given enough thought to providing~~ the missing link. Perhaps the writer has used an important word incorrectly by not taking the trouble to look it up ~~and make sure.~~ He may think that "sanguine" and "sanguinary" mean the same thing, but ~~I can assure you that~~ the difference is a bloody big one ~~to the reader.~~ The reader ~~He~~ can only ~~try to~~ infer ~~what~~ (speaking of big differences) what the writer is trying to imply.

Faced with these ~~such a variety of~~ obstacles, the reader is at first a remarkably tenacious bird. He ~~tends to~~ blames himself. ~~He~~ obviously missed something, ~~he thinks,~~ and he goes back over the mystifying sentence, or over the whole paragraph,

6 --

piecing it out like an ancient rune, making guesses and moving

on. But he won't do this for long. ~~He will soon run out of patience.~~ (The writer is making him work too hard ~~-- harder than he should have to work --~~ and the reader will look for

~~a writer~~ one who is better at his craft.

The writer must therefore constantly ask himself: What am

I trying to say? ~~in this sentence?~~ (Surprisingly often, he

doesn't know.) ~~And~~ Then he must look at what he has ~~just~~

written and ask: Have I said it? Is it clear to someone

encountering ~~who is coming upon~~ the subject for the first time? If it's

not, ~~clear,~~ it is because some fuzz has worked its way into the

machinery. The clear writer is a person ~~who is~~ clear-headed

enough to see this stuff for what it is: fuzz.

I don't mean ~~to suggest~~ that some people are born

clear-headed and are therefore natural writers, whereas

others ~~other people~~ are naturally fuzzy and will ~~therefore~~ never write

well. Thinking clearly is ~~an entirely~~ conscious act that the

writer must force ~~keep forcing~~ upon himself, just as if he were

embarking ~~starting out~~ on any other ~~kind of~~ project that requires ~~calls for~~ logic:

adding up a laundry list or doing an algebra problem ~~or playing chess.~~ Good writing doesn't ~~just~~ come naturally, though most

people obviously think it does. ~~it's as easy as walking.~~ The professional

Two pages of the final manuscript of this chapter. Although they look like a first draft, they have already been rewritten and retyped—like almost every other page—four or five times. With each rewrite I try to make what I have written tighter, stronger and more precise, eliminating every element that is not doing useful work, until at last I have a clean copy for the printer. Then I go over it once more, reading it aloud, and am always amazed at how much clutter can still be profitably cut.

FIGURE 4.1. Two edited manuscript pages from Zinsser's book, *On Writing Well*. Manuscript pages produced by kind permission of the publisher and of the author, William Zinsser, from *On Writing Well: An Informal Guide to Writing Nonfiction*, 2nd ed., Harper and Row, New York, 1980.

that one claims it means the "Uncomplicated Superficial Superior Surface Lateral Left Lobe Amoebic Liver Abcess Syndrome." Perhaps so, but the string of assorted modifiers also forms one of the longest and most useless "freight trains" on record.

FUGITIVE THOUGHTS: A POTPOURRI

Discovering an unmet need, P. W. Merrill once gave advice on ways to write poorly. "To do a consistently poor job," he said, "one must grasp a few essential principles: I. Ignore the reader. II. Be verbose, vague, and pompous. III. Do not revise."[22] He might have added, "IV. Write effortlessly." In fact, the problem starts with the first experiment, not when writing begins. Well-designed experiments make for clear description, but tortured studies torture the writing and the reading. Incidentally, papers written for publication are rarely interchangeable with papers intended for oral delivery. Listen carefully at a professional meeting, and you will see why. If the differences in structure, content, and delivery of spoken and written material interest you (as they should), read the informative discussion by Roy Meadow.[23]

Some readers and writers deserve each other. The producers concoct muddy elixirs that the consumers imbibe indiscriminately. The consumers later become producers, and so the elixirs remain muddy. A favorite bit of muddy prose, a variant I call "insider" writing, is the following sentence from a book review in the *British Medical Journal*. " ... Thomas Trapham ... was a demy at Magdalen College, Oxford, from 1645 to 1658, when he was a senior collector of determining bachelors."[24] Understandable, perhaps, to some Oxonians, but to no one else; the reviewer ignored his audience. Robert Graves and Alan Hodge, in *The Reader Over Your Shoulder*, suggest that " ... whenever anyone sits down to write he should imagine a crowd of his prospective readers ... looking over his shoulder. They will be asking such questons as 'What does this sentence mean?' 'Why do you trouble to tell me that again?' ... 'Must I really read this long, limping sentence?' 'Haven't you got your ideas muddled here?'"[25] Try asking and answering these and similar questions in preparing a paper, and abjure the obtuse.

In one of William Steig's cartoons, a finger-wagging housewife lectures her dog: "I never am trying to get anything across. It ruins writing to have purposes like that." She is right. We all know colleagues whose writing is memorable only in hiding the point. They confuse words with thoughts, Samuel Johnson's phrase for a syndrome that probably appeared with the printing press.

In his "Politics and the English Language", Orwell castigates a "catalogue of swindles and perversions" that muddle writing and befuddle readers.[16] To emphasize his point, he translates a passage of good English into bad modern prose. From Ecclesiastes (9:11) comes the following:

> I returned and saw under the sun that the race is not to the swift, nor the battle to the strong, neither yet bread to the wise, nor yet riches to men of understanding, nor yet favor to men of skill, but time and chance happeneth to them all.

Compare this with Orwell's "translation" into modern language:

> Objective consideration of contemporary phenomena compels the conclusion that success or failure in competitive activities exhibits no tendency to be commensurate with innate capacity, but that a considerable element of the unpredictable must invariably be taken into account.

You may contend that Orwell's "translation" is a parody, and that no one writes that way in biomedical publications. Not so. The following real excerpt from the literature (1978) intends to say something about breast cancer. "Therefore, while the validity of a lethality process model based upon a continuous exponential growth function cannot be excluded, it remains reasonable to consider it doubtful and to consider other types of process dynamics for the course of breast cancer as likewise admissible." As Zinsser says, writers "sit down to commit an act of literature," and the author of the foregoing passage succeeded admirably. Graves and Hodge insist that good prose should be "cleared of encumbrances for quick reading: that is, without unnecessary ornament, irrelevancy, illogicality, ambiguity, repetition, circumlocution, [and] obscurity of reference." A "classical" education is not, however, a panacea, for when the classical education was common years ago, medical writing was as bad—perhaps worse—than now.[15,25]

Style in writing bothers many, especially if they think they do not have any. Style in biomedical writing, however, is prose unencumbered and unambiguous. Writing that is gussied-up with adjectives and adverbs, deadened by the passive voice, and rendered like a disjointed fugue, achieves no standard of style. Clarity, logic, brevity, and precision, the elements of scientific writing, contribute to the directness and simplicity called style. Nathaniel Hawthorne wrote that style makes "...the words disappear into the thought." I wish I had said that.

Scientific papers, while not meant to entertain, need not bore. Noel Coward admonished playwrights to "consider the public...coax it, charm it, interest it, stimulate it...but above all...never, never, never bore the living hell out of it." Wait, you say, Coward was talking about the theater, not biomedical journals. Yes, but now consider the advice given to the editorial staff of *Lancet* by no less a figure than its editor-in-chief: "Be accurate if you can; but whatever happens don't be dull." One would not have thought that the theater and our journals have so much in common.

Some thoughts, finally, in praise of editors. Editors labor over onerous decisions and run exacting operations. They occupy powerful positions and bear heavy responsibilities. They must choose articles and correspond with authors; ride herd on referees; work in consonance with their associate editors, editorial boards, and publications committees; maintain channels with news outlets; watch over ethics, circulation, business, and production; and occasionally devise new ways for their journals to lead or serve the biomedical community. Editors are also the people who separate the wheat from the chaff and frequently publish the chaff.

REFERENCES

1. Lock, S. 1976. How editors survive. Brit. Med. J. 2:1118–19.
2. Trelease, S. F. 1958. How to Write Scientific and Technical Papers. Cambridge, Mass.: M.I.T. Press.
3. Woodford, E. P., ed. 1976. Scientific Writing for Graduate Students: A Manual on the Teaching of Scientific Writing. Council of Biology Editors. New York: Rockefeller University Press.
4. Dirckx, J. H. 1977. Dx and Rx: A Physician's Guide to Medical Writing. Boston: G. K. Hall.
5. Council of Biology Editors. 1978. Council of Biology Editors Style Manual. 4th ed. American Institute of Biological Sciences.
6. O'Connor, M., and Woodford, P. 1978. Writing Scientific Papers in English. London: Pitman Medical.
7. Day, R. A. 1979. How to Write and Publish a Scientific Paper. Philadelphia: ISI Press.
8. Strunk, W., Jr., and White, E. B. 1976. The Elements of Style. 3rd ed. New York: Macmillan.
9. Zinsser, W. 1980. On Writing Well: An Informal Guide to Writing Nonfiction. 2nd ed. New York: Harper and Row.
10. Chernin, E. 1975. A worm's-eye view of biomedical journals. Fed. Proc. 34: 124–30.
11. Ziman, J. M. 1969. Information, communication, knowledge. Nature 224: 318–24.
12. Ziman, J. M. 1978. The paradoxical conventionality of the traditional scientific paper. In Coping with the Biomedical Literature Explosion: A Qualitative Approach, pp. 20–24. Working Papers. New York: Rockefeller Foundation.
13. Lederberg, J. 1979. Discussion. In Claude Bernard and the Internal Environment, edited by E. D. Robin, pp. 10, 270. New York: Marcel Dekker.
14. Garland, J. 1952. Annual oration: The New England Journal of Medicine and the Massachusetts Medical Society. N. Engl. J. Med. 246: 801–6.
15. Pickering, G. 1961. Language: The lost tool of learning in medicine and science. Lancet 2: 115–19.
16. Orwell, G. 1954. Politics and the English language. In A Collection of Essays by George Orwell, pp. 162–67. New York: Doubleday Anchor.
17. International Steering Committee. 1979. Uniform requirements for manuscripts submitted to biomedical journals. Brit. Med. J. 1: 532–35.

18. Radovsky, S. S. 1979. Medical writing: Another look. N. Engl. J. Med. 301: 131–34.
19. Roody, P.; Forman, R. E.; and Schweitzer, H. B. 1977. Medical Abbreviations and Acronyms. New York: McGraw-Hill.
20. Hart, C. W., Jr., and Ursomarso, B. 1964. Literature citation abbreviations—a waste of time. Assoc. S.E. Biol. 11: 71–73.
21. Kapoor, O. P. 1979. Amoebic Liver Abscess. S.S. Publishers, India.
22. Merrill, P. W. 1947. The principles of poor writing. Sci. Monthly 64: 72–74.
23. Meadow, R. 1969. Speaking at medical meetings. Lancet 2: 631–33.
24. Ashcroft, M. T. 1979. Tercentenary of the first English book on tropical medicine, by Thomas Trapham of Jamaica. Brit. Med. J. 2: 475–77.
25. Graves, R., and Hodge, A. 1979. The Reader over Your Shoulder. 2nd ed. New York: Vintage.
25. Blake, J. B. 1971. Literary style in American medical writing. JAMA 216:77–80.

5

JOURNALS

Arnold S. Relman

A chapter about medical journals might logically begin with a definition. For present purposes, a journal is an unbound periodical usually containing multiple articles on different subjects by different authors that is published under the general editorial supervision of an identified editor or group of editors. But that definition—or any other I might attempt—fails to include the wide variation in publications subsumed under this heading. Journals have many differing purposes and styles; they contain various kinds of material and they exhibit a broad range of quality and usefulness.

A brief taxonomic description of medical journals therefore seems in order. Let me begin by considering some of the different types of material currently published in medical journals and saying something about their purpose.

TYPES OF ARTICLES

There are, first of all, *articles that present data*. Much of this material would be called "research," in the sense that these articles describe the results of planned research studies, whether carried out in the laboratory, the clinic, or on large population groups. Also included under this heading would be retrospective clinical surveys; case reports; and behavioral, social, and economic studies of all types, many of which might not be considered "research" by most biologic scientists. It is not the experimental design, methodology, or the nature of the subject material that defines this category of article but rather the presentation of observations that are intended to add something to the recorded store of information on the subject under discussion, or possibly even to generate new knowledge never before recorded in the literature. The essential purpose here is to provide information through experimentation or observation. To achieve this purpose, presentation of data is required.

Comprising another large category are the *articles that teach*. Under this heading belong reviews of the literature and didactic articles of all types. (See Chapter 6.) These articles may deal with basic or applied biological or behavioral science, practical clinical matters, or anything in between. Their primary purpose is to improve the understanding, dissemination, and use of existing knowledge in a field, rather than to add to that knowledge.

Then there are *articles that analyze, speculate, comment, or editorialize*. They may offer new ideas or give fresh perspective, but they differ from both the "research" and the "teaching" articles described above in that they are intended mainly to express personal opinions or to clarify ideas, rather than add information or summarize what is already in the literature.

These three types are not always clearly separated. Articles often cannot be described as either "research," "teaching," or "opinion and analysis" because they may serve more than one purpose. For example, many research reports include a survey of the literature, and many review articles contain opinion or analysis. However, in almost all cases, articles can be classified by their chief purpose. They mainly add information, or they teach, or they express opinions.

This list by no means exhausts the material that medical journals may contain. Some journals have *letters to the editor*, some publish *abstracts* of papers submitted to scientific meetings, and some offer *news stories* about current events in the organization or professional field represented by the particular journal. And then there is a final, *miscellaneous* category for all the other kinds of articles that may appear in medical journals, including humor, history, book reviews, poetry, fiction, public notices, and almost anything else that might conceivably be of interest to physicians.

TYPES OF JOURNALS

One useful way to classify medical journals, therefore, is by the types of articles they publish. There is a very large group of journals that publish only articles containing data. Other journals may contain only didactic articles, reviews, or abstracts, and so on. The subject matter may include many different fields in medicine, or it may be more or less narrowly confined to a particular clinical or scientific discipline. In fact, the field of interest may be so narrow as to be limited not just to a discipline, or a subdivision thereof, but to one special topic or one technique. At the opposite end of the spectrum are the general journals, which offer virtually all types of articles on all kinds of subjects. The great majority of journals are more or less specialized in terms of subject matter and style of article. Relatively few are general in subject matter; and fewer still, general in subject and style of article.

Science and Nature are examples of the most general kind of basic-science journal, while the New England Journal of Medicine (NEJM) and the Lancet are examples of the most general kind of clinical journal. These journals do not maintain a rigid distinction between "basic-science" and "clinical" subjects. Science and, to a lesser extent, Nature occasionally publish articles about "clinical" subjects, while NEJM and Lancet will sometimes offer material on topics that might easily be classified as "basic science." Of course, Science and Nature are not simply biomedical journals; a large part of their content deals with the other natural sciences. Most of the journals that limit their content to general biomedical subjects at the basic-science level do not have the variety of article styles found in Science or Nature. They usually confine themselves to one type of format, such as research articles (for example, the Journal of Clinical Investigation and the Proceedings of the National Academy of Sciences) or abstracts (for example, Federation Proceedings). Whether at the basic-science or clinical level, however, the great majority of journals restrict their content not only to a particular field (for instance, neurophysiology, orthopedic surgery, or immunology) but to a particular kind of article ("research," review, abstract, and so forth).

Medical journals are also classifiable by their intended readership. Some journals are aimed more or less exclusively at working investigators; others are written primarily for clinical specialists; and still others orient their content toward the general physician and family practitioner. Some journals are intended to be read mostly by medical students or house officers; and others, by medical educators or hospital administrators. Some journals clearly have a very local or parochial orientation in that they are published for the members of a particular institution or professional society or represent a special geographical, religious, ethnic, or demographic perspective. Some journals take the opposite stance and direct their articles to the broadest possible national or international readership. Finally, there are those courageous journals that struggle to bridge the broadest of all schisms—those between medicine and other disciplines, such as law, economics, sociology, philosophy, and so forth.

Medical journals differ according to sponsorship and financial structure. Some are owned by nonprofit, scientific or professional societies or institutions, and their sole purpose is to facilitate the dissemination and storage of information. Many such journals carry no advertising—not necessarily because they would not like the financial help that advertising income would provide but usually because their circulation is simply too small and their readership too unpromising to attract the interest of advertisers. They meet their operating expenses either entirely through voluntary subscription revenues and page charges or through a combination of such revenues, membership dues (involuntary subscriptions), and direct subventions from their sponsoring organization. On the other hand, many other nonprofit journals can and do attract advertisers and thereby generate advertising income, sometimes enough to meet a large fraction of operating expenses.

Despite the economic perils, many private publishing businesses own and manage medical journals, and some even manage to be profitable. In fact, the majority of journals are operated as profit-making enterprises. These would include virtually all of the controlled-circulation periodicals as well as some of the better, peer-reviewed, specialty journals. Proprietary journals all carry advertising, which is usually their major source of income.

A brief further digression on the economics of journals may help to explain the preceding paragraphs as well as some of the current vagaries of the journal-publishing business. Subscription revenues can be "voluntary" or "involuntary," depending upon whether the subscriber freely chooses to subscribe to the journal or is required to as part of the obligations of membership in the sponsoring society. Without additional income from advertising, revenue from subscriptions, whether "voluntary" or "involuntary," is rarely enough to meet publishing costs. "Page charges" are a device used by many nonprofit, basic-science journals (which have little or no advertising income) to help make up their operating deficits. Under this system, journals charge authors a certain fee per published pages. Since this cost is usually funded from research grants and contracts, the page charge is in effect a subsidy of the basic-science journals by the agencies and institutions that support medical research. The only other source of support for the nonprofit, basic-science journal is income from sale of reprints—another cost usually borne by the agencies that fund research. Only a very few basic-science journals—those with the largest circulation and the broadest appeal—carry advertising. Clinical journals, on the other hand, even those with a relatively small circulation and narrowly focused interest, are likely to contain advertising.

Whether proprietary or not, the majority of clinical journals published in the United States today depend heavily on advertising. Advertising income is usually taxable in any case, but net revenue after taxes may still be substantial, particularly for clinical journals with wide circulation among practitioners. Despite their dependence on advertising, most reputable clinical journals maintain high editorial standards. The best of the proprietary clinical journals have an editorial policy that is more or less independently determined by a professional organization or a group of physician-editors, and the scientific quality of their content may be quite comparable to that of nonprofit journals in the same field. On the other hand, in many proprietary journals, editorial direction is controlled by the entrepreneurial owners.

While in some cases a conscientious effort is made to maintain professional quality, far too many such journals are little more than conveyances for advertisements, with the profit motive dominating other considerations. They almost never publish original research articles or clinical studies, and virtually all of their material is solicited or written by members of their staffs.

An important example of this kind of journal is the so-called throw-away—the controlled-circulation periodical that is distributed gratis to large segments of the physician population. In these journals, advertising material is not simply interspersed between articles or confined to the front and back section of the journal. As if to make the journal's purpose unmistakably clear, the ubiquitous advertising is interleaved with the textual material in the body of individual articles and may sometimes even share the same page with the text.

A variety of throwaway literature needing special mention is the medical newspaper or newsmagazine. These are periodicals, usually weeklies, that specialize in news items about professional meetings, health politics and economics, organizations, personalities, and so forth. At their best, they provide readable coverage of health-related news that would not ordinarily be found in either the lay press or the primary biomedical literature. At their worst, they try to "scoop" the regular journals by carrying brief, superficial stories about new developments in clinical medicine or medical research. Many of these stories are based on presentations at meetings, press conferences, and interviews and are therefore liable to be biased, premature, and unsupported by data. These medical newspapers resemble the popular press in that they often entertain readers more than they inform them.

There are two characteristics of medical journals that may not be as readily apparent to the reader as those discussed above but are nevertheless important. One has already been alluded to: the mode of acquisition of material, that is, whether manuscripts are largely solicited or unsolicited, remunerated or not. Research articles and clinical studies are rarely solicited, and their authors are almost never paid. Journals publishing only material of this kind therefore depend almost entirely on unsolicited manuscripts. Of course, editors of such journals—particularly early in the journal's history—may cast about among their professional colleagues to encourage submissions, but there is no systematic or sustained effort to commission manuscripts, and the ultimate goal of the editor is to be able to select material from among a plethora of unsolicited submissions. Journals publishing more varied types of articles, particularly reviews, editorials, and articles of opinion, will usually have to solicit at least some of their material and may remunerate authors. Almost all of the articles published in the controlled-circulation journals are solicited and remunerated.

Lest there be any misapprehension, I should say here that solicited articles, whether remunerated or not, are not necessarily inferior in quality to unsolicited ones. Some excellent teaching articles appear in the throwaway periodicals, and many of the best scientific reviews and editorials published in other kinds of medical periodicals are also of the solicited (and even remunerated) variety. The quality of the editing is more important than the mode of acquisition of manuscripts in predicting the quality of a journal. However, with rare exceptions, journals that must depend totally on solicited material cannot be expected to have much scientific or archival merit, whatever their educational or entertainment value may be.

Finally, there is the distinction between journals on the basis of their editorial policies. Are the editors free to exercise their best editorial judgment, or must they follow the policies of the owners? Do the editors have the advantage of being able to select from among a large amount of material offered for publication, or are they constantly struggling simply to fill their pages? And how are manuscripts actually selected—solely by in-house editorial judgment or with the help of outside referees and consultants? Most of the reputable clinical and basic-science journals in the biomedical field have autonomous editorial management and enjoy considerable freedom in the selection of material. They receive, unsolicited, many more manuscripts than they can publish, and, in making their choice, they rely heavily on the advice of consultants. Many have well-organized peer-review systems, with editorial boards and many outside reviewers. Not all quality journals depend on peer review, however, One notable exception is *Lancet*, which uses outside consultants for only a fraction of its manuscripts and depends mostly on its own full-time editorial staff[1].

The percentage of unsolicited manuscripts ultimately accepted and published varies considerably from journal to journal. The most selective journals publish only 15 or 20 percent of what they receive, and only after considerable revision. There are no data, but I would imagine that the average acceptance rate among the well-known journals is approximately 40 to 60 percent. More importantly, there is no information on the selectivity of the medical-journal network as a whole. Many articles rejected by one journal will be resubmitted to others and ultimately accepted. Follow-up studies by the *Journal of Clinical Investigation* and *NEJM* have shown that about 85 percent of manuscripts initially rejected by these journals were published elsewhere, often in other journals of excellent repute [2,3]. Almost certainly, therefore, the average acceptance rate of the many individual journals underestimates the ultimate acceptance rate of the journal network as a whole. I suspect that the great majority of manuscripts submitted for publication are ultimately published somewhere. The selection exercised by editors and reviewers apparently has much more influence on *where* an article will be published than *whether* it will be published at all. Viewed as a whole, the total network of medical journals may be more of a sponge than a filter for submitted manuscripts—which may explain why the size of the medical literature continues to grow exponentially[4].

All of the characteristics discussed above—subject and format of articles, intended readership, sponsorship and financial management, mode of acquisition of manuscripts, and editorial management and policies— produce a vast variation among journals. Knowledgeable readers use these differences to identify journals that will be of greatest interest to them. Collectively, these characteristics accurately predict the nature and quality of journal content and can be used as a reliable guide on which to base reading habits. This subject will be discussed further in the last section of the chapter.

EDITORS AND THEIR ROLE

Medical editors may be physicians or editors by training but are rarely both. Most physicians who take up editorial duties do so on a part-time basis and for relatively short tenure. Conversely, most career editors have spent their professional lives in the publishing field and have little or no medical training. Almost all editors of established medical journals that publish research articles are professional biomedical scientists, serving in their editorial roles on a part-time basis. Many are quite innocent of training in publication and communication skills, having been appointed to their editorial posts primarily because of biomedical competence and prior service as reviewers or members of editorial boards. Most of the full-time medical editors are employed by controlled-circulation journals, and none are physicians. I am aware of only three medical journals in the United States that employ full-time physician-editors: *NEJM*, the *Journal of the American Medical Association* (*JAMA*), and *Annals of Internal Medicine*.

This circumstance is not as troublesome as it would at first appear. It may, in fact, be entirely appropriate to the needs of the medical publishing enterprise. Journals publishing mainly original scientific articles and clinical studies need editors who can supervise the selection of material on the basis of technical quality—a task well suited to the part-time editor still actively pursuing a biomedical professional career. By contrast, journals publishing a broader variety of material requiring more editorial attention and initiative, particularly if they are weekly journals, can hardly make do with less than full-time editorial supervision. Journals publishing mainly general material may not need medically or scientifically trained editors, but those that publish both technical and general articles will require full-time editors who are medically or scientifically qualified.

Whether full-time or part-time, medically trained or not, editors of medical journals play a critical role in determining their quality. What should the editor's function be? At least four models can be suggested: censor, critic, judge, and facilitator. In exercising their responsibilities editors can be censors; that is, they can make firm decisions about acceptance, based on their own tastes and judgments or on the tastes and judgments of their colleagues and consultants. To the degree that those decisions are made capriciously, arbitrarily, or through personal bias, editors become censors. No matter how talented the editor, that is clearly a baleful situation, one that is not in the best interests of science communication and tends inevitably to be repressive. Fortunately, such editorial control occurs only rarely and, when it does, almost never endures for very long.

At the other pole are the facilitator-editors: editors who see their job to be mainly that of encouraging and facilitating the free exchange of scientific information. Such editors are concerned more with style than substance. They welcome most contributions, are critical of few, and reject virtually none. That kind of editor may be more popular but is not any more useful than the censor. Like censors, facilitators fail to understand their main function, which is to improve both the quality and readability of published material by presiding over an orderly process of review, selection, and revision.

Ideal editors, therefore, should be, in the first place, constructive critics. They usually need help in this role and should get advice from experts when technical subjects are under review. But experts often disagree—not so much on technical details as on the evaluation of the relevance, interest, and importance of the research and on the overall priority that it should be given. Model editors, therefore, must also be wise judges who weigh the evidence and then make a fair decision. Since they are fallible and will inevitably make mistakes, they must be open to appeal and willing to reexamine their decisions when these are seriously challenged. Only after editors have considered the substance of a manuscript and made their judgment about acceptability should they turn their attention to the facilitating function. Of course, this injunction applies primarily to scientific articles. Reviews, editorials, commentary, and didactic material need to be judged as much on their clarity of thought and felicity of expression as on their substance.

REVIEWERS AND THE PEER-REVIEW SYSTEM

Most of the reputable medical journals that publish research and clinical studies, and at least some of those that publish other kinds of articles, have a peer-review system. Manuscripts submitted to them are independently reviewed by referees who have been selected for this task by the editor because they are experts in the field.

Journals differ in their peer-review processes, but a common technique, used by the journal I formerly edited (*Journal of Clinical Investigation*), the one I now edit (*NEJM*), and many others, is to send each manuscript needing review to at least two referees. They are asked to give their appraisal of overall merit and acceptability in a separate letter to the editor and to summarize their detailed criticisms and comments about substance and style on another form for transmittal to the author. Editors, often with the aid of assistants, then attempt to reach a decision based on the advice and criticisms of their referees as well as their own best judgment. The latter is called into play more often than is generally appreciated because reviewers frequently disagree. Sometimes, when disagreements concern technical matters, editors may decide to seek advice from more experts. However, the issue often hinges on the interest or relevance of the work, and the decision then becomes simply a matter of editorial judgment. Under these circumstances, editors have nowhere to turn, and the responsibility for assigning publishing priorities is clearly theirs.

When technical manuscripts are under consideration, knowledgeable and judicious reviewers are the key to an effective peer-review system. If they do their job well, they make the editor's task relatively easy. However, a discouragingly large number of scientists and clinicians, although expert in their field, are either unwilling or unable to meet their responsibilities as referees. They may be too lenient and superficial in their comments. Some reviewers appear to be so grateful for any work published in their special field of interest that they will enthusiastically endorse almost anything. Other reviewers, more dour and suspicious by nature, appear to resent anyone working in their territory and find nothing of value in any work not originating from their own laboratory or clinic. Even reviewers who make a conscientious effort to analyze a paper on its merits sometimes make impetuous comments that are either so glowing or so abusive and harsh that they cannot be transmitted without offending the author or compromising the editor. In either case, rational dialogue between editor and author is made more difficult. In short, the peer-review system does not automatically produce editorial judgments, let alone good ones. The process must be carefully monitored, moderated, adjudicated, and sometimes even circumvented by the editor.

Reviewers are consultants to the editor, not the author, and should not communicate directly with the latter without the editor's approval. They may, however, wish to sign the comments that are to be transmitted to the author. There has been much debate on this question. Some critics think that the signed review is more likely to be responsible, temperate and constructive [5,6], but I agree with those who contend that anonymity encourages reviews that are forthright and unconstrained by personal or political considerations. However, the editor must see to it that reviewer anonymity is not abused.

Intemperate or unreasonable comments, whether signed or not, should not be transmitted. The policy of *NEJM* is to leave the matter of anonymity to the discretion of the reviewer. Those who wish to do so may sign their reviews, but we insist that all communications between reviewer and author about a manuscript prior to its publication pass across the editor's desk and be monitored by the editor. About 15 percent of our reviewers choose to sign their reviews.

Papers that pass the peer-review process must not be assumed to have received editorial endorsement or some sort of scientific seal of approval. Publication of a manuscript in the most selective and carefully edited of journals does not guarantee its validity or durability. Reviewers and editors, however capable and conscientious, make mistakes and may overlook serious flaws. Furthermore, new evidence may soon invalidate or modify even a flawless study. All that a good peer-reviewed journal can do is make reasonable efforts to winnow out unsound work and repair correctable defects. But readers of the literature should understand that scientific journals are records of work, not of revealed truth. The better the journal, the better— and the more worthy of reading—the published work is likely to be.

SELECTING MEDICAL JOURNALS: A READER'S GUIDE

This section briefly considers three ways in which one can use the periodical literature: by browsing, by keeping up, and by searching.

Browsing is the most fun. It is the least efficient of the three methods and yet invaluable as a catalyst for new ideas and fresh perspectives. It is best done in the current periodical room of a library, where the reader can pick up and peruse the journals displayed on the shelves. One can also browse through journals, old and new, that have been acquired in the course of a literature search. Sometimes an article discovered this way proves to be much more interesting than the one that first brought the particular issue or volume of the journal to hand. There are no guides to the art of browsing; the main requirements are time, curiosity, and access to a library.

However, browsing should not be an entirely random process. The universe of medical periodicals is too vast to expect that aimless wanderings will often lead to useful discoveries. One must have some sort of map. For this purpose, a working knowledge of the taxonomy of journals, as outlined earlier in this chapter, is invaluable. The essence of browsing lies in finding the unexpected, but knowledgeable readers learn to browse in the journals most likely to be rewarding and to avoid those that will simply waste their time.

"Keeping up" is a much more serious and purposeful kind of reading. Every physician needs to read the periodical literature regularly in order to keep abreast of new developments. Textbooks and monographs are useful as references but inadequate as timely chronicles of recent developments. Only monthly or weekly periodicals can provide the coverage that practitioners need.

However, the periodical literature is so vast that practitioners' reading must be selective. The task is simpler than it looks. To stay well informed, the average practitioner only needs to read a few, well-chosen periodicals: one or two general medical journals (weeklies) plus two or three specialty journals (usually monthlies). Naturally, not everything of interest will be published first in those few journals, but, over the course of a year or two, nothing of importance is likely to be overlooked. Sooner or later, every significant development will have been covered, either in original research reports or in editorials, reviews, and other didactic articles.

There is such an enormous amount of duplication, overlap, and fragmentation in the clinical literature that it is not only impossible but quite unnecessary to read *all* the original articles on a given subject in order to be well informed. For most practical purposes, one or two good research articles (which usually have an introduction, discussion, and bibliography that will put the new development in perspective) are all that is necessary to read at first, perhaps to be supplemented later by an authoritative review or other didactic article that gives a follow-up on the original development. The quality of these articles is far more important than their number. Careful reading of a few, high-quality journals is therefore much more useful in "keeping up" than the hasty and superficial scanning of many more journals of lesser quality. The trick, of course, is to select the right journals and to get in the habit of reading them regularly.

"Searching" is the most focused and businesslike way in which one can use the periodical literature. In this kind of activity, one is asking a specific question, such as "What has been written on subject X since 1970?" Elsewhere in this book (Chapters 10, 11, and 12) are discussed the various methods by which this kind of question can be answered. Suffice it to say here that the end result of such a search is likely to be a long list of references from a great many journals of highly variable style, content, and quality. Most of the important original research articles are to be found in a relatively few journals. The reliable reviews will probably also be similarly restricted. A knowledge of the various kinds of journals and their important characteristics as described in this chapter should therefore be helpful in sorting out priorities. What one needs always to keep in mind is that most of the important business of scientific communication in medicine is conducted in a very small sector of top-quality journals. The farther one's reading strays from these journals, the less rewarding it is likely to be.

REFERENCES

1. Douglas-Wilson, I. 1977. Editorial review: Peerless pronouncements. N Engl J Med 297:724–25.
2. Wilson, JD. 1978. Peer review and publication. Proceedings of the American Society for Clinical Investigation.
3. Relman, AS. 1978. Are journals really quality filters? In Coping with the Biomedical Literature Explosion: A Qualitative Approach, edited by KS Warren and W Goffman. Rockefeller Foundation, New York, pp. 54–60.
4. Durack, DT. 1978. The weight of medical knowledge. N Engl J Med 298:773–75.
5. Ingelfinger, FJ. 1974. Peer review in biomedical publication. Am J Med 56:686–92.
6. Gordon, M. 1977. Evaluating the evaluators. New Scientist 73:342–43.

GENERAL REFERENCES

7. Houghton, B. 1975. Scientific Periodicals: Their Historical Development, Characteristics, and Control. Linmet, Hamden, Conn.
8. O'Connor, M. 1979. The Scientist as Editor. Wiley, New York.

6

REVIEWING REVIEWS

Edward H. Kass

Reviews (and I shall consider the word review to be a generic term covering reviews, monographs, and those books that explore more circumscribed subjects or serve as how-to-do-it manuals, in contrast to textbooks) serve two functions that are critical to the development of science. The first is that they provide an opportunity for a synthesis of the state of knowledge in a given field. A synthesis may serve primarily to permit the formulation of new hypotheses or new viewpoints that are essential to the development of the field. Alternatively, a synthesis may serve to summarize the state of knowledge in an aspect of a field, particularly when there has been a surge of rapid progress or when the field may have been a relatively obscure one to which the author would like to call greater attention. These two functions are self-evidently important. The development of new hypotheses, a reshaping of data that lead to the hypotheses, and the predictions that may be drawn from such hypotheses are part of the fabric of science, of course. Sometimes a primary research paper that developed new data permits the formulation of such hypotheses. Often, however, the theoretical and expository aspects of the new formulations are sufficiently broad to demand presentation in a review.

Those reviews that serve primarily to synthesize the state of knowledge in a given field are increasingly necessary. The explosion of information makes it physically impossible to keep abreast of important developments in a wide variety of fields.

At its best, a review article is a transient miniature of the end product desired in an information transfer system; it is a high quality, analytic,

79

organized, and compacted current synthesis of information in a given area. Drawing on personal knowledge and experience, the expert selects from the massive published information available and presents to the reader a highly organized, concise, analytic summary. To bolster credibility of his or her views, the expert cites the highest quality and most relevant literature and, because of usual constraints on page space, severely limits the numbers (and redundancy) of citations [1].

A second function of reviews, which is often overlooked, is the opportunity for an author to express in more personalized terms the manner in which a given line of thought or series of discoveries actually developed. One can cite one of the most charming examples of this type of writing from Claude Bernard's Traité, in which he wrote:

> One day rabbits from the market were brought into my laboratory. They were put on the table where they urinated...the urine was clear and acid. This fact struck me, because rabbits, which are herbivora, generally have turbid and alkaline urine; while on the other hand carnivora, as we know, have clear and acid urine. This observation of acidity in the rabbits' urine gave me an idea that these animals must be in the nutritional condition of carnivora. I assumed that they had probably not eaten for a long time, and that they had been transformed by fasting into veritable carnivorous animals, living on their own blood.... I gave the rabbits grass to eat...their urine became turbid and alkaline. I then subjected them to fasting...their urine became clearly and strongly acid; then after [the rabbits ate] grass their urine became alkaline again, etc. I then repeated this experiment on a horse...[and] thus reached the general proposition which was then still unknown, to wit, that all fasting animals feed on meat, so that herbivora then have a urine like that of carnivora....I fed rabbits cold boiled beef, which they ate very nicely when they were given nothing else. My expectation was again verified, and as long as the animal diet was continued, the rabbits kept their clear and acid urine....
>
> In sacrificing the rabbits which I had fed on meat, I happened to notice that the white and milky lymphatic were first visible in the small intestine at the lower part of the duodenum...[coincident] with the position of the pancreatic duct....In fact, pancreatic juice obtained in suitable conditions from dogs, rabbits, and various other animals, and mixed with oil or melted fat, always instantly emulsified, and later split these fatty bodies into fatty acids, glycerin, etc. etc. by means of specific ferment [2].

In these few paragraphs, Bernard shows how a simple observation, made by a prepared mind with a quick imagination, led to two major discoveries of physiology. The first was that the protein of the body is not an inert matrix but is in a dynamic metabolic state. This later became generalized into his concept of the milieu interieur and was followed by Walter B. Cannon's statement of homeostasis. The second discovery was that the pancreas elaborates lipolytic enzymes that enter the duodenum through the pancreatic duct, and from this came a more complete appreciation of the exocrine function of the pancreas and the relation of enzymes to digestion.

The scientific papers that announced these discoveries, or that later built upon them, start with the discoveries themselves, omitting mention of the unique circumstances by which the discoveries evolved. Such omissions are the rule in scientific presentations. Constraints of space and the tradition of sparse and impersonal presentation of salient facts create a method of presentation in research papers that often omits the human processes of discovery and sometimes reviews the literature post hoc, creating a somewhat distorted picture of the process as it actually occurred. Such distortions have several disadvantages. By serving a series of idealized myths about the scientific process, they produce attitudes that are fundamentally untrue and therefore a cause of discomfort in scientists who know better. Perhaps of greater moment is that a younger investigator, not being brought in contact with the process as it actually had occurred, tends to view much scientific exploration as representing inspirational leaps of the imagination such as are given to few mortals, a view that might inhibit all but the most perceptive and most ambitious. Even in translation, Bernard's capacity to transform simple observations into major generalizations becomes delightful, inspirational, and not at all inhibitory. It is doubtful that this tale could be published today in a research paper, but it finds a ready home in a review or monograph that permits a more leisurely and expository approach to the analysis of a problem.

The opportunity to develop a subject from this more personalized point of view is a regular feature of writing in the humanities. There is a reasonable case for excluding such expositions from the scientific journals that exist primarily to present new data. Reviews, monographs, and the personal book can serve a unique purpose in giving some insight into the self-perceived thought processes of scientists. Of course, these are subject to all of the caveats about personal expositions and about the deletions, alterations, and adjustments that are almost inevitable during retrospection. Nevertheless, these are forms of written communication in science that provide a human dimension that often otherwise becomes part of the oral tradition.

To the student, this form of communication has a special function. Students are often awed by the process of discovery as delineated through a series of logical steps or flashes of insight in most scientific papers, whether primary or review. To recognize that often authors reshape the steps in a discovery to suit a logical and rational framework, rather than state the actual processes as they occurred, is a revelation that may escape the aspiring novitiate in a field of science. The consequence is often despair on the part of the younger person, who has not been struck with bolts of blue lightning and has not perceived that much of discovery is a painful, disciplined, and laborious building of one step upon the preceding.

However, this more personalized function of reviews is an uncommon one and is only occasionally displayed in monographs as well. Most reviews necessarily serve the more general functions of critical synthesis and exposition of major advances in a given field.

This latter type of review is the one most desired by information technologists and is also the kind that can be most easily abused. The most common source of abuse is also the only forseeable source of relief from the weight of the expanding literature, and therein lies a major contradiction that is difficult to resolve. It is relatively easy to order up from a computerized file all titles that have in them a certain number of key words relevant to the subject under review. Other disregarded, thereby, are the contributions that antedated the advent of the computer-based memory, and one consequence of the computer will undoubtedly be that much of science will stand still while well-known facts of the past are rediscovered and inserted into the memory system. Similarly, contemporary authors and those of the future will be constrained to write short research reports that can be adequately described in their titles, so that important information will not be lost to the all-powerful memory of the future. Now that abstracts and key words can be filed and recalled with relative ease, it may become desirable for those who wish to be referred to with some frequency not only to make useful contributions, whether original or repetitive, but also to couch these in a basic language that will minimize exclusion from the process of recall. Authors with an urge for expository writing, or who feel that they may have something different to say, may need reviews more than ever.

It can reasonably be argued that the advent of computer technology, and its growth in the forseeable future, may make reviews that synthesize the state of knowledge in a given field obsolete and unnecessary. The argument is cogent if the reviews that emerge from the use of the newer technologies limit themselves to what is little more than a listing of work in the given field with a brief description of the salient points, particularly those that appear in the abstracts. Therefore, for reviews of the future to have any useful role, other than to add to a bibliography or to be profitable to a publisher (scientific publications other than textbooks are rarely profitable to the author), they must be critical, selective, and, whenever possible, must attempt to bring new insights into the field. The temptation for a writer of a review, who is also a primary contributor, to cite excessively his or her own work is apparent. We are faced with the thought that reviews will need to be evaluated as critically as are primary scientific papers but with slightly different guidelines that encompass some of the considerations that have been discussed.

These guidelines will need to stress completeness, perspective, and critical analysis of a given subject. Moreover, one hopes that they will emphasize the lack of value of mere compendiums or of considering every printed article and/or paper equally acceptable regardless of the nature of the evidence, experimental design, or cogency of the analysis. Newer information exchanges necessarily stress the need that each review present as ideal a synthesis as possible. To the degree that a review falls short of the ideal, important work may be overlooked, and so a certain amount of redundancy and overlap in reviews by different authors is both desirable and necessary. Obviously, an information-transfer system can cope only with a limited amount of redundancy without losing the efficiency that is a major reason for its existence. Therefore, the review function of journals and of certain types of books requires critical editorial judgment and careful peer review if the projected newer systems of information transfer are to be more than mere catalogs. The burdens on writers, editors, and editorial consultants to achieve these ends are lightened only by the knowledge that the scientific objectives that are being served are likely to be of increasing importance in the future.

Several potential contradictions can readily be perceived as the role of reviews in the future is contemplated. Since peer review and a certain amount of collective judgment constitute a critical feature of the information technology of the future, there may be a tendency for peer reviewers to look a little less kindly on syntheses that express hypotheses that break sharply from the conventional wisdom of the time. Editors always must try to separate the unusual from the bizarre.

Of still greater importance is the problem of profitability. As long as reviews and monographs may sell at a profit, there will be pressure for publication of increasing numbers of these. This, in turn, leads to publications that may not have received peer review or that have been judged by those who feel excessive pressures from the marketplace. Ultimately, it can be argued, poor quality publications will wither, as will publishers with lowered standards. On the other hand, understanding of the media, advertising revenue, and alert merchandising practices can go a long way toward selling marginally adequate publications to unwary readers.

What guidelines can be offered to the reader? One is to concentrate on those publications that are organs of reputable organizations. Such organizations, because of their size and standards, are responsible for the choice of editors and for the surveillance of the editorial function. Members of a society, or faculties of an institution, tend to watch more closely the publications emanating from their own establishment, and this is a safeguard.

Another important marker is the peer recognition of the editors and editorial consultants. Still another is the presence or absence of a large amount of advertising revenue over which the editors or the sponsoring institution exert no influence. Publications whose editors are not well-recognized experts in the field need careful scrutiny. Publishers differ in the degree to which careful editorial standards are used and peers consulted.

A publication, whether of reviews or of other types of articles, must be economically viable to continue. It may receive hidden or overt subsidies in order to remain viable. A balance must be struck, difficult as it sometimes may be, between achieving sufficient profitability to permit continuation of publication and keeping the economic aspects from running away with the editorial standards. Over the long run, the effect of individuals in maintaining these standards tends to decline; and the effect of organizations, to persist. Therefore, publications that receive the backing and support of reputable organizations will tend, despite occasional exceptions, to maintain standards more effectively than those that are primarily published with the expectation of profit.

In more empirical fields, such as clinical medicine, reviews serve an added instructional function, and the relation of reviews to information transfer is more complex. Effective clinicians try to develop as many reliable generalizations as possible in order to minimize the mountain of minutiae that would otherwise need to be stored in their memories. The nature of an empirical field is such that it does not permit a large number of sweeping generalizations, and the nature of human memory is such that regular reminders help to keep certain facts within ready recall. Reviews, case reports, rereading of textbooks, and a variety of other devices that are well-known to all who attend medical conferences and grand rounds serve to keep much clinical material fresh and often to provide details about a relatively uncommon aspect or illness. Although many clinical reviews lend themselves to the type of efficient information transfer that has been advocated for scientific subjects, many unsolved problems remain. Literature searches for clinical purposes often seek information on relatively uncommon associations or manifestations of a disease, and these may be published in relatively obscure journals or may have been observed many years before the scope of the usual retrospective scientific review article.

At the moment, citation frequency and newer information-transfer techniques have a considerable relevance to the empirical aspects of clinical medicine but must be used with much more caution than in the more scientifically established aspects of a clinical field, since much empirical material can be found only after the widest possible search and with useful, but more limited, assistance from the computer. A somewhat different technology will need to be developed for empirical clinical medicine.

The usefulness of selective literature for most scientific purposes is evident. The shortcomings will need to be addressed in the future, as the technology evolves. Certain incongruities have appeared, most of them minor, and these also need to be recognized and corrected. For example, indexing of books and monographs is less well developed than is indexing of works in scientific journals. Some reviews that appear in books are forever lost to the computer and therefore may have only transient value. A better means for indexing reviews and aspects of the contents of these reviews needs to be developed.

Moreover, at the present level of technology, those who had the misfortune to do seminal work before the onset of computers may be condemned to a kind of technological limbo, unless they or their colleagues have chosen to mention the earlier work in more recent reviews. The occasional scholarly person who investigates earlier discoveries often finds that much rich and useful material has been lost from the common perception. It may be a subtle recognition of the wasteful disregard of the past that there is now a resurgence of interest in medical history and the history of science among students and established individuals alike.

A minor, but irritating, incongruity in the current literature is the practice, in certain journals and in many indexing services, of citing only the first three authors of a given publication. This practice is difficult to understand. Computer technology is not limited any longer to listing some but not all authors. The expense to journals is not great but the cost to complete information processing of omitting authors who happen to be fourth or fifth in a listing, may be substantial.

Briefly, reviews serve a necessary function that is likely to grow as dependence on selective information processes grows. Reviews provide a format in which selective and critical summaries of a given field may be presented, and the use of such reviews provides information processing with a basis for selective retention of certain scientific reports and not others. The ability of a given review to acomplish this selective and critical purpose is therefore a necessary condition for the use of selective information storage. However, it is difficult to insure the existence of such reviews. Critical editorial standards, freedom from external pressures, and careful and complete peer review are the minimum necessary conditions for attempting to assure adequate coverage of a topic. Peer review, for all of its inadequacies,* is the most important single element and has thus far functioned reasonably well. However, a peer-review system, as stressed earlier, makes severe demands on those who must review and edit the reviews, and better methods must still be developed in order to assure optimal function of reviews.

Reviews that devote themselves to certain clinical subjects, particularly to the more descriptive and instructive aspects of medicine (rather than the more mechanistic aspects), are less easily used for selective information processing. Nevertheless, information-processing systems are essential for

---

*Like democracy, as defined by Winston Churchill, the peer-review system is the worst of all systems, except for all the others.

the future of scientific inquiry, and the need for constant improvement in their function as well as in their content will surely continue to stimulate new advances in the approach and the technique of information processing.

Little has thus far been said about books. It is apparent from the foregoing discussion that there is a thin and nebulous line between reviews in a journal and bound monographs or bound collections of reviews that are sold as books. Space, marketability, uniqueness, and the reputation of the author or authors are among the considerations that will govern the decision to publish a given work in a journal or in a book. How does the sorting-out process actually occur?

The stimulus to write a review may come from several sources. On the one hand, a group of authors may feel that the development of their own work or the development of their field of interest has reached a point at which the formulation of a general statement of progress or a reshaping of hypotheses would be worthwhile. They may prepare such a work with a given journal in mind. The more widely read journals differ in editorial policies, and not all take review articles. Those that do publish reviews generally publish original articles also. Therefore, editors will reject a certain number of reviews simply because of limitations to the amount of space that can be allotted to reviews in their journals.

Generally, review articles may undergo peer reviews, and these reviews assist the editorial staff in determining whether a given work is accurate and comprehensive, whether it reasonably reflects the field or provides unique insight, or whether it deals with a subject that has already been amply reviewed in recent publications elsewhere. Often an editor will express a desire to publish a review if the authors agree to reduce it or otherwise to modify it to encompass criticisms that have arisen in the editorial process. Moreover, a work often may be judged meritorious but rather more specialized than is desired by the editors of a journal dealing with more general topics. The authors must decide whether the editorial suggestions that have been made are valid. They then may revise the review in accordance with these comments or may choose to send the review elsewhere.

Many reviews are solicited. These solicited reviews may take the form of articles in a series that reflect a systematic approach to a larger subject, may represent a summary of progress in a given geographic area or given institution, or may be a portion of a presentation at a meeting. Most recently, "controlled-circulation" periodicals, also known as the "throwaway" journals, have arisen. These are privately owned periodicals that carry a great deal of advertising and that try to present the textual material in a manner that will be visually attractive and will make for relatively easy reading. Articles for such periodicals are almost always solicited, and it is a widespread practice for editorial writers employed by the periodical to interview the "author," obtain that author's scientific views, and then rewrite these in the style that is characteristic of the publication involved. In general, reviews in most journals (as well as original articles) are not paid for. Occasionally, however, an honorarium may be given to an author whose review is part of a symposium. Of course, in the more entrepreneurial press, a fee is customarily paid.

Frequently, a collection of reviews will be published as a book, and some of these books are serials that come out regularly, whereas others represent individual publishing enterprises. Of course, books and journals must be paid for. When a journal is an official publication of a society, the members of the society may assume a certain amount of financial obligation, or a publisher may assume the financial obligations independently of the society. In such arrangements, the editorial content of the journal is under the direct control of the society involved. Some journals and review publications are directly owned by publishers, and representatives of the publishers choose editors, approach prospective authors, and make whatever arrangements are necessary, including the transfer of the fee when a fee is involved. Similarly, publishers may publish the proceedings of given meetings or may publish various serial review books that attempt periodically to review progress in certain fields. Obviously, the continued publication of such journals and books depends upon their financial success.

A prospective author who would like to develop a book or monograph either alone, or with other authors, has several choices. The author may approach the so-called scholarly presses, which, generally speaking, are the presses attached to universities. These, too, have been subject to financial pressures but tend to be somewhat more permissive of books in special fields in which sales are not likely to be high. Certain foundations will assist in the publication of scholarly books that may or may not become commercial successes, and some foundations work particularly closely with certain publishers. Most of the university presses are in touch with such foundations. Alternatively, a prospective author may approach a publisher directly, and, at least as often, the publishers will try to judge what books may be desirable and approach individuals or groups of individuals to fashion such books. Publishers vary widely in their practices. Some are more critical than others, and some have a network of editorial consultants, while others have none. It is this range of quality, and the relative absence of peer review, that makes the book market somewhat more hazardous than the journal market for the purchaser.

Certain books have an appeal because they focus on techniques and are essentially "how-to-do-it" books. Others are straightforwardly written as textbooks for students at different stages of development in a field, and still others are written as textbooks but also attempt to serve as reference volumes. The choices are vast, and profitability seems to be relatively high, if the large numbers of publishers of medical and scientific books are to be taken as an index. The fact that the National Library of Medicine last year received approximately 14,000 titles gives some indication of the magnitude of the problem.

For the reader who is beginning to fashion an approach to the literature, a few guidelines are useful. The first is that peer-review journals will tend to be more reliable than those that are not subject to peer review. Secondly, journals that are official publications of recognized societies will generally reflect higher standards than those journals that are not associated with such societies. After a manuscript is submitted, an average of about two years is required to publish a book. Therefore, a book that stresses synthesis of existing knowledge, or that gives new insights, will be more desirable than a book that claims to be up-to-date. On the other hand, in regularly published journals and review sources, only about six months are needed to bring an article (once it has been accepted) out in print.

Only rarely can a general textbook be more than an introductory text to a given subject. The constraints of space and the variety of topics that must be covered necessarily lead to summarized presentations. When greater depth is needed, recourse to journals and review mechanisms becomes necessary. Recently, an old idea has been rejuvenated, and loose-leaf texts have once again surfaced. Their ultimate success will depend upon the rapidity, timeliness, and economic feasibility of revisions. Even revisions will tend to suffer from the defect of textbooks in general, namely, the constraints that lead to truncated, rather than in-depth, presentations.

There is an incongruity between the proliferation of books and the limitations on what a medical student, house officer, or practicing physician can reasonably be expected to know. This incongruity is partially due to the important archival function of scholarly books that become reference works for a special field, but it also stems from the profitable nature of publishing. At present, there tends to be a relatively fixed institutional sale that will accompany most books. Medical librarians need assistance in weeding out the unwanted growths and fertilizing the sprouts that represent quality and critical analysis. Books that are written for one's colleagues are not always books that are suitable for students or for individuals not in that special field of interest.

Multiauthor books are convenient and occasionally intellectually essential. In teaching students that it is impossible for one individual to know everything about a broad subject, such as internal medicine or general surgery, a basic humility is introduced that is essential for future growth. On the other hand, the student and graduate physician are justified in asking what the requisite body of knowledge is that it is reasonable for individuals in their position to grasp and understand. If such a requisite body of knowledge can be defined, is there an individual in academic medicine able to assemble it in a readable form? Until this question is answered in the affirmative, and a sufficient number of books that exemplify this response become available, a certain amount of skepticism will continue to exist among those who buy and use multiauthor texts, not as reference material, but as delineation of bodies of knowledge that ought to be at the command of each of the readers.

Book reviews have been used as a means for informing potential purchasers of the desirability or lack of desirability of a given volume. Publishers seem to feel that sending their products for review is economically justified. Large numbers of volumes are sent for review, and publishers request that a book be listed even if it is not reviewed. Unhappily, a large number of book reviews follow such a stylized form that they are rendered almost completely useless to the critical reader.

Occasionally, a critical book review appears that puts a book into perspective, indicates precisely where its strengths and deficiencies lie, and compares it with other volumes in the field. Such reviews may be unpopular, and sometimes unjust, but they do help to sort the wheat from the chaff. In medical publication, however, there is generally a lack of the broader critical book reviews that analyze a group of related works and try to put them into perspective in a manner that is more common in literary and historical criticism than in scientific writing. Such a format for criticism for medical books should be developed soon.

In the meantime, medical librarians with shrinking budgets, increasing numbers of books from which to choose, and with generally inadequate book reviews to assist them, must necessarily depend on their constituencies— faculties, student bodies, members of their appropriate societies, and so forth—to help them in making judgments. It seems appropriate that libraries stock those books that are archival in function, in the sense of storing away important knowledge, and particularly those books that are inspirational— that present new and unusual reformulations of ideas in a field. Large reference works that are too expensive for most individual purchasers constitute an essential component of a well-stocked library. On the other hand, the more topical books—proceedings of meetings, many multiauthored textbooks, and books from publishers whose review practices have been faulty or nonexistent—are just as well avoided.

One of the trends of the past several decades has been the rise of increasing subspecialization in medicine and in most scientific work. The intensity of this growth has put severe pressures on the journals with multiple uses. Therefore, some general journals have quite specifically chosen to convey news in the sense of original articles that seem to present new and interesting material and brief reviews that are topical and usually related to one of the original articles in a particular issue. Other journals have attempted to publish a mix of original articles and review articles but to select the latter through editorial and peer-review mechanisms in order to give a broad picture of the entire field. With the rise in subspecialty areas and the greater numbers of individuals wanting more detailed information about many subjects that cannot be covered regularly in the journals dealing with general topics, there have arisen both journals that carry original articles in subspecialty areas and journals or books that regularly try to review progress in subspecialty fields. In many ways, these are among the most valuable of publications.

A system of selective information technology necessarily will depend upon critical reviews, and these, in turn (as has been outlined above), depend upon peer review and careful editorial consideration. The student who develops the habit of reading regularly a small number of general journals, who becomes familiar with subspecialty review journals and books, and who uses the latter intelligently will find this type of approach to be more intellectually satisfying than an approach that is limited to textbooks and related publications. There should be continued alertness to the trends in the material that is being read. If a general journal is judged, in time, unable to keep up or to satisfy other needs of the reader, the reader necessarily looks elsewhere.

The evolutionary process in the publication of journals is a dynamic one. At present, about 3 percent of journals discontinue publication each year, and an approximately equal number are created each year. Similarly, books have a short life, except for the few that set a new tempo in a field or the many textbooks or reference works that serve those who do not have the time or inclination to dig more deeply into the definitive literature on a subject.

The abiding problem in developing an approach to the biomedical literature of reviews and books has to do with the quality of a publication, and, in part, quality control depends upon the objective of the publication.

If the primary purpose of a publication is to stimulate the creative process, certain books and monographs that permit expository writing, analyze a process in detail, and give insight into the manner in which a field has developed can be unusually rewarding to the reader and can provide a basis for thinking through a problem in a way that had not existed earlier. If the objective is to stimulate awareness of the literature in scientific subjects, the use of citation analyses, other information-processing techniques, and, particularly, selective reading offers the greatest reward. However, such reading will be generally more rewarding if it is limited to sources in which peer review plays a central role, in which reputable societies act as governing forces on the content of the publication, and in which the economic pressures are contained within reasonable limits. If the objective is to impart information to students and younger members of the field, publications that have undergone peer review offer safeguards, but there is the complex problem that many such publications appeal more to colleagues than to students. There are serious inadequacies at present in the nature of textbooks that are presented to students. The student would do well to concentrate on a limited number of journals and to become familiar with the review journals and books that cover a variety of subspecialty areas. Once again, such reading is best limited to those journals and books that are directly connected with reputable societies, with authors who have demonstrated critical approaches, and in which the objectives and purposes are clearly defined.

At present, technological advances have made it possible to retrieve information at a rate equal to that at which the information is being generated. Therefore, it is more necessary than ever that reviews and critical books provide the basis for reducing this vast amount of information to a size that can be encompassed by one individual. In doing so, the new technology offers for each individual a wider range of knowledge than ever before.

REFERENCES

1. Bernstein, LM; Siegel, ER; and Goldstein, CM. The Hepatitis Knowledge Base. Annals of Internal Medicine 92:165–222,1980.
2. Bernard, C. Introduction á l'étude de la médecine experimentale, 1875. Edited by PF Cranefield. Science History Publications, New York, C1976.

PART III

UTILIZING BIOMEDICAL INFORMATION

7

HOW TO READ A PAPER

Oscar D. Ratnoff

Some years ago, a much publicized best-seller bore the catchy title, *How to Read a Book*. Its popularity baffled me. Aside from its turgid prose, suggesting that the author might well have consulted a volume on *How to Write a Book*, it carried a depressing message. Only if one dissected the text into little pieces would one learn what a book was all about. It was a recipe for the destruction of pleasure.

This memory provides me with a certain diffidence in approaching the subject of how to read a scientific paper. As will become evident, I have to a large extent turned the question around. A paper, to be read well, must first be written well. The process of reading should be a joy, and should fill the reader with the satisfaction that comes from assimilating one more bit of the endless information at his disposal, from acquiring one more stimulus to his research. This provides my first homily. You can't read it all, and still retain your sanity. You must pick and choose with an eye to your interests. You must read selectively and with an eye to proportion.

How one reads depends upon immediate goals. Are you perusing a current journal to find out what's going on? This sort of reading is much like looking at the morning newspaper; a general blur may be all that you want. Are you trying to teach yourself about a subject? This will take more care, but can often be done with minimal effort through the use of reviews. Or are you digging in to examine some problem with the thought of pursuing it or extending your own previous research? This may take the fine-toothed comb approach, in which every fragment that a particular article provides is gleaned.

What brings an article to my attention in my random reading is that I am attracted to its title. Well, attracted to it if the title is written correctly. Early in my own career, I made what I like to think of as a significant discovery about a particular infectious disease. The results were published in a prestigious journal, and I was pleased as punch. Alas, the several confirmatory papers that have since appeared have never quoted my original work. Although this has bruised my fragile ego, the fault was mine. The title of my paper, scientifically correct, gave no hint of the meaning of the work I'd performed. No one reviewing the appropriate indexes would ever have surmised that the newer papers were but replays. This provides another rule. The title of a paper should tell us why we want to read it. I've learned to write long titles, with as many "key words" as I can get away with.

When I'm perusing a journal, I may get no further than the title. "A New Cure for Australian Dingbat Fever." Hurray, I may say, but unless I think it likely that I'll see a patient with this extraordinary disease, or that I'll investigate the well-known infectious agent that causes it, I'll stop here. If I have a good memory, I'll recall this article the next time I see a case of Australian dingbat fever, and I'll read it then.

I may go no further into an article that is closer to home if the title doesn't excite me. But the names of the authors, if I know they avoid trivia and have a good reputation, may change my mind. If William Osler thought the paper was worth writing, perhaps I'd better not be too off-hand.

Past this hurdle, I'll read the Abstract or Summary. I don't know who the genius was who started the practice of putting the Abstract at the beginning instead of the end of an article, but I doff my hat to him; I do know the *Journal of Laboratory and Clinical Medicine* has done this for 20 years. Reading a scientific article isn't the same as reading a detective story. We want to know from the start that the butler did it. Again, it is the writer and not the reader who holds the key. If the Abstract is well written, it will describe successively the problem posed by the author, the general method of approach, the solution of the problem, and the lesson to be drawn. It should never be filled with minutiae, an often violated rule; it should be expository, avoiding where possible numerical data. I don't want to know here the standard deviation of the difference between two groups of observations; I'll learn about that if I read the article. Least of all should the Abstract be enigmatic: "The cure of Australian dingbat fever will be described."

Reading the Abstract may be all I want to do in my random reading, or even when I am trying to explore a subject. In the latter case, I may realize that the author's observations or conclusions are not as novel as he thinks, or that his point is irrelevant to my purposes. But, either because I've been excited in a non-specific way, or because I think that the article will help me in some specific fashion, I may want to learn more. My next step is twofold. I'll read the Introduction to the paper and the Discussion. These days, the structure of a paper is so stereotyped, it won't be accepted for publication unless it is divided up in a rigid way. Gone is the easy style that makes reading eighteenth-century William Hewson on blood clotting so delightful. Indeed, if you try to emulate these elders you may get a letter from the editor, as I did recently, asking you to remove the extraneous writing and stick to the scientific "facts."

A great help to me is an Introduction that sets forth the problem to be discussed in just a few brief sentences.

> To date, no cure for Australian dingbat fever has been found, despite earlier claims by Aristophanes, Marco Polo, and Chiang Kai-shek. An accidental observation has led to the discovery that 100 percent of cases are cured permanently by administration of 5 grams of aspirin a day. The present study provides data in 75 cases in which the diagnosis was well established, and outlines the technique of administering aspirin and the side-effects that are encountered.

Note, then that the paper's introduction tells the reader the answer as well as the question. It is, if you please, an abstract of the Abstract.

Having digested the Introduction, I turn to the Discussion. Properly written, this should set forth the nature of the problem in much greater detail, citing all pertinent previous work. In another place, I noted that there are two sorts of scientists, those who look in the bibliography to see if they're quoted, and liars; the Discussion is no place to overlook one's peers. Nothing bothers me quite so much, too, than to find that the author cites the moppers-up, and forgets (or does not know) the originator of an idea.

Reading on into the Discussion, I should find a step-by-step interpretation of the authors' observations, how they confirm old ideas or plow new ground. A Discussion need not be long, but the author who does not mention a key result is unfair both to the reader and to himself. If he really thinks his work means anything, he should close the Discussion with a sentence or three outlining where he thinks we go from here.

A carefully designed Discussion, then, may tell me all I need to know about the author's thoughts; of course, if I'm at all excited, I shall have sneaked looks at his tables and figures on the way, to convince myself that he's quoting himself correctly.

For random reading, or to acquaint myself with a subject when I must read many articles, that's about as far as I may go. Of course, I'll still retain a healthy skepticism about what I've read. At this point, what I've acquired is a concept of how the author decided to study Australian dingbat fever, what the prognosis of this disorder is when untreated or with previous therapeutic regimens, how the author came to choose aspirin as the preferred form of treatment, and what he thinks the results of this dramatic therapy were. Note,

I haven't concerned myself too deeply with the validity of the observation, or such details as the selection of cases, the means of diagnosis, the way the drug was administered, the way cure was established, nor the means of statistical analysis.

Either because, in my random reading, the author has inspired me to go further, or because the answer to such specific questions is needed, I'll then go on to read his section on Results. Here I have to be careful. Careless reading may lead to misinterpretation, or, worse yet, to a failure to pick out flaws in the author's logic. I'll probably intersperse my reading of Results with an examination of Methods, for sometimes the text will otherwise be opaque. As I read, I fervently pray that the writer has followed the dictum of Hale Ham, a noted hematologist who was the architect of Case Western Reserve University's "new curriculum" for the medical school. Hale taught us to tell our story logically and not in the disordered way we did our experiments. I realize that this provides rewritten history, but the reader is better served by *post hoc* rationalization.

When I read the Results section, I'll undoubtedly spend much of my time looking at the tables and figures. Once again, it's the author and not the reader whom I've really got to write about here. Even the "best" journals forget that every table and figure should stand by itself. One ought to be able to get the writer's point without reference to the text. That means that every table and figure should tell you all you need to know to get the author's message. You shouldn't have to guess that those numbers in parentheses mean the numbers of patients or observations. I review a lot of manuscripts for journals, and I think the structure of tables and figures is the commonest source of my editorial confusion. A good book to read to learn how to do it right is Robert Day's *How to Write and Publish a Scientific Paper*, published in 1979 by ISI Press in Philadelphia. As a matter of fact, that's a good book to read to learn how to write the rest of the paper as well.

I'll look carefully in the Results section for measures of statistical validity, because I've now reached the point where I care about detail. I'll worry a lot about control experiments or data, the more so if I'm reading about a subject with which I'm familiar enough to care. Now, indeed, I need to know how the patients with Australian dingbat fever were selected. How, I must ask, did the author decide which of his patients had this exotic disease? If the diagnosis was based on a laboratory procedure, I need to know the limits of accuracy of the test in reaching this conclusion. How, for example, did the author decide what was a "normal" result, and were his control subjects truly appropriate? My concern will be even greater if the diagnosis is made on purely clinical grounds. Perhaps the rash we all associate with Australian dingbat fever is hard to distinguish from that of rubella, and our author is, in fact, so color blind (like a dermatologist I know) that he can't tell the two diseases apart. We also need to know how those patients who were to receive the innovative therapy were selected. Were those who were given aspirin chosen by a valid randomization technique? Were there patients who refused to be part of a controlled experiment, or who were eliminated from consideration before or during the study? Did the patients or the physicians know who got what? Could the patients have been aware that they were getting aspirin by its taste? Did the author worry about such things? In one therapy for hemophilia, to provide a homely example, the physicians were unaware of which drug the patient received, but the patients could easily tell. Happily, this was described in the paper. How did the author decide that a patient was cured? How did the author know that his patients took the prescribed therapy? How long and how complete was the follow up? I recall one paper on amebiasis in which the diagnosis was made by finding the offending organism in one of three consecutive stools: cure was determined by observing one negative stool. It does pay to read with care.

I'll look at the Methods section still more closely if I am deeply interested in the scientific area and particularly if I plan to attempt to repeat or extend the observation. I do mean closely, and here we must face the continual war between authors and editors. A good author tries to describe his methods in detail. An editor wants to save space. I've prided myself over the years in being absolutely explicit in my description of experimental technique. If a critical method has been published before, I'll describe its principle, and not leave it to the reader to search in the 1909 German literature. If I deviate from the published method, however slightly, I avoid writing, "by a minor modification of the method of Galen," without telling the reader what this modification was. Particularly important in reading many papers is to examine the statistical techniques used. If they're obscure to me, and I think this information is important, I'll take the paper to my statistician friends for help. Different problems require different methods of analysis, and the appropriateness of the methods used must be assessed. All may stand or fall on the numbers game.

Sounds pretty exhausting, and that's why I reserve thorough reading only for selected papers. I suppose this represents a sacrifice of quality of reading for quantity.

I've described the way I approach an article that deals with original observations, either clinical or investigative. Of course, all of us build or supplement our knowledge by reading reviews. Again, I'm more likely to read a review if it's by someone whose name rings a bell, but this is a rule to be violated since (to paraphrase E. B. White) there are new babies being born every minute. Here the thoroughness of my reading depends in large measure on the literary capacity of the writer. Reviews vary widely in their styles, sometimes because the editors apply strictures of space or of the number of bibliographic citations that the author may use. I'm particularly attracted to reviews in which the writers provide their own slant on controversial issues.

If I'm reading the latest review of what's known about Australian dingbat fever, I'll be upset if I read that Jones said this disease occurred only in men and Smith reported that it occurred only in women, while the reviewer provides no guidance. It is the reviewer's duty to tell me that Jones limited his observation to Army personnel, while Smith was the doctor for a convent. He mustn't leave it to me to figure this out by getting Jones's and Smith's articles from the library. Another cause of great distress I've touched on before. It's disconcerting to read a review that ignores all work earlier than five years ago, or that is naively provincial. It really isn't true that everything we know about Australian dingbat fever was learned in the last few years in Boston, New York, or Baltimore and was published in the *New England Journal of Medicine*. A good review has another characteristic I cherish. You ought to be able to pick it up in the middle to read about the one part you're interested in, without reference to the rest of the review.

That brings me to a favorite peeve about modern medical literature in general. Editors nowadays seem to allow authors to use long strings of abbreviations to replace words. A few of these make sense, like min. for minute, but most of them are really an exercise in argot, the secret language of thieves. One certainly knows that the writer is an in-person if he can disguise his thoughts in arcane abbreviations. You, dear reader, are not an in-person, and this you will recognize immediately as you spend more time deciphering the abbreviations than the author saved in writing them. Dear author, give me a break and write out all those words. English is a wonderful language (WL to you). While I'm on the subject, I'm often turned off by the persistent use of jargon. It may be too much to ask, but particularly in the Discussion the author ought to write for an audience of intelligent ignoramuses, a phrase I suspect I borrowed from C. P. Snow.

I haven't touched yet on how to keep track of what one reads. There are two parts to this, note-taking and reprint-gathering. When I was much younger, I used to fill index cards with brief abstracts of the articles I wanted to remember. As I look around, this seems to be the way most of my colleagues keep notes. Many years ago, I found this was too cumbersome for my needs, and I turned to another technique suggested to me by an old friend, a pathologist who I only later found was a pioneer in my own field. In brief, I write my abstracts on loose-leaf notebook sheets that I can file away in something like logical order. I use a fresh page for each subject (there'd be one for Australian dingbat fever, and if I have a lot of information about this disorder, perhaps it will be a page devoted exclusively to "Therapy of Australian Dingbat Fever"). I'll duplicate my efforts on another page entitled "Aspirin, Unusual Therapeutic Uses." In this way I can retrieve the information in two ways. I carefully choose notebook paper that is subdivided horizontally into one-inch segments, and I try to keep each abstract within this small space. This is good exercise, for ordinarily, if you have to use more than an inch you have not gotten the point of the article. I file my entries into my notebooks by subject, and within each subject, in chronological order. I then take advantage of the author's scholarship by transcribing onto the appropriate sheets his references to earlier literature in their chronological sequence. I usually fortify this entry with a sentence or two stating what the quoted article is alleged to say. Thus, I gradually build up a section of my notebook that will provide me with a chronological, and sometimes rather complete, bibliography of a particular field. I make a check next to the articles I've read so that I can keep track of what is just secondhand (and not necessarily accurately quoted) information.

Ultimately, of course, this admittedly idiosyncratic method of mine takes reams of paper and shelves of notebooks, but the value of this obsessive behavior has been immense. It has made it easy for me to write a plethora of review articles with a minimum of strain. To supplement my random bibliography, I use two tools described elsewhere in this book. I'll select one or more early references and enlist the librarian to prepare a list of the articles in which it is quoted. And I'll use Medlines or some other indexing method to find other articles I may have missed.

Of course, no abstract will help me as much as the original article. Where I have no pressing need to refer to a paper soon, if the article is longer than a few pages, and not too "old," I may write for a reprint. Like everyone else, however, I've turned more and more to the use of duplicating machines. They've revolutionized the process of recall.

I must here mention one of the failures of modern library technology. If I ask our librarian to find me an article on Australian dingbat fever that was published some years ago, I sometimes get in the mail a trim photocopy. I've been robbed of a great aid to one's general education. The late Dr. David Seegel taught us students at Columbia University to look through every journal we picked up. In this way one can sometimes find by serendipity (and here I use the word correctly) a plum waiting for the picking. It's a technique that provides a little extra to the task of reading.

Finally, I have another secret method of understanding what I read. Sometimes a crucial bit of technical information is not recorded because it seems obvious to the writer or it's so much a part of his daily life he doesn't realize that the reader was not trained in his laboratory. I fill the gap by writing or phoning the author. He always responds with the glow of satisfaction that comes from knowing someone out there cares.

Reading the literature is a daily task. "Keeping up" is impossible except in narrow areas. Perhaps others have simpler ways than I have outlined. My aim has been to describe what I do, and not some theoretical scheme. The real answer, of course, is to be blessed, as too few of us are, with a photographic memory. Such individuals can check the box, "None of the above applies."

8

EVALUATION: REQUIREMENTS FOR SCIENTIFIC PROOF

Frederick Mosteller

Large chunks of this book devote themselves to the statistical aspects of the biomedical literature. In a world of microscopes, stethoscopes, and computers, readers may wonder how statistics managed to intrude in such a work. The word *statistics* has two aspects, both important for progress in medicine and health: statistics as number and statistics as method.

STATISTICS AS NUMBER

The first meaning comes from counting "for the state." That original meaning connected statistics with censuses for tax purposes. In modern times, we have broadened official statistics to include education, births, taxes, causes of death, frequency of hospital admissions, and expenditures for various purposes. Although these columns of figures repel many of us, they often largely determine both public policy and directions of biomedical research. These numbers, for example, tell us of the burden of illness, both of its extent and of its costs, as measured by money, extent of morbidity, mortality, or even impact on family.

Although Florence Nightingale is better known as "the Lady with a Lamp," a biographer, Sir Edward Cook (1913), also labeled her "a Passionate Statistician" (II, p. 395). Her appreciation for the need for statistics as number in hospital care makes her one of the founders of the modern statistical profession. She pursued these matters with such leaders in social statistics as Adolphe Quetelet and Francis Galton, and barely failed to establish what would have been the first statistical chair at any university.

The great problems of statistics as number come in specifying the measures to be collected, in carrying out the collection, and in processing, organizing, and interpreting the resulting data. We know that definitions matter enormously. For example, the frequencies of diseases wax and wane with changes in preferences for particular diagnoses. For instance, formerly, when someone dropped dead at a street corner, the cause of death would be labeled apoplexy (stroke). Now, such an incident is more likely to be called a heart attack.

STATISTICS AS METHOD

Statistics as method deals more with the design, execution, data analysis, and interpretation of studies. Some researchers have the impression that statistics is limited to data analysis and so may not go to statisticians for consultation until too late, since the design may already have ruined a study. Statistical methods do not intrude on biomedical research because bio-statisticians like to proselytize. Instead, biomedical researchers have demanded these methods to help them solve their problems. Early twentieth-century contributors, such as Student (William S. Gossett, who worked for a brewer), Francis Galton, Karl Pearson, and R. A. Fisher (the geneticist), founded the modern field of statistical methods, even though such early workers as Karl Gauss and Pierre de Laplace knew a great deal about data analytic tools. Fisher more or less single-handedly established the area of design of experiment as a discipline.

DESIGN

Although comparative investigations have many possible designs, two stand out, and a third has some supporters. The most common controlled experimental design compares the performances of independent groups, each group treated by a different therapy. This design is illustrated in Chapter 9, especially in David Sackett's snow-shoveling examples. Even when the investigation is not a controlled experiment, comparative studies try to emulate controlled experiments as closely as they can. Again, Sackett's snow-shoveling examples offer illustration.

The second main type of controlled experiment uses the crossover design. When two therapies can be and are applied in succession in either order to the same patient, individuals behave as their own controls. (Studies of identical twins come close to this, but they are rare.)

The third method is that of historical controls. If historically the rate of cure has been 30 percent, and the new therapy cures 60 percent, the new therapy looks good. One problem is that of comparability of groups, which is discussed in Chapter 9.

Reiffenstein, Schiltroth, and Todd (1968) scored clinical trials on the basis of the presence of four properties: (1) controls, (2) randomization, (3) objective measures, and (4) statistical analysis, in that order. They reviewed many clinical investigations according to the number of properties that appear in unbroken succession. Thus, if a study has properties 1, 2, and 4, it would be scored as having controls and randomization. Table 8.1 shows the distribution of scores for comparative clinical investigations in two medical journals. Note that relatively few studies have all four properties. The hope is that the percentage will increase. Between the two time periods reported, the percentage with all four approximately tripled in the *Canadian Medical Association Journal*.

Statistics as a Means for Understanding Variation

Biological variation generates much of the need for these statistical methods. Although some features, such as circulation of the blood, are common to all living humans, when we go a step further and ask about pulse rate, blood pressure, or counts of red corpuscles, we find variation both among people and within a person from time to time. Given the large variation among individuals, systematic methods are required to discover causes of disease or relations between biological or social variables. Efficient discovery requires even more carefully designed methods. When measurements become expensive, we hunt for ways to make one measurement do the work of several.

TABLE 8.1 Use of Standards by Reported Clinical Trials (in Percentages)

Strengthening Properties	Canadian Medical Association Journal 1956-60	1961-67	New England Journal of Medicine 1963-67
None	66	56	48
C*	24	21	18
RC*	3	5	3
ORC*	2	3	12
SORC*	5	16	20
N (total papers)	203	264	103

*C = controls, R = randomization, O = objective measures, and S = statistical analysis.
Source: R. J. Reiffenstein, A. J. Schiltroth, and D. M. Todd "Current Standards in Reported Drug Trials," *Canadian Medical Association Journal* 99 (1968):1135.

In many problems, variation has more than one source. Nutrition and exercise help determine physical well-being. When we try to sort out the impact of changes in such input variables, statistical methods may be required to aid in their untangling or to discover that in some circumstances the untangling may not be possible.

Statistics for Strengthening Arguments about Causation

Systematic quantitative methods have been developed and used more and more because researchers have demanded stronger and stronger proofs. One might at first suppose that it would be easy to tell whether a new therapy is better than an old one or better than none at all. Citing a few obvious sources of difficulty will clarify the problem. An innovator's enthusiasm for a new invention may generate more glowing reports than are appropriate; a patient's eagerness to please the physician also may lead to overrating the gains; and inadvertent or even deliberate selection of healthier patients for treatment can produce extraordinary cure rates and thus mislead. The placebo effect—gain from treatment alone, even if the treatment is well-known to have no medical value—has misled many investigators. Its ability to relieve a variety of symptoms is documented by Henry K. Beecher's collection of findings from studies by many investigators as shown in Table 8.2.

A slightly more complicated trap also lurks under the title of regression

TABLE 8.2 Beecher's Summary of Relief from Placebos

Condition	Number of Patients	Percentage Relieved by a Placebo
Severe postoperative wound pain	455	31
Cough	45	40
Experimental cough	s.e.*	37
Mood changes	50	30
Pain from angina pectoris	112	36
Headache	199	52
Seasickness	33	58
Anxiety and tension	31	30
Common cold	158	35
Average		35

*Scores of experiments.

Source: H. K. Beecher, *Measurement of Subjective Responses: Quantitative Effects of Drugs* (New York: Oxford University Press, 1959), pp. 66–67.

effect. The general idea relates to quantities (such as a patient's temperature) that vary up and down from time to time. Such quantities tend to return toward the middle of their range. Thus, if we look at such a quantity when it is high, we could predict that it will likely go down. If we think of the well-being of an individual as such a quantity, then a patient is likely to present when feeling ill and be somewhat restored a little later. Any treatment given at the time of presenting is likely to be credited with the results of such natural restoration as well as its own effect. Thus, with the best will in the world, investigators have a severe struggle to keep themselves, their colleagues, their patients, and nature from misleading them about the merits of a treatment. The constraints on design, execution, and analysis of investigations have been created over several decades to help honest investigators assure themselves of the reality of the effects their treatments produce. (For more detail and examples, see Chapter 9, which takes up a variety of sources of bias and describes useful preventive steps.)

To hunt out dishonest investigators probably requires methods different from those discussed in this book. The discussion in both this chapter and Chapter 9 focuses on unconscious bias and well-intentioned error. Before appealing to fraud, it is well to keep in mind the old saying that most institutions have enough incompetence to explain almost anything.

Statistics as a Means of Deciding Whether a Difference is Real

A paradigm of the controlled experiment is shown in the following diagram:

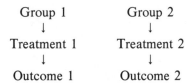

Ideally, the groups are equivalent before treatment. The outcomes might be averages for some appropriate measure or proportions with certain properties. Usually because of sampling error and other variation, investigators use statistical tests to compare the outcomes.

For example, Corey et al. (1978) compared the safety and efficacy of topical diethyl ether with no treatment for genital infections due to herpes simplex virus. They report (p. 238) that "comparisons between groups were evaluated by Student's t-test or chi-square analysis." Moreover, in reporting results, they use such language as "The mean number of lesions present when therapy started was 7.4 for the ether group and 5.9 for the control group

$(P > 0.05)$" and "the duration of new-lesion formation during episodes was actually longer for both men and women with ether therapy (4.8 vs. 1.8 days, $P < 0.01$ by t-test)." We turn now to discuss this language.

The Language of Testing Hypotheses

For any kind of statistical investigation, it helps to be aware of some of the jargon. Since much of statistical analysis used in straightforward investigations is intended to confirm or establish a value, the language of testing hypotheses or testing significance is frequently used.

In everyday language, the idea is this: even if a treatment has no medical effect on patients, patients vary in their performance following treatment and might by chance variation alone produce what looks like a healing effect. Investigators try to control for this by setting criteria that require effects to be large enough so that chance variation would rarely exceed the criteria and thus be declared "statistically significant." The treatment may actually have a substantial effect. If so, then the criteria are likely to be exceeded, though unfortunate chance variation might negate this.

The ideas just expressed can profitably be thought of as parallel to the "diagnostic test versus the truth" as presented early in Chapter 9. Table 8.3 displays these ideas. The heading labeled "the truth" corresponds to a

TABLE 8.3 Analogy between Statistical Hypothesis Testing and Diagnostic Testing

		The Truth (Patient Does/Does Not Have Disease)	
		A Difference Does Exist	A Difference Does Not Exist
Investigator's conclusion (outcome of diagnostic test)	A difference *does* exist	Great!	Bad. Frequency of this "Type I error" controlled by choice of statistical significance level α, sometimes chosen as 0.05.
	A difference does *not* exist	Bad. Ideas of power, $1-\beta$, control frequency of this "Type II error"	Great!

patient having or not having the disease. The investigator's conclusion corresponds to the outcome of the diagnostic test. The approach is crude in the sense that it regards agreement with the truth as favorable and disagreement as unfavorable but does not formally consider:

the value of the gains from being correct, or the losses from the two kinds of mistakes; or

the frequencies with which the two forms of truth hold; or

the likelihood of various sizes of difference.

We turn next to ideas of significance and power.

We can now translate the above discussion into the generalized statistical jargon. The investigation tests whether the *null hypothesis*—no treatment effect—is true or whether an *alternative hypothesis*—some treatment effect—is true. The criterion is set so that if the null hypothesis is true, the probability of exceeding the criterion (by chance) is small. The value of that probability is called the *significance level* of the test. Sometimes the Greek letter α is used to label the significance level. Making the statement that there is an effect when none exists is called a Type I error. If the treatment has an effect, the probability that the criterion is exceeded in the investigation is called the *power* of the test for that size of effect. The power tells how much chance a given size of effect has of being detected by the investigation, given the criterion. Sometimes the greek letter β is used in connection with power, $1-\beta$ being the power. The mistake of saying that there is no effect when one is present is called a Type II error, and β is associated with its frequency. (Unfortunately the names Type I and Type II are so faceless that few can recall their meaning.) The significance level is often chosen as 0.05 or 0.025 (equivalently, 5 percent and 2.5 percent). Thus, if there is no effect, a 5 percent significance level means that only 5 investigations per 100 would exceed the criterion.

The origin of the widely used 5 percent level may be due to wanting a small round number, such as 1 percent, 5 percent, or 10 percent, and wanting a round value for the t-statistic like 1, 2, or 3. When 1.96 gave a 2-sided, 5 percent level (see bottom line of Table 8.4), perhaps the choice was automatic. It is also true that, if in a college class one tosses a penny repeatedly and after each toss asks the class if there is anything suspicious about the reporting, when the fifth head in a row is reported, hands suddenly go up all over the room. The chance of the first 5 tosses being 5 heads in a row is 1/32, and so the chance of 5 tails or 5 heads in a row is 1/16, or 0.0625. This is also near 0.05, and so we have some behavioral grounds to support a number near 5 percent. The choice does not matter much, and there is some benefit in a standard value as long as it is used, not for making decisions, but for reporting.

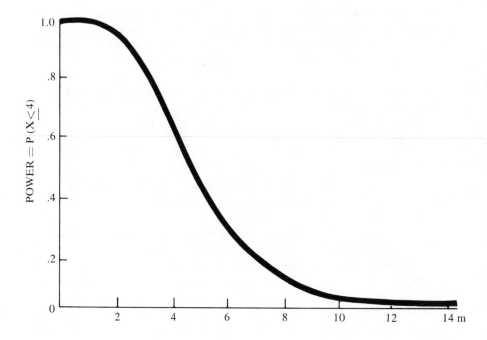

FIGURE 8.1. Power of the Test for a Reduction of Angina Attacks from an Average of 9 per Week Following a Change of Therapy.

Source: Compiled by the author.

In the opening comparison in the herpes example, the investigators want to check the equivalence of the groups in terms of number of lesions before therapy. They essentially ask whether it is reasonable that the mean numbers of lesions in the populations from which these groups are drawn are equal. Their null hypothesis is that they are equal, the alternative that they are not. They apparently are using a 0.05 significance level. They report $P > 0.05$, presumably implying thereby that since they could not reject the hypothesis of equality at the 0.05 level, the agreement was satisfactory. (In some studies, corrections might later be made for the observed difference. Since these investigators find few and small differences, a later correction would probably not be important.)

Few authors discuss power. It is a very neglected area in medical research design. One good source is Cohen (1977). George W. Snedecor and William G. Cochran (1980) also have good discussions in sections on power and sample size.

Freiman et al. (1978) document that perhaps 70 percent of randomized trials that reported "no effect" had insufficient power to detect changes in effect amounting to 25 percent of the risk, and half of these trials could not detect a 50 percent reduction in risk. Thus, an investigation reporting "no effect" may well be overlooking improvements of considerable clinical importance because of inadequate design.

Corey et al. (1978, p. 239) say, "The likelihood that our study would not have detected a 50 percent reduction in any of the symptoms or signs of genital infection due to herpes simplex virus outlined in Table 1 was less than 5 per cent." (Table 1 included 6 items each for primary and recurrent episodes.) Thus, their power to detect a 50 percent improvement is 95 percent, or 0.95. the 5 percent here is β, not the significance level.

The power of a test can usually be increased by increasing the sample sizes used. Another way is to reduce the natural response variability by improving the method of measurement. Physical scientists often feel that by this second route they can avoid the problem of variation. Expense and feasibility are common obstacles.

Power depends on the actual difference, which can rarely be observed. Indeed, if we knew it, we would not be making an empirical investigation. Let us illustrate with an oversimplified example. A patient suffers an average of 9 angina attacks per week. A new medication is prescribed for him. The physician decides that, if the report on the first week is 4 or fewer attacks, the treatment is having a favorable effect. Using a mathematical model for the variability, called the Poisson distribution, we can relate the probability of detecting an improvement to its size. Let m be the true rate per week. Then the probability of getting 4 or fewer attacks is shown in the graph of Figure 8.1. For this problem, the significance level is 0.055. The power is the whole curve. Each rate m has a different power. At m= 3, the power is 0.82.

Some Common Tests of Statistical Significance

The principal statistical tests in common use can be applied to many different problems. Some standard uses are very frequent, and a reader may be helped to know what these are.

When the data come in the form of continuous measurements (like weight or height), the t-test is used for testing the difference between two means or for comparing a mean with a standard known value. If t is large, either positively or negatively, then the null hypothesis is rejected. Just how large t needs to be for "statistical significance" depends on the significance level one selects and on the effective number of independent measurements in the study, called the degrees of freedom (abbreviated d.f. or df). When the degrees of freedom is large, say over 30, the two-sided, 5 percent level is about ±2. Moreover, since a t-value measures a difference in terms of its standard

TABLE 8.4 Sizes of t-Values Associated with Degrees of Freedom (for the 2-sided 5 percent level of statistical significance.)

Degrees of Freedom	Critical Value of t
1	12.71
2	4.30
3	3.18
4	2.78
5	2.57
10	2.23
30	2.04
100	1.98
1,000	1.96
∞	1.96

deviation, people often mention two standard deviations as a criterion. For smaller degrees of freedom and other significance levels, tables are available. No natural line divides large samples from small samples, but the criteria for small degrees of freedom are very different from those over 30, as Table 8.4 shows.

Table 8.4 shows that the giant steps come in the early degrees of freedom. The move from 1 to 2 df cuts the size needed for significance from 12.7 to 4.3, roughly a reduction of two-thirds. For a sample size 30, the t-value is within 4 percent of its value for an infinite sample size which can be interpreted as exact knowledge of the standard deviation.

Figure 8.2 shows two probability distributions. The one on the left shows the distribution of the statistic when the null hypothesis is true, together with the cutoffs $t_{\alpha/2}$ and $t_{1-\alpha/2}$, which cut a probability of $\alpha/2$ off each tail, corresponding to a significance level of α. The right-hand distribution represents the distribution of the t-statistic when an alternative hypothesis is true—one where the mean difference is larger than zero. The area $1-\beta$, to the right of $t_{1-\alpha/2}$, is the power of the test when this alternative hypothesis is true.

The official close of a test of significance rejects or accepts the null hypothesis. "Reject" means the evidence is strongly against the null hypothesis, and "accept" means the evidence is not strongly against it. In most problems, the null hypothesis is a point on a continuous scale—the difference is zero—more particularly 0.000000.... Naturally, we don't believe a real-life situation is correct to infinitely many decimals. If we have lots of data, then we are saying (when we say "accept") that the truth is not far from the

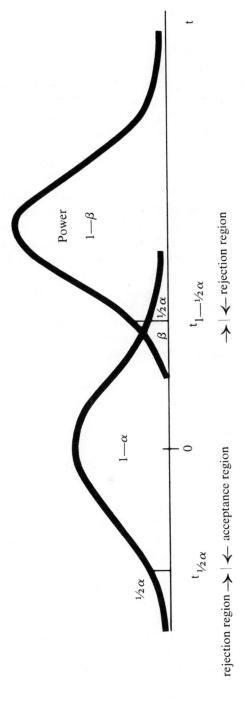

FIGURE 8.2 Schematic Diagram Showing Distribution Corresponding to Null Hypothesis (left) and Alternative Hypothesis (right), Critical Value of t, Significance Level, and Power for a Two-Sided t-Test

null hypothesis. We can better say this with confidence intervals, which are described below.

The t-test may also be used to test whether a regression coefficient differs significantly from zero.

The F-test compares the alikeness of means of several groups, or it compares variation. It is much used in the analysis of variance that generalizes the idea of comparing two means to comparing many means. If the F-statistic is large or (rarely) very near zero, the null hypothesis is rejected. Roughly speaking, F-values near 1 mean little evidence against the null hypothesis. One needs a table to check an F-value.

In comparing the telephonic interviewing done by pediatric nurse practitioners, house officers, and practicing pediatricians, Perrin and Goodman (1978) developed scores for various aspects of the interviews. They used the F-test to test whether the mean scores of the three groups of interviewers might reasonably have come from the same population. Because F was large, they rejected this hypothesis and concluded that the nurse practitioners were better at the telephonic interviewing. They did not report the value of F, only a P-value.

The χ^2 (chi-squared) test is used for tables of counts, often called contingency tables, to see whether they conform to some theory. In a two-way table of counts, we often ask whether, except for sampling variation, the rows are proportional. For example, do two treatments achieve the same percentage of cures?

When the statistic χ^2 is large, the null hypothesis is rejected. It essentially measures the distance from a null position but in an unusual way, just as do t and F.

Creagan et al. (1979), preliminary to a study of the effect of vitamin C (ascorbic acid) therapy on advanced cancer, compared, among other things, the age, sex, and performance score of the vitamin C and placebo group by χ^2.

Age	Age Vita-min	Age Pla-cebo	Sex	Sex Vita-min	Sex Pla-cebo	Score	Performance Score Vita-min	Performance Score Pla-cebo
≤ 45	2	4	Male	37	39	2	12	13
46–65	26	27	Female	23	24	3	39	43
> 65	32	32				4	9	7

These tables give χ^2 values of 0.61, 0.00, and 0.42. These values are all small, indicating close agreement between the two groups. The statistical significance levels, instead of being near zero, are near one. Specifically the P's are approximately 0.74, 1.00, and 0.81. These P's are called P-values.

They give the probability that a larger value of the statistic would be observed when the null hypothesis is true and only chance effects are operating.

When the counts are small, the approximation employed by the χ^2 test may not be satisfactory, and then Fisher's exact test may be used. In studying cimetidine for anastomotic ulcers after partial gastrectomy, Gugler et al. (1979) found the following:

	Cimetidine	Placebo
Healed	7	1
Not healed	0	7

Using Fisher's exact test, they reported $P < 0.01$. The actual P-value is 0.0012 substantially smaller than the bound given, and so the result is more impressive than the report. It is better to give the actual P-value than the bound, not only because the bound may be conservative but because the P-value may be useful to others in later research.

An author sometimes chooses a t-test to be one-sided and sometimes two-sided. If we ask whether an effect is favorable, we may not be interested in knowing that it turned out to be definitely unfavorable. Thus, in large samples, the criterion might be set at some number like $t = 1.65$ (as opposed to ± 1.96), and, if the t-statistic observed exceeded 1.65, then the result would be declared statistically significant at the one-sided, 5 percent level. Often investigators fail to report the "one-sidedness" of the test. If we want to know whether the treatment effect differs from zero, then in large samples, if the observed t is less than -1.96 or greater than 1.96, an effect would be declared statistically significant at the 5 percent, or 0.05, level of significance. In the herpes example, it seems likely that the initial test was two-sided, although this is not stated. Sometimes a great fuss is made about the decision to use one or two sides. This should be regarded primarily as a reporting problem rather than a moral issue. Multiplying or dividing by 2 is not hard if one knows which to do.

In the second illustration of the herpes example, the statistical significance of the duration of new lesion formation was reported as $P < 0.01$. The authors thus have not chosen the 0.05 level once and for all. Instead, they are using 0.05 and 0.01 as baselines for reporting.

Although the 5 percent level is an arbitrary criterion, it is widely employed as a device for concluding that an effect is actually present. This conclusion might be changed by other data from other sources. A conclusion that something differs does not settle that a new therapy is better than an old because we have to consider the many ways such data can arise through "troubles in design" as discussed earlier. The reader should ask what causes other than improvement in therapy could produce the observed effect: lack of equivalent groups, lack of blindness in the investigation, regression effect, and so on. (See Chapter 9.)

Pitfalls in Interpreting Tests of Statistical Significance

Difficulties can arise also through troubles in analysis. Sometimes investigators have choices among several outcome variables and, by choosing the one that most favors the new treatment, will be able to reach an impressive level of significance. Thus, if a curious or unusual outcome variable is used, the reader should be concerned

In many investigations, several outcomes will be reported. In the herpes illustration, the authors report mean duration of symptoms after therapy started; high temperatures with headache, malaise, or myologia; mean duration of pain; mean duration of pruritus; mean duration of virus shedding; mean duration of lesions; mean time to next recurrence; and at least five other properties, not including data on recurrent episodes. Presumably, these are all of interest to the therapist. The herpes study is an example where no one variable is the key that would settle the value of the therapy. The danger occurs when the investigators review many variables and report on only favorable ones, unlike these authors, who report that "topical ether, though dramatically painful, did not shorten the duration of either primary or recurrent genital herpes, and did not prevent or delay recurrent episodes" (p. 239).

Similar potential biases can occur by applying several different statistical tests of the same hypothesis and choosing to publish only the test that most favors the new treatment. That this has been done may be hard to detect because an investigator may have an excellent reason for using a special test, even one devised specifically for the study. If a special test is used, the report should explain why. In writing a report, when several measures or several tests have been employed and a selection made, good reporting will discuss this.

Even when design and analysis seem satisfactory and the new therapy has advantages, the decision to use it is a separate matter. Concerns about cost, availability, method of administration, side effects, addiction, irreversibility of treatment, or incompatibility with other therapies may deter the use of the therapy.

An Alternative Way of Reporting Statistical Results: Confidence Statements

Although the approach of testing hypotheses sounds like a decision mechanism, it can profitably be regarded as a way of reporting data in a standardized manner. An alternative method of reporting is through the method of confidence intervals. To report an estimate for a population based on a sample, the investigator gives an interval together with a confidence coefficient. For example, the report may read as follows: The 95 percent confidence interval for the population mean is

sample mean $\pm$ 2(standard deviation of the mean)

example: 85 ± 15, or 70 to 100.

The 85, the sample mean, estimates the population mean, and the 15 is approximately 2 standard deviations of the sample mean (or 1.96 for large samples). The investigator says that the true mean is between 70 and 100, which is true or false. If in many samples statements are constructed in this manner, 95 percent of the statements will be true, 5 percent false.

The confidence interval has the advantage of announcing the uncertainty of the estimate along with the estimate itself. Confidence intervals are also called interval estimates. In some problems, special tables are required for constructing the intervals.

Confidence intervals can be used to test hypotheses, because, if a value to be tested falls outside the interval, we can reject it at a significance level equal to

100 percent minus the confidence level.

In our example above, the hypothesis might be that the population mean is 105, but it falls outside the 95 percent confidence interval and so would be rejected at the 5 percent level of statistical significance.

(For the reader who would like one good practical book on statistical methods, Snedecor and Cochran's *Statistical Methods* is excellent.)

REPORTING ON THE DESIGN, EXECUTION, AND ANALYSIS OF A RANDOMIZED CLINICAL TRIAL

Without knowing much about the kind of study being done, the reader can get some idea of the quality of the reporting, which, in turn, is one way to appreciate a study. If a study has been done well, then it deserves a good write-up so that its strength can be assessed.

Randomization. If the patients were not randomized to treatment, then the biases described in Chapter 9 may be present.

Description of randomization. The danger for the reader is that the investigator says the study was randomized but means that the assignment to treatment was haphazard. A study is better reported if it says a word about how the randomization was achieved.

Degree of blindness. Although an investigation may have several degrees of blindness, some important features, not always feasible, are that

the patient does not know the treatment,
the administrator of treatment does not know the treatment, and
the evaluator of the outcome does not know the treatment.

Many randomized trials are said to be double-blind, usually meaning that the patient and the evaluator do not know the treatment. A few words in the report about how the blindness was achieved lend added credence to the claim.

What is tested? The paper should report what the statistical analysis was designed to test—difference in survival, difference in recurrence rate, or difference in proportion cured.

Statistical procedure. It should report the test procedure actually used, for example, a t-test for the difference of means.

Values. The study should give the numerical value of the statistic used as well as its P-value, because this is more complete reporting and the results may be of value to others later trying to gather data for survey articles or for comparison. Ideally, the major component quantities, such as the means themselves, will be given for the same reason. They may also help knowledgeable physicians to decide whether their patients are similar to those in the study.

TABLE 8.5. Percentages of Papers Reporting Statistical Methods and Informed Consent in Cancer Trials

Item Reported/Not Reported	Studies of Multiple Myeloma and Chronic Myelocytic Leukemia	Studies of Gastrointestinal Cancer	Studies of Breast Cancer
Survival	47	47	51
Randomization	16	25	39
Source of P-value	16	20	42
Informed consent	5	15	10
Power	0	0	2
Average percent	17	21	29
Number of papers	19	20	93

Source: F. Mosteller, J. P. Gilbert, and B. McPeek, "Reporting Standards and Research Strategies for Controlled Trials: Agenda for the Editor," *Controlled Clinical Trials* (1980):48.

Reporting on topics such as these is not frequent even in the field of cancer trials, in which the statistical sophistication is rather high. For example, Frederick Mosteller, John P. Gilbert, and Bucknam McPeek (1980) reviewed random samples of several kinds of cancer trials, 132 papers in all, and found the results given in Table 8.5. Because the cancers studied were often fatal, survival was generally an issue. Randomization, source of P-value, and power have already been discussed. Although informed consent may have been required for most studies, it was not often reported (the papers were mainly from the period 1972–77). Note that we are emphasizing reporting and its absence. In these cancer studies, about 24 percent of the five items were reported. This does not mean that in 76 percent of the papers the items were not executed. No doubt many papers executed and did not report.

Although the criticism might be made that excellent reporting of a study with basic flaws in design and execution will not save it, the reader in our complex world often must judge, at least temporarily, on the basis of matters readily appraised. Good reporting is one hallmark, though no guarantee, of good work. Poor reporting of good work leaves the reader with ambiguities or misimpressions.

SIDE BENEFITS OF A STUDY

Although most studies have some primary goal, such as comparing therapies or contributing to the understanding of a biochemical process, sometimes they make additional long-run contributions. This is true both of statistics as number and as method. As an example, *The National Halothane Study* was primarily concerned with comparing the safety of anesthetics, with special emphasis on the anesthetic halothane. In the course of the investigation, information became available about institutional differences in outcome of surgical operations, mortality rates following certain operations when several variables (such as sex, age, and physical status) were controlled, and new methods of analysis. These additional materials are often used in the current literature. The point is that large-scale studies often have the opportunity to make special contributions that go beyond their primary mission. Once a few facts are solidly established, they can lead to the dismissal or support of many speculations.

SUMMARY

This article provides a biomedical reader with some equipment for reading about quantitative methods.

1. It explains the main experimental designs: independent groups, crossovers, and historical controls.
2. It mentions major features of good comparative investigations and shows that relatively few studies provide them all.
3. It warns about placebo effect and regression effect.
4. It provides the ideas that are in back of the statistical testing of hypotheses.
5. It provides the language of statistical testing and reporting: null and alternative hypotheses, significance level, power, Type I and Type II errors, reject, and accept.
6. It illustrates the common statistical tests: t, χ^2, and F.
7. It emphasizes that statistical testing can best be thought of in terms of reporting on outcomes, rather than in terms of making clinical decisions, and suggests confidence intervals as often a better method of reporting.
8. It warns about problems of multiplicity.
9. It suggests that poor reporting of randomization and its description, of blindness, of the statistical testing, and of the values of the statistics often goes with a poor paper.
10. It suggests that the lasting value of a study is often different from the purpose of the original investigation, and so care in reporting may have value for a long time.

REFERENCES

Beecher, HK: *Measurement of subjective responses: Quantitative effects of drugs.* Oxford University Press, New York, 1959.

Cohen, J: *Statistical power analysis for the behavioral sciences.* Rev. ed. Academic Press, New York, 1977.

Cook, Sir Edward: *The life of Florence Nightingale.* 2 vols. Macmillan, London, 1913.

Corey, L; Reeves, WC; Chiang, WT; Vontver, LA; Remington, M; Winter, C; and Holmes, KK: Ineffectiveness of topical ether for the treatment of genital herpes simplex virus infection. *New England Journal of Medicine* 299:237–39, 1978.

Creagan, ET; Moertel, CG; O'Fallon, JR; Schutt, AJ; O'Connell, MJ; Rubin, J; and Frytak, S: Failure of high-dose vitamin C (ascorbic acid) therapy to benefit patients with advanced cancer. *New England Journal of Medicine* 301:687–90, 1979.

Freiman, JA; Chalmers, TC; Smith, H., Jr.; and Kuebler, RR: The importance of beta, the type II error, and the sample size in the design and interpretation of the randomized control trial. *New England Journal of Medicine* 299:690–94, 1978.

Gugler, R; Lindstaedt, H; Miederer, S; Möckell, W.; Rohner, H-G; Schmitz, H; and Székessy, T: Cimetidine for anastomotic ulcers after partial gastrectomy. *New England Journal of Medicine* 301:1077–80, 1979.

Mosteller, F; Gilbert, JP; and McPeek, B: Reporting standards and research strategies for controlled trials: Agenda for the editor. *Controlled Clinical Trials* 1: 37–58, 1980.

Perrin, EC, and Goodman, HC: Telephone management of acute pediatric illnesses. *New England Journal of Medicine* 298:130–35, 1978.

Reiffenstein, RJ; Schiltroth, AJ; and Todd, DM: Current standards in reported drug trials. *Canadian Medical Association Journal* 99:1134–35, 1968.

Snedecor, GW, and Cochran, WG: *Statistical Methods*. 7th ed. Iowa State University Press. Ames, Iowa, 1980.

9

EVALUATION: REQUIREMENTS FOR CLINICAL APPLICATION

David L. Sackett

INTRODUCTION

This chapter has been summarized for those clinicians who are behind in their clinical reading. As nearly as we can tell from several informal polls, this includes all of us. Accordingly, our recommendations in this chapter stress efficiency as well as validity and applicability, and many of our prescriptions for the busy clinical reader call for tossing an article aside early rather than devoting time to its detailed study, only to reject it later.

We confront a given article in two different ways. First, it may find us, as a result of our subscribing to its parent journal or because someone gave it to us. Second, we may find it, as a result of trying to track down information that will help us to evaluate or manage a particular patient. Both routes acknowledge our priority for keeping up with developments in medicine.

There are many reasons why we read (or at least "flash") clinical journals, and most of them are not pertinent to the topic of this chapter. Rather, we shall focus on four distinct reasons: to find out whether to use a (new) diagnostic test, to learn the clinical course and prognosis of disease, to

This chapter was prepared by D. L. Sackett, R. B. Haynes, P. X. Tugwell, and their colleagues from the Department of Clinical Epidemiology & Biostatistics, MacMaster University Health Sciences Centre, Ontario, Canada. It is a condensation of a series of clinical epidemiology rounds that appeared in Volume 124 of the *Canadian Medical Association Journal* in 1981. The author wish to acknowledge, with thanks, the suggestions and criticisms of earlier versions of these ideas that have been received from students, housestaff, and clinical colleagues.

determine etiology and causation, and to distinguish useful from useless (or even harmful) therapy.

The strategies we shall suggest assume that clinical readers are already behind in their reading and that they will never have more time to read than they do now. For these reasons, and because the rules that follow call for closer attention to materials and methods and other matters that usually appear in small type, many of these strategies recommend tossing an article aside as not worth reading, usually on the basis of preliminary evidence. It is only through such early rejection of *most* articles that busy clinicians can focus on the *few* that are both valid and applicable in their own practices.

THE FIRST FOUR RULES

Figure 9.1 is a flowchart of rules for reading clinical journals and shows that the first four rules are common to all of the reasons for reading clinical journals that will be discussed in this chapter. Oscar Ratnoff has made similar recommendations in his earlier chapter.

The first rule calls for you to *look at the title*. Is it potentially interesting or possibly useful in your practice? If not, reject it and go on to the next article, to some other task, or to the hockey rink.

The second rule is to *review the list of authors*. In addition to the occasional recognition of a former classmate, the seasoned reader will know the track record of many authors. If this track record is one of careful, thoughtful work that has stood the test of time, read on. If, on the other hand, the track record is a series of unsupported conclusions that remain in vogue only until letters to the editor catch up with them or, worse yet, the repeated presentation of a prejudice in search of supporting data, reject the article. Like the work of unknown sculptors, however, that of unknown authors deserves at least the following passing glance.

Rule three exhorts you to *read the summary*. The objective here is simply to decide whether the conclusion, *if valid*, would be important to you as a clinician. At issue here is, *not* whether the article's results are *true* (for you can rarely tell this by reading an abstract), but whether the results, *if* true, are *important*.

Finally, the fourth rule is to *consider the site*. Is it sufficiently similar to your own so that its results, if valid, would apply to patients in your practice? There are several issues here. First, is your access to the facilities, expertise, and technology sufficient to permit you to implement the maneuvers described in the article? Second, are the patients in the article similar to your patients in terms of disease severity, comorbidity, treatment, age, sex, race, or other key features that have an important bearing on their clinical outcomes? Finally, and not so obviously, were the article's patients assembled and studied in a

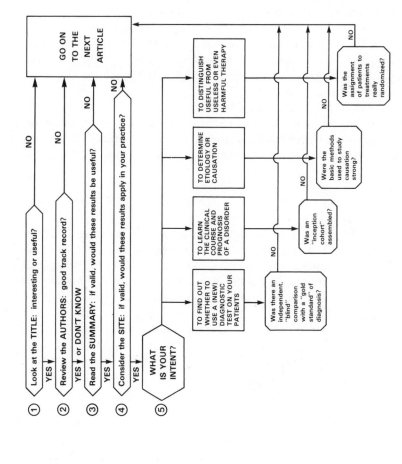

1. Look at the TITLE: interesting or useful? — NO →
   YES ↓
2. Review the AUTHORS: good track record? — NO →
   YES or DON'T KNOW ↓
3. Read the SUMMARY: if valid, would these results be useful? — NO →
   YES ↓
4. Consider the SITE: if valid, would these results apply in your practice? — NO →
   YES ↓
5. WHAT IS YOUR INTENT?

GO ON TO THE NEXT ARTICLE

TO FIND OUT WHETHER TO USE A (NEW) DIAGNOSTIC TEST ON YOUR PATIENTS → Was there an independent, "blind" comparison with a "gold standard" of diagnosis? — NO →

TO LEARN THE CLINICAL COURSE AND PROGNOSIS OF A DISORDER → Was an "inception cohort" assembled? — NO →

TO DETERMINE ETIOLOGY OR CAUSATION → Were the basic methods used to study causation strong? — NO →

TO DISTINGUISH USEFUL FROM USELESS OR EVEN HARMFUL THERAPY → Was the assignment of patients to treatments really randomized? — NO →

FIGURE 9.1. Rules for Reading Clinical Journals

125

fashion and at a site sufficiently similar to your own to render the results transferable?

THE PARTING OF THE WAYS

Thus we must view published experience critically (if not
biblically), for too often the "Conclusion" giveth, but the
"Materials and Methods" taketh away [1].

The review and editorial policies of even the most respected journals provide incomplete protection from error, and a single subscription can provide both truth and a parade of bias. Accordingly, we know of no alternative for clinical readers (once they are satisfied with the title, authors, summary, and site) but to invest time early in reviewing the methods section of an article so as to avoid wasting time later in the execution of useless or even harmful clinical procedures.

The rules branch at this point, depending upon the clinical reader's intent. This arborization is shown in Step 5 of Figure 9.1. The next section of this chapter will consider rules to use when reading a clinical journal in order to decide whether to use a new or existing diagnostic test.

READING TO LEARN ABOUT A DIAGNOSTIC TEST

When encountering an article that looks as if it might be describing a useful diagnostic test (that is, the title is interesting, the authors include a bright former classmate, the summary shows it would be very helpful if it really works as claimed, and the site is similar to your own), what should the reader seek in the methods portion of the paper? The eight elements of a proper clinical evaluation of a diagnostic test appear in Table 9.1. They constitute guides for the clinical reader and will be considered in order.

Was there an independent, "blind" comparison with a "gold standard" of diagnosis?

Patients shown (by application of an accepted "gold standard" of diagnosis) to have the disease of interest, plus other patients shown (by application of this same gold standard) not to have the disease of interest, should have had the diagnostic test carried out and interpreted by clinicians who did not know (that is, they were "blind" to) the results of the gold standard of diagnosis. Once completed, the results of the diagnostic test and those of the gold standard should be compared.

TABLE 9.1 Guides to Reading Articles about a Diagnostic Test

1. Was there an independent, "blind" comparison with a "gold standard" of diagnosis?
2. Did the patient sample include an appropriate spectrum of mild and severe, treated and untreated disease, plus individuals with different, but commonly confused, disorders?
3. Was the setting for the study, as well as the filter through which study patients passed, adequately described?
4. Were the reproducibility of the test result (precision) and/or its interpretation (observer variation) determined?
5. Was the term normal, if used, defined sensibly?
6. If the test is advocated as part of a cluster or sequence of tests, was its individual contribution to the cumulative validity of the cluster or sequence determined?
7. Were the tactics for carrying out the test described in sufficient detail to permit its exact replication?
8. Was the "utility" of the test determined?

TABLE 9.2 A Fourfold, Blind Comparison with a Gold Standard

		Gold Standard		
		Patient Really *Does* Have the Disease	Patient Really Does *not* Have the Disease	
Conclusion drawn from the results of the test	Positive: Patient appears to have the disease	a	b	a + b
	Negative: Patient appears *not* to have the disease	c	d	c + d
		a + c	b + d	N

Note:

Stable properties: $a/(a + c)$ = sensitivity
$d/(b + d)$ = specificity
Frequency-dependent properties: $a/(a + b)$ = positive predictive value
$c/(c + d)$ = negative predictive value
$(a + d)/N$ = accuracy
$(a + c)/N$ = prevalence

The most straightforward method of displaying this comparison of a diagnostic test and a gold standard is a "two-by-two," or "fourfold," table, such as Table 9.2. The key words in such comparisons are *sensitivity*, *specificity*, and *predictive value*. If you do not see at least the first two of these words in the abstract or can not find a fourfold table in a sneak preview of the results of the article, it is probably not worth your time to read any further. Toss it!

If the article survives the quick "screening" test mentioned above, a great deal of useful information can be derived from the comparison of diagnostic test results and the gold standard. The basic concepts follow.

First, the "gold standard" refers to a definitive diagnosis attained by biopsy, surgery, autopsy, long-term follow-up, or other acknowledged standards. If you can not accept the gold standard (within reason, that is— nothing is perfect!), then you should abandon the article. If you do accept the gold standard, then consider the diagnostic test. Does it have something to

TABLE 9.3 Postexercise Electrocardiogram as Predictor of Coronary Artery Stenosis When Latter is Present in One-Half of Patients

		≥ 75% Stenosis		
		Present	Absent	
Postexercise Electrocardiogram	Positive	55	7	62
	Negative	49	84	133
		104	91	195

(Note: cells are labeled a, b in the Positive row and c, d in the Negative row, at the intersection between the Present/Absent columns.)

Note: Positive predictive value $= \dfrac{a}{a+b} = \dfrac{55}{62} = 89\%$

Negative productive value $= \dfrac{d}{c+d} = \dfrac{84}{133} = 63\%$

Sensitivity $= \dfrac{a}{a+c} = \dfrac{55}{104} = 53\%$

Specificity $= \dfrac{d}{b+d} = \dfrac{84}{91} = 92\%$

Source: Adapted from D. L. Sackett, "Clinical Diagnosis and the Clinical Laboratory," *Clinical and Investigative Medicine* 1 (1978):37–43, and M. H. Sketch et al., "Significant Sex Differences in the Correlation of Electrocardiographic Exercise Testing and Coronary Arteriograms," *American Journal of Cardiology* 36 (1975): 169–73.

offer that the gold standard does not? For example, is it less risky, less uncomfortable or embarrassing, less costly, or applicable earlier in the course of the illness? Again, if the proposed diagnostic test offers no theoretical advantage over the gold standard, why read further?

Having satisfied yourself that it is worth proceeding, you are now ready to study the comparison between the diagnostic test results and the gold standard. There are several useful elements in this comparison, and we will cover them one by one, introducing their associated terms along the way.

The first two elements of this comparison consider how well the diagnostic test correctly identifies patients known to have, and known not to have, the disease of interest. Consider the vertical columns of Table 9.2. The gold standard has identified (a+c) patients as really having the disease of interest, and "a" of these had positive diagnostic test results. Thus, an index of the diagnostic test's ability to detect the disease when it really is present is the fraction $a/(a+c)$, usually expressed as a percentage, and for purposes of quick communication referred to as "sensitivity." Similarly, the ability of the diagnostic test to correctly identify the absence of the disease is shown in the next vertical column as $d/(b+d)$, and this index goes by the name "specificity."

Sensitivity and specificity can be considered the "stable properties" of the test because they do not change when different proportions of diseased and well patients are tested. This is an important issue, and we will come back to it.

But stop a moment to consider the usual clinical situation. When we attempt to diagnose a patient's illness, we do not have the results of a gold standard to go by. (If we did, we would not bother to order the less definitive diagostic test because we would already have more information than it can provide.) We are operating "horizontally" in Table 9.2, not vertically." What we must do is order the test and act upon its results (for example, by ordering other tests or prescribing therapy). Thus, in judging the value of a diagnostic test, what we wish to know is not its sensitivity and specificity but how well its results will predict the results of applying the gold standard. If the prediction is good enough, we will add the test to our bag of diagnostic tricks.

Accordingly, we are primarily interested in the horizontal properties of the diagnostic test. Among (a+b) patients with a positive diagnostic test result, in what proportion, $a/(a+b)$, have we correctly predicted, or "ruled in," the correct diagnosis? This proportion, $a/(a+b)$, again usually expressed as a percentage, goes by the name "positive predictive value." Similarly, we want to know how well a negative test result correctly predicted the absence of, or "ruled out," the disease in question. This proportion, $d/(c+d)$, is named the "negative predictive value" of the diagnostic test.

If a diagnostic test's predictive value constitutes the focus of our clinical interest, why waste time considering its sensitivity and specificity? The reason is a fundamental one that has major implications not just for the rational use of diagnostic tests but for the basic education of clinicians. Put simply, a diagnostic test's positive and negative predictive values fluctuate widely, depending on the proportion of truly diseased individuals among those patients to whom the test is applied. (In Table 9.2, this is the proportion $(a+c)/(a+b+c+d)$, a property called "prevalence.")

Whereas a diagnostic test's sensitivity and specificity remain constant with changes in the proportions of diseased and well people who are tested, its predictive values change quite markedly when the prevalence of illness changes [2]. This is not a theoretical concern. In the "real world," the prevalence of a given condition varies quite considerably between the primary- and tertiary-care levels. Furthermore, to achieve certain statistical gains, most diagnostic tests are initially evaluated among equal numbers of individuals with and without the disease of interest (that is, a contrived prevalence of 50 percent).

Because an understanding of the "stable" and "unstable" properties of diagnostic tests is central to their rational use, and because the authors of this chapter are convinced that active problem solving beats passive absorption, we invite you to work through the following example [2].

A group of investigators carefully studied a group of men referred with chest pain and, following graded treadmill stress testing and selective coronary arteriography, obtained the results shown in Table 9.3 [3]. The ability of the postexercise electrocardiogram (ECG) to predict the results of selective coronary angiography was revealed in its positive predictive value of 89 percent (the percentage of men with positive ECGs who had greater than or equal to 75 percent stenosis at arteriography) and its negative predictive value of 63 percent (the percentage of men with negative ECGs who had less than 75 percent stenosis). Accordingly, the authors concluded that, in men, a positive multistage stress test is useful in predicting the presence of significant coronary artery disease, although a negative stress test cannot be relied upon to rule out the presence of significant disease.

As you can see from the gold standard results, 104/195 or 53 percent of the patients had coronary artery disease on angiography, a highly selected group of patients indeed. What would happen if enthusiasts adopted the multistage stress test for wider use in an effort to detect significant coronary disease in men, regardless of whether they had any chest pain? (Please note that the authors of the work cited in this example made no such recommendation.) Would a positive stress test still be useful?

The results of applying this test to a less carefully selected group of men are entirely predictable and are shown in Table 9.4. If the true prevalence of marked coronary artery stenosis, as assessed by the gold standard of angiography, was only one in six (17 percent), rather than better than one in

TABLE 9.4 Postexercise Electrocardiogram as Predictor of Coronary Artery Stenosis When Latter is Present in One-Sixth of Patients

		≥ 75% Stenosis		
		Present	Absent	
Postexercise Electrocardiogram	Positive	55 a	42 b	97
	Negative	49 c	478 d	527
		104	520	624

Note: Positive predictive value $= \dfrac{a}{a+b} = \dfrac{55}{97} = 57\%$

Negative predictive value $= \dfrac{d}{c+d} = \dfrac{478}{527} = 91\%$

Sensitivity $= \dfrac{a}{a+c} = \dfrac{55}{104} = 53\%$

Specificity $= \dfrac{d}{b+d} = \dfrac{478}{520} = 92\%$

Source: Adapted from D. L. Sackett, "Clinical Diagnosis and the Clinical Laboratory," *Clinical and Investigative Medicine* 1 (1978):37–43; and M. H. Sketch et al., "Significant Sex Differences in the Correlation of Electrocardiographic Exercise Testing and Coronary Arteriograms," *American Journal of Cardiology* 36 (1975):169–73.

two (53 percent), the test's positive predictive value will fall from 89 percent to 57 percent, and its negative predictive value will rise from 63 percent to 91 percent, just the reverse of the original situation.

We said that this result could be forecast from Table 9.3, and it is this forecasting feature that permits you to translate the results of a diagnostic test evaluation to your own setting. All you need are a rough estimate of the prevalence of the disease in your own practice (from personal experience) or practices like it (from other articles) and some simple arithmetic. For example, as we have charitably estimated for Table 9.4, approximately one-sixth of all men sent for angiography from a primary-care setting might ultimately be found to have severe coronary artery stenosis.

Thus, if we started with the original number of patients with coronary artery disease (104), five times this number (520) would be free of the disease. Because sensitivity remains constant, 55 (53 percent) of the 104 diseased men would have positive exercise ECGs. Similarly, because specificity remains at 92 percent, 478 of the 520 undiseased men would have negative tests. The rest of the table can then be completed by adding or subtracting to fill in the appropriate boxes, and the predictive values and accuracy can then be calculated.

Having discussed the fourfold comparison with a "gold standard," what about the element of "blindness"? This simply means that those who are carrying out or interpreting the diagnostic test should not know whether the patient being tested really does or does not have the disease of interest; that is, they should be "blind" to each patient's true disease status. Similarly, those who are applying the gold standard should not know the diagnostic test result from any patient. It is only when the diagnostic tests and gold standard are applied in a "blind" fashion that we can be assured that conscious or unconscious bias (in this case the "diagnostic suspicion" bias) has been avoided [4].

Did the patient sample include an appropriate spectrum of mild and severe, treated and untreated disease, plus individuals with different, but commonly confused, disorders?

Florid disease usually presents a much smaller diagnostic challenge than the same disease in an early or mild form, and the real clinical value of a new diagnostic test often lies in its predictive value among members of this latter group. Moreover, the apparent diagnostic value of some tests actually resides in their ability to detect the manifestations of therapy (such as radiopaque deposits in the buttocks of elderly syphilitics) rather than disease, and the reader must be satisfied that the two are not being confused. Finally, just as a duck is not often confused with a yak, even in the absence of chromosomal analyses, the ability of a diagnostic test to distinguish between disorders not commonly confused with one another is scant endorsement for its widespread application. Again, the key value of a diagnostic test often lies in its ability to distinguish among otherwise commonly confused disorders, especially when their prognoses or therapies differ sharply.

Was the setting for the study, as well as the filter through which study patients passed, adequately described?

Because a test's predictive value changes with the prevalence of the target disease, the article ought to tell you enough about the study site and patient-selection filter to permit you to calculate the diagnostic test's likely predictive value in your own practice.

The selection of "control" subjects who do not really have the disease of interest should be described as well. Although lab technicians and janitors may be appropriate control subjects early in the development of a new diagnostic test (especially with the declining use of medical students as laboratory animals), the definitive comparison with a gold standard demands equal care in the selection of both patients with and patients without the target disease. Furthermore, the reader deserves some assurance that differences in diagnostic test results are due to a mechanism of disease and not simply differences in the age, sex, diet, mobility, and so forth, of case and control subjects.

Were the reproducibility of the test result (precision) and/or its interpretation (observer variation) determined?

Validity demands both the absence of systematic deviation from the truth (that is, the absence of bias) and the presence of precision (the same test applied to the same, unchanged patient must produce the same result). The description of a diagnostic test ought to tell readers how reproducible they can expect the test results to be. This is especially true when expertise is required in performing the test (abdominal ultrasound is a current example) or in interpreting it (observer variation is a major problem for tests involving Xrays, ECGs, and the like) [5].

Was the term "normal," if used, defined sensibly?

There are several definitions for the word *normal* that can be used in clinical medicine [2,6]. They can be based on statistics (for example, the mean plus or minus two standard deviations), on cultural norms (for example, body mass), on the risk of subsequent illness (for example, coronary risk factors), or, more appropriately, on clinical properties, such as the ability to identify (with known levels of accuracy) whether patients have given diseases or whether they are likely to benefit from certain treatments. The decision about which definition of normal to use will have a profound effect upon diagnosis, and this must be confronted whenever one reads about new tests.

Although the normal ranges derived from any definition can be compared to an appropriate gold standard, the diagnostic definition of normal has this comparison as its essence. As a result, it makes no assumptions about distributions or social norms and has considerable utility in everyday clinical practice. As we have seen, however, its clinically useful dimension, predictive value, is quite susceptible to differences in disease prevalence.

Finally, increasing attention is being given to a definition of normal based on whether intervention has been shown, in proper experiments, to do more good than harm. Such a definition protects the patient from needless and possibly harmful labeling when no benefit can result from the act, but its use does require keeping up with advances in therapeutics, which brings us back to the reason behind this chapter!

When reading a report of a (new) diagnostic test, then, you should satisfy yourself that the authors have defined what they mean by normal and that they have done so in a sensible and clinically useful fashion.

If the test is advocated as part of a cluster or sequence of tests, was its individual contribution to the cumulative validity of the cluster or sequence determined?

In the diagnosis of many conditions, an individual diagnostic test examines but one of several elements or manifestations of the underlying disorder. For example, in diagnosing deep vein thrombosis, the impedance plethysmograph (IPG) examines venous emptying, whereas the 125 I-fibrinogen leg scan (LS) examines the turnover of coagulation factors at the site of thrombosis. Furthermore, IPG is much more sensitive for proximal, than distal, venous thrombosis, whereas the reverse is true for LS. As a result, these tests are best applied in sequence. If the IPG is positive, the diagnosis is "made," and treatment begins at once. If the IPG is negative, LS begins, and the diagnostic and treatment decision await its results. This being so, it is clinically nonsensical to base a judgement of the value of leg scanning on a simple comparison of its results alone against the "gold standard" of venography. Rather, its agreement with venography among suitably symptomatic patients with negative impedance plethysmography is the appropriate examination for its validity and clinical usefulness.

Were the tactics for carrying out the test described in sufficient detail to permit its exact replication?

If the authors have concluded that you should use their diagnostic test, they have to tell you how to do it, and this description should cover patient issues as well as the mechanics of performing and interpreting the test. Are there special requirements for fluids, diet, or physical activity? What concomitant drugs should be avoided? How painful is the procedure, and what is done to relieve this? What precautions should be taken during and after the test? How should the specimen be transported and stored for later analysis? The advocates of a diagnostic test ought to provide information to potential users on all of these points.

Was the "utility" of the test determined?

The ultimate criterion for a diagnostic test or any other clinical maneuver is whether the patient is better off for it. If you agree with this point of view, you should scrutinize the article to see whether the authors went beyond the foregoing issues of accuracy, precision, and the like to explore the longer-term consequences of their use of the diagnostic test.

In addition to telling you what happened to patients correctly classified by the diagnostic test, the authors should describe the fate of the false positives (positive test results but the patients really do not have the disease) and the false negatives (negative test results but the patients really do have the disease). Moreover, when the execution of a test requires a delay in the initiation of definitive therapy (while the procedure is being repeated, the test is incubating or the slides are waiting to be read) the consequences of this delay should be described.

Use of These Guides to Reading

By applying the foregoing guides, you should be able to decide whether a diagnostic test will be useful to you in your practice, whether it will not, or whether it still has not been properly evaluated. Depending on the context in which you are reading about the test, one or another of the eight guides will be the most important one, and you can go right to it. If this guide has been met in a credible way, you can go on to the others. If it has not been met, you can discard the article right there and go on to something else. Thus, once again, you can improve the efficiency with which you use your scarce reading time.

READING TO LEARN THE CLINICAL COURSE AND PROGNOSIS OF DISEASE

The clinical management of patients with a first urinary stone; a ten-degree scoliosis; or quiescent, left-sided, ulcerative colitis includes, as one central theme, making judgments about the likely time course of their illnesses. Will the urinary stone recur, or does it portend serious disease requiring immediate and extensive diagnosis? Will the ten degrees of scoliosis progress to a frank physical or physiologic derangement? Do patients with left-sided colitis face an increased risk of colorectal cancer?

Each of these patients is experiencing a natural history of their disease—that is, the time course of the interaction between man, causal factors, and the rest of the environment, beginning with the biologic onset of disease and ending with the outcomes of recovery, death, or some other state of physical, social, or emotional function. The subset of that natural history of special interest to us is the portion that begins with the first unambiguous signs or symptoms of illness: the clinical course. Still more specifically, we are called upon to make judgments about prognosis, that is, the probability of developing one or another of the outcomes of the natural history and clinical course of these illnesses.

In reading articles about the clinical course of urinary stone, scoliosis, or ulcerative colitis, whether the papers have come to us or we have sought them out, we will wind up examining reported case series of patients with urinary stones, spinal curves, and ulcerative colitis in order to arrive at some conclusion about their likely outcomes.

But can we accept published reports at face value? The reported rates of stone recurrence range from 40 percent [7] (where we might forgo a workup following a first stone) to "nearly 100%" [8] (where we might as well get on with it). The published spontaneous recovery rates for scoliosis exhibit a sevenfold range [9], and those for cancer risk in ulcerative colitis vary threefold, from 3 percent [10] to nearly 10 percent [11]. With this much inconsistency in the clinical journals, how are we to use them sensibly in making clinical decisions about the clinical course and prognosis of human illness?

As it happens, most of the inconsistencies among the published studies of clinical course and prognosis are due to the different ways (many of them wrong and some of them merely different) that their authors selected and followed the patients. Nonetheless, the requirements for the proper study of clinical course and prognosis are relatively straightforward, involve the sort of "applied common sense" we have called upon earlier in this chapter, and can be translated into a brief set of guides or "diagnostic tests" that can be applied quickly to published articles [12].

These guides are six in number, can be posed as questions, and are listed in Table 9.5. Once again, they focus on how the clinical study was carried out and are therefore applied to the article's section on patients and methods.

TABLE 9.5. Guides to Reading Articles about the Clinical Course and Prognosis of Disease

1. Was an "inception cohort" assembled?
2. Was the referral pattern described?
3. Was complete follow-up achieved?
4. Were objective outcome criteria developed and used?
5. Was the outcome assessment "blind"?
6. Was adjustment for extraneous prognostic factors carried out?

Was an "inception cohort" assembled?

The first guide deals with the fact that patients should be identified at an early and uniform point ("inception") in the course of their disease (such as when they first develop unambiguous symptoms or first receive definitive therapy), so that those who succumb or completely recover are included with those whose disease persists.

Many studies of prognosis are done backwards, for some or all of their patients. For example, several studies of the risk of stone recurrence ask *currently* symptomatic patients if they have had stones *previously*, failing to realize that recurrent stone formers (with positive past histories) have multiple chances to be included in such studies but patients without recurrences (with negative past histories) have only one chance of being included. No wonder that recurrence rates vary all over the map. Similarly, in one recent study of cancer risk in ulcerative colitis, the reason for inclusion in the study of several patients was that they already had cancer [11]. Because colitis patients who remained cancer-free could not be entered under this circumstance, the apparent risk of cancer in colitis patients would become spuriously elevated [12].

The failure to start a study of clinical course and prognosis with an inception cohort has an unpredictable effect on the study's results. In the examples cited above, the effect was to make prognosis appear gloomier than it really is. The opposite error can occur as well, however.

Thus, the failure to assemble a proper "inception cohort" of patients who are at an early and uniform point in the course of their disease usually constitutes a fatal flaw in studies of prognosis. Application of this standard to an article can increase your efficiency as a reader of the clinical literature. If the author should have assembled an inception cohort but failed to do so, discard the article early and go on to something else!

Was the referral pattern described?

The second guide points out that the pathways by which patients entered the study sample should be described. It must be possible for you, the reader, to be able to tell whether the results apply to patients in your practice. Did they come from a primary-care center? Were all hospitals in a defined region scoured for cases? Or, were they assembled in a tertiary-care center that attracted the hopeless, wealthy, and bizarre? It is in the assembly of patients that studies of the course and prognosis of disease often flounder, for it is here that four types of bias are most pervasive [4].

Because a major clinical center's reputation results in part from its particular expertise in a specialized area of clinical medicine, it will be referred problem cases likely to benefit from its special expertise (the *centripetal bias*), and its experts may preferentially admit and keep track of these cases over other, less challenging or less interesting ones (the *popularity bias*). In any event, the selection that occurs at each stage of the referral process can generate patient samples at tertiary-care centers that are much different from those found in the general population (the *referral filter bias*). Finally, patients differ in their financial and geographic access to the clinical technology that identifies them as eligible for study of the course and prognosis of disease. If this degree of access is linked to the risk of a poor outcome, the resulting *diagnostic access bias* will distort the conclusion of the study.

Thus, sampling biases can distort both the timing and the absolute rates of important prognostic outcomes. Despite this serious drawback, the study of inception cohorts at tertiary-care centers can provide useful information on the potential importance of prognostic subgroups as long as sampling biases affect each of the prognostic subgroups equally. However, this equality may be difficult to show and risky to assume.

These sampling biases are largely responsible for the chaos that characterizes most discussions of the course and prognosis of human disease, and these pitfalls are not easily avoided. Short of the Framingham-type of study, in which a large population of individuals is assembled and closely followed for decades, the sampling approach with greatest promise systematically gathers eligible cases from *all* clinical facilities in a given catchment area.

Was complete follow-up achieved?

The third guide asks that all members of the inception cohort be accounted for at the end of the follow-up period and that their clinical status be known. Patients do not disappear from a study for trivial reasons. Rather, they leave the study because they refuse therapy, recover, die, or retire to the Sunbelt with their permanent disability. All of these reasons represent important prognostic outcomes, and, if you are to use the results of the article in making prognostic judgments about your own patients, you deserve to know how *all* the members of the inception cohort fared.

Of course, it is difficult for the authors to achieve perfection; they are bound to lose a few members of their inception cohort. There are, however, some rough rules of thumb that you can apply here. The loss to follow-up of 10 percent of the original inception cohort is cause for concern. If 20 percent or more are not accounted for, the results of the study are probably not worth reading. Thus, this rule provides you with yet another tactic for increasing your efficiency. If less than 80 percent of the inception cohort are accounted for in a study of clinical course and prognosis, discard the article!

Were objective outcome criteria developed and used?

According to the fourth guide, the prognostic outcomes should be stated in explicit, objective terms, so that you, as the reader of the subsequent report, will be able to relate them to your own practice. Suppose that you came upon an article about the prognosis of patients with transient ischemic attack (TIA). If the article describes the risk of "subsequent stroke" without presenting the explicit, objective criteria for what constituted a "stroke," you are in a quandary. Are these "strokes" limited to severe derangements of sensation or motor power such that their victims require assistance in dressing, feeding, and toileting? Or, are the majority of these "strokes" merely patients with transient or trivial changes in sensation or in deep or superficial reflexes? The implications for counseling patients or initiating therapy are obvious.

The article's failure to describe explicit, objective outcome criteria raises a second problem in the application of these criteria: the incorrect or inconsistent diagnosis of important prognostic outcomes. Even experienced clinicians will disagree with themselves or other clinicians about key manifestations of disease. As a result, one clinician's stroke becomes another clinician's observer variation, and a patient's apparent prognosis will be determined, not by biology, but by the luck of the draw in who is selected to perform the final examination.

Was the outcome assessment "blind"?

The fifth guide points out that the examination for important prognostic events should be carried out by clinicians who are "blind" to the other features of these patients. This is essential if two additional sources of bias are to be avoided [4]. First, the clinician who knows that a patient possesses a prognostic factor of presumed importance may carry out more frequent or more detailed searches for the relevant prognostic event (the *diagnostic-suspicion bias*). Second, pathologists and others who interpret diagnostic specimens can have their judgments dramatically influenced by prior knowledge of the clinical features of the case (the *expectation bias*).

The diagnostic-suspicion bias can be avoided by subjecting *all* patients to the *same* diagnostic studies, perhaps at prescribed intervals and by all means at the end of the study. In order to reduce expectation bias, many clinical centers recognize the need, even in routine practice, for an initial "blind" assessment of diagnostic test data [1].

Was adjustment for extraneous prognostic factors carried out?

The sixth guide asks whether adjustment for extraneous prognostic factors was carried out. Suppose you wanted to know whether the duration of your ulcerative colitis patient's disease was an important determinant of the risk of developing cancer. In order to get a "clean" answer to this question, you would like to be sure that there would be no interference from other factors that might both accompany disease duration and also have an effect on prognosis (such as age at onset, the number of courses of therapy, and so forth). The failure to meet this standard can result in assigning causal roles to factors that are merely "markers" for other factors of real importance.

These, then, are six standards that a busy clinician can apply to an article on the clinical course and prognosis of disease. Their application should have two results. First, many, if not most, of the prognosis articles you come across can be discarded early on, increasing the efficiency with which you spend your precious reading time. Second, the articles that do pass muster will provide you with prognostic information that is increasingly reproducible, valid, and applicable in your own clinical practice.

READING TO LEARN THE CAUSATION AND ETIOLOGY OF DISEASE

Perusal of a grab sample of issues from any clinical journal reveals that its readers are faced with claims for causation every time they read. When we add to the foregoing the bevy of claims for causation that our patients, to their distress, have come upon in the lay press and on television, it becomes clear that clinicians are called upon to make judgments about causation all the time.

To help meet these demands for instant sagacity, we have brought together some "applied principles of common sense" that should help the busy clinician assess an article that claims to show causation. They are distilled from the work of a number of methodologists, most notably Sir Austin Bradford Hill [13].

The application of these commonsense principles involves two steps. First, readers scan the methods section of the article to see whether the basic methods used were strong or weak. Second, readers apply a set of "diagnostic tests" for causation to the methods and to the results.

Step One: Deciding Whether the Basic Methods Used Were Strong or Weak

Sometimes, you can learn the basic method used in a study from its title. At other times, you must examine its abstract or methods section. Thus, step one, deciding whether the basic methods used were strong or weak, can be accomplished quickly, without having to read the introduction or discussion. Readers are also referred to Chapter 8 for some very useful comments on this issue.

Suppose, for example, we really wanted to find out whether snow shoveling was a cause for heart attack in middle-aged (your age plus five years) men. What would be the most powerful sort of study we could find in the clinical literature?

Most of you, we hope, will have selected a true experiment in humans— that is, a study method in which middle-aged men would have been randomly allocated (by a system analogous to tossing a coin) to habitually shovel or not shovel snow each winter and then followed up to see how many in each group went on to sudden death. Evidence from such a *randomized trial* is the soundest evidence we can ever obtain about causation (whether it concerns etiology, therapeutics, or any other causal issue), and the reasons for this, if not already clear, will become apparent as we proceed. The basic architecture of the randomized trial is shown in Figure 9.2.

Although the true experiment (randomized trial) would give us the most accurate (or valid) answer to a question of causation, and therefore represents the strongest method, we will not find it very often in our clinical reading. In many cases (incuding the present example), it is not feasible to do a randomized trial to determine etiology, and, in some, it is downright unethical. For example, who would ever consider carrying out a true experiment that would deliberately cause viral encephalitis in a random half of a group of humans to see whether they were rendered more likely to develop parkinsonism?

Thus, we are much more likely to encounter subexperimental studies into the risk of heart attack from snow shoveling. The next most powerful study method (the *cohort study*) would identify two groups (or cohorts) of middle-aged men, one who did and the other who did not make a practice of shoveling snow each winter. Such a study would then follow these two cohorts forward in time, counting the heart attacks that occurred in each. This is depicted in Figure 9.3. If the heart-attack rate was higher in the cohort who shoveled snow, this would constitute reasonably strong evidence that snow shoveling precipitated heart attacks. However, the strength of such a cohort analytic study is not as great as that of a randomized trial, and the reason for this difference in strength is apparent if we consider the middle-aged man with angina pectoris. Is he likely to avoid snow shoveling or other activities

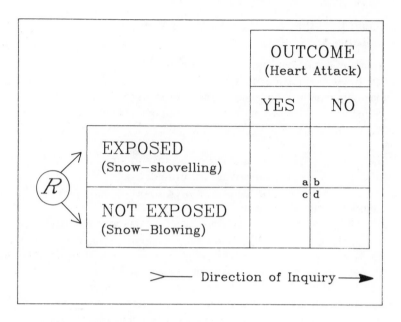

FIGURE 9.2.   A Randomized Control Trial.

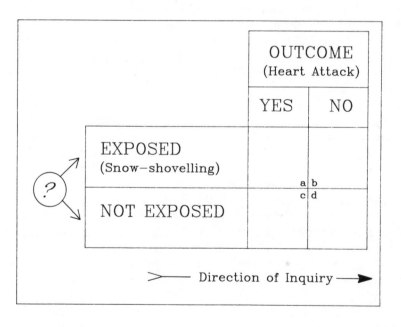

FIGURE 9.3.   A Cohort Study

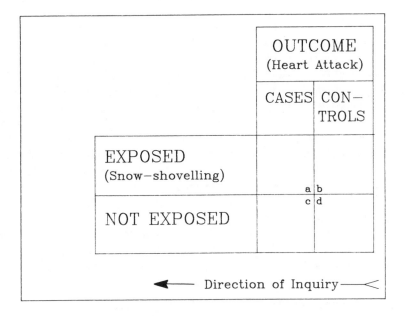

FIGURE 9.4.   A Case-Control Study

that precipitate angina? Yes. Furthermore, is he at high risk for heart attack? Yes again. Thus, the cohort analytic study could provide a distorted answer to the causal question if men at high risk of heart attack for extraneous reasons were not equally distributed between the cohorts of those who did and did not shovel snow. We see, then, that we must view a subexperimental study, such as the cohort analytic study, with some caution and suspicion.

A second type of subexperimental study deserves to be interpreted with even greater caution. This is the *case-control study*. In a case-control study, the investigator gathers "cases" of men who have suffered a heart attack and a "control" series of men who have not had a heart attack. Both groups of men are then questioned about whether they regularly shovel snow each winter. If those who had heart attacks were more likely to be regular snow shovelers, this would constitute some evidence, though not very strong, that snow shoveling might precipitate heart attack. Thus, in this case, the direction of inquiry is backwards, as shown in Figure 9.4.

Why is the case-control analytic study low on the scale of strength? This is because it is so very liable to bias. Not only is the case-control study susceptible to the bias from the angina patient we noted with the cohort study; it is susceptible to several other sorts of bias [4]. For example, if snow shoveling precipitated not only heart attack but sudden death, many victims would not survive long enough even to be included in a case-control study, much less be interviewed. As a result, snow shoveling could appear to be a benign pastime when, in fact, it was lethal for some middle-aged men. Accordingly, the results of case-control studies are tenuous at best.

One final type of subexperimental study deserves mention. This is the *case series*, in which an investigator might simply report that 60 percent of his male heart-attack patients were shoveling snow just before onset of their infarcts. No comparison group of any sort is provided, and about all that the reader can conclude is tht heart attack *can* (but not necessarily *does*) follow snow shoveling. Such case reports are generally thought provoking, but the thoughts they provoke are sometimes extreme. In terms of strength, such studies are best used to provoke other, more powerful investigations. All too often, however, they provoke authoritarian (rather than authoritative) clinical advice about prevention and therapy.

In summary, then, readers of reports purporting to show etiology or causation should begin by deciding whether the basic methods used were strong or weak.

Step Two: Applying the Diagnostic Tests for Causation

Having decided from the foregoing that the article warrants further consideration, the reader should then turn to the results and the discussion to see how the data fit some commonsense rules of evidence.

In making a causal decision, information should be sought in terms of the diagnostic tests that are listed in Table 9.6. They are discussed in order of decreasing importance, and we have suggested their impact upon the causal decision in Table 9.7.

You must first consider whether there is *evidence from true experiments in humans*; that is, whether there are investigations in which identical groups of individuals, generated through random allocation, are and are not exposed to the putative causal factor and are followed up for the outcome of interest. As

TABLE 9.6. Diagnostic Tests for Causation

---

1. Is there evidence from *human experiments*?
2. How *strong* is the association?
3. Do other investigators *consistently* find this same result?
5. Is there a *gradient*?
6. Does the association make *epidemiologic sense*?
7. Is the association *biologically sensible*?
8. Is the association *specific*?
9. Is the relationship *analogous* to another, well-accepted relationship?

TABLE 9.7. Importance of Individual Diagnostic Tests in Making the Causal Decison

Diagnostic Test	Effect of Test Result on Causal Decision		
	Test Result Positive	Test Result Neutral	Test Result Reverse of Hypothesis
Human experiments	++++[a]	———[b]	————
Strength from cohort study	+++	——	———
Strength from case-control study	+	0[c]	—
Consistency	+++	——	———
Temporality	++	——	————
Gradient	++	—	——
Epidemiologic sense	++	—	——
Biologic sense	+	0	—
Specificity	+	0	—
Analogy	+	0	0

[a]+ = causation supported.

[b]— = causation not supported.

[c]0 = causal decision not affected.

Note: The number of +'s or —'s indicates the relative contribution of the diagnostic test to the causal decision.

we learned in the previous section, this is the best evidence we will ever have, but it is not always available and is rarely the initial evidence for causation. Nonetheless, any consideration of an issue in causation should begin with a search for a proper randomized trial.

Second, the *strength of association* must be determined. What are the odds favoring the outcome of interest with, as opposed to without, exposure to the putative cause. The higher the odds, the greater the strength. There are two strategies for estimating the strength of association. In the randomized trial and cohort studies, patients who were and were not exposed to the putative cause are carefully followed up to find out whether they develop the adverse reaction or outcome. Both randomized trials and cohort studies permit direct calculations of relative risk (strength) by comparing outcome rates in exposed and unexposed persons, or

$$[a/(a + b)] \div [c/(c + d)]$$

In case-control studies, however, relative risk can only be indirectly estimated as follows:

$$ad \div bc$$

As we have seen, cohort and particularly case-control analytic studies are vulnerable to a series of systematic distortions (biases) that may lead to invalid estimates of relative risk (strength) and therefore to incorrect conclusions about causation.

Third, there must be *consistency*, the repetitive demonstration of an association between exposure to the putative cause and the outcome of interest, using different strategies and different settings. Much of the credibility of the causal link between smoking and lung cancer arises from the repeated demonstration of a strong statistical association in case-control, cohort, and other study designs. Similar credibility is now being gained for the link between oral contraceptives and thromboembolism, with consistent findings from both the earlier case-control and more recent cohort studies [14].

A fourth consideration concerns *temporality*, a consistent sequence of events of exposure to the putative cause, followed by the occurrence of the outcome of interest. Although this diagnostic test looks easy to apply, it is not. What if a predisposing factor of a very early stage of the adverse effect is responsible both for exposure to the causal factor and for the full-blown outcome? This yardstick is, of course, easier to apply to cohort than to case-control data.

Fifth, you must determine if there is a *gradient*, the demonstration of increasing risk or severity of the outcome of interest in association with an increased "dose" or duration of exposure to the putative cause. An appropriate contemporary example is the recent report linking conjugated estrogens with endometrial carcinoma [15]. The point estimate of relative risk of developing endometrial cancer rose from 5.6 for those who used the drug from one to 4.9 years, to 7.2 for users from five to 6.9 years, and, finally, to 13.9 for users for seven or more years. Reverse gradients are useful, too.

Sixth, the association must make *epidemiologic sense*; that is, there must be agreement with current understanding of the distributions of causes and outcomes. For example, Renwick summarized the distribution of exposure to potato "blight" by country, climate, socioeconomic status, and other sociodemographic factors and found remarkable congruence with the occurrence of neural-tube defects [16]. Recognizing the need to test the resulting causal hypothesis with a more powerful strategy, he subsequently called for a randomized trial of a nutritional replacement [17].

A seventh consideration is whether the association makes *biologic sense*; that is, there must be agreement with current understanding of the responses of cells, tissues, organs, and organisms to stimuli. It is with this yardstick that nonhuman experimental data should be measured. Although virtually any set of observations can be made biologically plausible (given the ingenuity of the human mind and the vastness of the supply of contradictory biologic facts), some biologic observations are compelling, such as the production of limb hypoplasia in hybrid rabbits given thalidomide.

An eighth concern is *specificity*, the limitation of the association to a single putative cause and a single effect. One of the minor diagnostic tests for causation, specificity is only moderately useful and then only when it is present. The weakness of this test is underscored when considering teratogens, where multiple effects in several organ systems are commonplace.

A ninth diagnostic test involves *analogy*, the similarity to another, previously demonstrated causal relationship. The last and least of the diagnostic tests, this yardstick is invoked whenever, for example, a baby is born with foreshortened limbs.

When confronted by a question of causation, these nine diagnostic tests can be used to distill your prior knowledge and, with the assistance of such judgments as those shown in Table 9.7, to reach a causal conclusion. Better still, these diagnostic tests can be used to increase the efficiency of a literature review, focusing attention on those publications that will shed the strongest light on the causal question and warning the user against accepting plausible, but biased, conclusions.

The diagnosis of causation is not simply arithmetic, and the strategies and tactics for making this judgment are still primitive. The diagnostic tests presented here constitute a start. It is suggested that their use, particularly when clearly specified before a review of relevant data, will lead to more rational—albeit less colorful—discussions of causation in human biology and clinical medicine.

READING TO DISTINGUISH USEFUL FROM USELESS OR EVEN HARMFUL THERAPY

We accept some treatments as clearly efficacious (that is, we are convinced that they do more good than harm to those patients who comply with them), are doubtful about others, and mock the consensus of a former era that embraced the gastric freeze and internal mammary ligation. Why is this? One major reason is because we *are* willing to learn from experience, and those treatments that do more harm than good are, we think, eventually unmasked. More important, however, is the growth of an attitude that a claim for efficacy needs to be backed up by solid evidence, ideally in the form of a randomized clinical trial, before clinicians will accept it.

This final section will show how to apply some rules of evidence to the claims for efficacy that appear in clinical journals. These rules can be summarized into six guides for the busy clinical reader. Once again, they constitute "applied common sense" and are designed to maximize the efficiency as well as the accuracy of your clinical reading. These guides are summarized in Table 9.8 and will be discussed in order.

Was the assignment of patients to treatments really randomized?

Every patient who entered the study should have had the same, *known* probability (typically 50 percent) of receiving one or the other of the treatments being compared. Thus, assignment to one treatment or another should have been carried out by a system analogous to flipping a coin. It is usually easy to decide whether this was done, for such key terms as *randomized trial* or *random allocation* should appear in the abstract, the methods section, or even in the title of such articles.

As a result, the busy clinical reader has the option of applying this guide rigorously. If you are reading a subscribed journal to "keep up with the clinical literature" (rather than searching the clinical literature to decide how to treat a specific patient), discard at once all articles on therapy that are not randomized trails.

Why such a strict criterion? Why should clinicians not accept the results of trials that are not randomized? A formal explanation for this strict rule is lengthy, involves the concept of confounding, and can be found elsewhere [4]. The brief explanation is pragmatic. We are very much more likely to help our patients, and very much less likely to harm them, if we select those therapies that have been shown to do more good than harm in proper randomized control trials.

The list of examples of how we have been misled by accepting less than randomized trial evidence is a long one. For example, clofibrate was growing in popularity before publication of the randomized clinical trial that showed that it actually increased mortality [18]. The drug has subsequently been

TABLE 9.8. Guides for Reading Articles about the Risks and Benefits of Therapy

1. Was the assignment of patients to treatments really randomized?
2. Were all clinically relevant outcomes reported?
3. Were the study patients recognizably similar to your own?
4. Were both clinical and statistical significance considered?
5. Is the therapeutic maneuver replicable in your practice?
6. Were all patients who entered the study accounted for at its conclusion?

banned or its use restricted in several countries. Furthermore, it has been estimated that 2,500 gastric-freezing machines had been purchased to treat tens of thousands of peptic ulcer patients by the time that a cooperative randomized clinical trial demonstrated the lack of efficacy of this procedure [19]. Finally, it took a randomized clinical trial, in which angina patients were randomly allocated to undergo or not undergo ligation only after the internal mammary arteries had been surgically exposed, to impress on us how often symptomatic improvement can follow placebo medications and procedures [20].

The situation can be summarized in a quotation attributed to various authors: "The studies with enthusiasm tend not to have controls, and the studies with controls tend not to have enthusiasm." This state of affairs was actually quantified for therapeutic maneuvers in psychiatry by Foulds, who simply classified articles on therapy by whether they had controls and whether they concluded that therapy was efficacious [21]. His results appear in Table 9.9.

Of course, the randomized clinical trial goes beyond merely assembling a control group of patients. It specifically avoids confounding by randomly allocating eligible patients to either an experimental or a control group. Thus, the comparability of experimental and control patients is insured, and such reports usually include a table confirming "baseline similarities" between these experimental and control patients. Indeed, randomized trials may go even further by stratifying potential study patients for important determinants of study end points prior to randomization (a process called "prognostic stratification") [22].

In summary, then, although the randomized control trial can sometimes produce an incorrect conclusion about efficacy (especially, as we shall find out shortly, when it is a small trial), it is by far the best tool currently

TABLE 9.9. Relation between Therapeutic Enthusiasm and Use of Control Groups

	Number of Studies	% Reporting Therapeutic Success
Studies without controls	52	85
Studies with controls	20	19

Note: $X_1^2 = 21$, $P < 0.001$.

Source: Adapted from G. A. Foulds, "Clinical Research in Psychiatry," *Journal of Mental Science* 104(1958):259–65.

available for identifying the clinical maneuvers that do more good than harm. Can we *ever* be confident that a treatment is efficacious in the absence of a randomized trial? Only when traditional therapy is invariably followed by death. Consider tuberculous meningitis. Before 1946, the outcome of this disorder was invariably fatal. Then, when small amounts of streptomycin became available for use in humans, a few U.S. victims treated with this new drug survived [23]. This remarkable survival following streptomycin was repeated shortly thereafter in the United Kingdom [24]. Thus, the ability to show, with replication, that patients with previously universally fatal disease can survive following a new treatment constitutes sufficient evidence, all by itself, for efficacy.

Insisting on evidence from randomized clinical trials can increase the efficiency with which you read a subscribed journal, for it will lead to the early rejection of most articles concerned with therapy. The rule requires some modification, however, when reading around a particular patient. In this latter instance, it will often occur that no proper randomized control trials have every been published. What should the clinical reader do then?

Two sorts of actions are appropriate when reading up on a specific patient. First, the initial literature search should seek out any randomized trials that do exist. Second, in the absence of any published randomized clinical trails, clinical readers have to use the results of subexperimental investigations. Before accepting the conclusions of such studies, clinicians should satisfy themselves that the differences in the reported results of therapy are simply so great that they are extremely unlikely to have been caused by any conceivable baseline differences between experimental and control patients. This second rule is obviously a judgment call and should be tempered by the recollection that this same sort of subexperimental evidence supported the earlier use of clofibrate, internal mammary ligation, and the gastric freeze.

Were all clinically relevant outcomes reported?

In dealing with the question of whether all clinically relevant outcomes were reported, consider Table 9.10, which summarizes the results of an important randomized trial of clofibrate among men with elevated serum cholesterol [18]. Some of the outcomes of therapy appear highly favorable. For example, serum cholesterol—a key coronary risk factor—fell by almost 10 percent, providing some biologic evidence for benefit. However, many readers will recognize this cholesterol change as an example of the "substitution game," in which a risk factor is substituted for its associated outcome [25] and will want to look further to see whether there were real changes in the occurrence of acute coronary events. Such evidence is also available in Table 9.10, in which we note reductions in both nonfatal myocardial

TABLE 9.10. Clinically Relevant Outcomes in a Randomized Trial of Clofibrate for Preventing Coronary Heart Disease

Outcome	Placebo Group	Clofibrate Group
Average change in serum cholesterol	+1%	−9%
Nonfatal myocardial infarcts/1,000 men	7.2	5.8
Fatal and nonfatal myocardial infarcts/1,000 men	8.9	7.4
Deaths/1,000 men	5.2	6.2

Source: M. F. Oliver et al., "A Cooperative Trial in the Primary Prevention of Ischaemic Heart Disease Using Clofibrate," *British Heart Journal* 40(1978):1069–1118.

infarctions (line 2 in the table) and in all infarctions, both fatal and nonfatal (line 3 in the table). Thus, the efficacy of clofibrate would appear to be supported in this study. However, when we consider clinically relevant outcomes, especially from the point of view of the patient [26], we must consider total mortality, and this is shown with disturbing effect in line 4 of Table 9.10. Total mortality rose with clofibrate therapy, a result that subsequently has profoundly affected both the use and availability of this drug. Thus, because judgment about the usefulness of clofibrate or other agents can depend, in a crucial way, on the clinical outcomes chosen for comparison, readers must be sure that all clinically relevant outcomes are reported.

Furthermore, because clinical disagreement is ubiquitous in medicine [5], readers should also recognize the necessity for explicit, objective criteria for the clinical outcomes of interest and their application by observers who are "blind" to whether the patient under scrutiny was in the active-treatment or control group.

Were the study patients recognizably similar to your own?

The guide that asks whether the study patients were recognizably similar to your own has two elements. First, the study patients must be *recognizable*; that is, their clinical and sociodemographic states must be described in sufficient detail for you to be confident that you could tell whether a patient in your practice would be eligible for inclusion in the trial. Second, the study results must be *applicable* to patients in your practice. This requirement goes beyond the fourth general guide for reading clinical journals ("the site") to encompass the precise features of individual patients rather than the general features of their referral network.

Were both clinical and statistical significance considered?

In determining whether both clinical and statistical significance were considered, it should be remembered that *clinical* significance here refers to the *importance* of a difference in clinical outcomes between treated and control patients and is usually described in terms of the *magnitude* of a result. Thus, in the bottom line of Table 9.10, we see that the clofibrate patients were $(6.2 - 5.2)/5.2$ or 19 percent more likely to die than were patients randomly assigned to receive placebos. Such a difference becomes clinically significant when it leads to changes in clinical behavior. Thus, this 19 percent difference in total mortality is confirmed as being clinically significant when its recognition is followed by sharp reductions in the prescribing of clofibrate for such patients.

By contrast, *statistical* significance merely tells us whether a difference is *real*, not whether it is important or large. More precisely, the statistical significance of a difference is nothing more than a statement about the likelihood that this difference is due to chance alone. Thus, if the 19 percent difference in total mortality between clofibrate and placebo takers in Table 9.10 is very unlikely to be due to chance alone (say, less than 5 percent, or < 0.05),* we refer to the difference as being statistically significant.

The determinants of clinical significance are therefore the determinants of changes in clinical action. If a result of a study leads to abandoning an old treatment for a new one, the difference in their effects is clinically significant. The determinants of statistical significance are not as immediately obvious. Simply stated, statistical significance rises (that is, the "P-value" falls) when the number of study patients rises, when the clinical manifestation of treatment effect shows less fluctuation from day-to-day, and when the measurement of this clinical effect is both accurate and reproducible.

On the basis of the foregoing discussion, the busy reader can develop two quick yardsticks for reading therapeutic articles. First, if the results are statistically significant ($P < 0.05$), is the difference clinically significant as well? If so, the results are both real and worthy of implementing in clinical practice. Second, if the results are not statistically significant, is the sample size big enough to show a clinically significant difference if it should occur? As discussed in the previous paragraph, the number of patients in a study is one of the determinants of statistical significance. Thus, if a study is huge, the difference in clinical outcomes can be statistically significant ("real") even when it is clinically trivial (too small to affect clinical behavior). Conversely,

---

*By convention, this likelihood is called the "P-value," "alpha," or "the chance of making a Type I error," in which we conclude that a difference exists when, in fact, it does not. See Chapter 8 for a comprehensive discussion of these issues.

however, if a study is too small, even large differences of enormous potential clinical significance may not be statistically significant.* Readers must therefore scrutinize the difference in clinical outcomes in studies whose results are not statistically significant to see whether they are of potential clinical significance. This admonition has received additional weight from the demonstration that a majority of recently published randomized trials whose results were not statistically significant had too few patients to show outcome differences of 25 and even 50 percent [27].

Is the therapeutic maneuver replicable in your practice?

In determining whether a therapeutic maneuver is replicable in your practice, there are three prerequisites. First, the therapeutic maneuver has to be described in sufficient detail for readers to replicate it with precision. Who did what to whom, with what formulation and dose, administered under what circumstances, with what dose adjustments and titrations, with which searches for and responses to side effects and toxicity, for how long, and with what clinical criteria for deciding that therapy should be increased, tapered, or terminated?

Second, the therapeutic maneuver has to be feasible. Readers must be capable of administering it properly, and their patients must find it accessible, acceptable, and affordable.

Third, when reading the description of the maneuver in the published report, readers should note whether the authors avoided two specific biases in its application: *contamination* (in which control patients accidentally receive the experimental treatment and thereby spuriously reduce the difference in clinical outcomes between the experimental and control groups) and *cointervention* (the performance of additional diagnostic or therapeutic acts on experimental, but not control, patients thereby spuriously increasing the difference in clinical outcomes observed between experimental and control groups). Once again, it should be apparent that cointervention is prevented by "blinding" both study patients and their clinicians as to who is receiving which treatment [28].

Were all patients who entered the study accounted for at its conclusion?

The canny reader will note how many patients entered the study (usually the numbers of experimental and control patients will be almost identical)

*This is what is meant by "low power" or the "beta error problem" or the risk of a Type II error," in which we conclude that no difference exists when, in fact, it does. See Chapter 8 for a more complete discussion.

and will tally them again at its conclusion to make certain that they correspond. For example, in a randomized trial of surgical, as opposed to medical, therapy for bilateral carotid stenosis, 167 patients entered the study [29]. Among 79 surgical and 72 medical patients "available for follow-up" (the total at the end of the study equaled 151), a risk reduction for continued transient ischemic attack, stroke, or death of 27 percent (P = 0.02) was reported, a difference that is both clinically and statistically significant. However, closer reading of the report reveals that 167 (not 151) patients entered this study, that 16 of them suffered a stroke or died during their initial hospitalization, and that these 16 were excluded from the foregoing analysis.

Furthermore, 15 of these 16 patients had been allocated to surgery; five of them died, and ten suffered strokes during or shortly after surgery. When they are reintroduced into the final analysis, the risk reduction from surgery is now only 16 percent, and it is no longer statistically significant (P = 0.09).

The authors of the foregoing report were careful to include outcome information on all patients who entered their trial. What can the reader do when outcomes are not reported for missing subjects? One approach (admittedly conservative and therefore liable to lead to the "Type II" error) is to arbitrarily assign a bad outcome to all missing members of the group with the most favorable outcomes and a good outcome to missing members of the group with the least favorable outcomes. If this maneuver has no effect upon the statistical or clinical significance of the results, the reader can accept the study's conclusions.

CONCLUSION

What proportion of papers will satisfy the requirements both for scientific proof and for clinical applicability described in the last two chapters? Not very many, although there is evidence that matters are improving. (Although cohort studies appear to be losing out to less powerful, cross-sectional studies in general medical journals, randomized trials of therapy are on the rise [30].) After all, there are only a handful of ways to do a study properly but a thousand ways to do it wrong.

Moreover, even if a study does satisfy all of these requirements, it will not settle a clinical question for all time. At best, it will contribute a small, sometimes only temporary increment to our ability to relieve suffering and promote health. Moreover, the results and conclusions of even the soundest studies may provoke sharp and continuing controversy.

The reasons for this slow progress and these disputes are several. First there is the possibility that, despite impeccable design and analysis, the study results are flat wrong. This, of course, is the inevitable (although rare) consequence of testing for statistical significance.

Second, the contemporaneous understanding of human structure, function, and mechanisms of disease that led us to group certain sorts of patients together or conclude that they had certain sorts of responses may be shown subsequently to have been seriously deficient, negating the results or interpretations of the original study.

Third, the study may be misunderstood or misinterpreted by those who read about it when an explanatory trial designed to answer the question "Can treatment X work under optimal circumstances (for example, compliant patients, elaborate dose-setting schemes, and a restricted set of clinical outcomes)?" is criticized for its inability to answer a management question, "Does treatment X do more good than harm under usual clinical circumstances (for example, all comers, usual dose-setting procedures, and the gamut of morbid and mortal outcomes)?" [26].

Fourth, controversy can arise over the interpretation of even a proper study when a trade-off must be made between the different sorts of results it produces. For example, studies of alternative approaches to managing patients with symptoms of appendicitis have shown that one could minimize deaths from this cause with a liberal policy of operating on all such patients, even those with mild symptoms [31]. On the other hand, if one wanted to minimize unnecessary surgery, hospital costs, or convalescence, one would adopt a more conservative policy and reserve surgery for patients with severe symptoms. Thus, there are, not one, but two, sharply contrasting "best answers," and controversy perhaps is inevitable.

Fifth, study results and interpretations, even those that satisfy the requirements set down in these two chapters, may meet considerable resistance when they discredit the only treatment currently available for a condition. Clinicians still may elect to do something, even if it is of no demonstrable benefit, rather than nothing. Finally, study results may be rejected, regardless of their merit, if they threaten the prestige or livelihood of their audience.

In summary, this section of the book is intended to help the serious reader afford time for the proper evaluation of that subset of biomedical literature most likely to yield valid, useful, new knowledge. Although it would be naive for us to expect the application of these guides to result in a great burst of speed in the acquisition of useful truth, we are confident that their adoption will insure that whatever momentum is achieved will be in a forward direction.

REFERENCES

1. Spodick DH: On experts and expertise: The effect of variability on observer performance. Amer J Cardiol 1975;36:592–96.
2. Sackett DL: Clinical diagnosis and the clinical laboratory. Clin Invest Med 1978;1:37–43.

3. Sketch MH, Mohiuddin SM, Lynch JD, Zeraka AE, Runco V: Significant sex differences in the correlation of electrocardiographic exercise testing and coronary arteriograms. Amer J Cardiol 1975;36:169–73.

4. Sackett DL: Bias in analytic research. J Chron Dis 1979;32:51–63.

5. Department of Clinical Epidemiology and Biostatistics: Clinical disagreement. Can Med Assn J 1980;123:499–504.

6. Murphy EA: The Logic of Medicine. Baltimore, Johns Hopkins University Press, 1976, pp 117–34.

7. Almby B, Meirik O, Schonebeck J: Incidence, morbidity, and complications of renal and ureteral calculi in a well defined geographical area. Scand J Urol Nephrol 1975;9:249–53.

8. Coe FL, Keck J, Norton, ER: The natural history of calcium urolithiasis. J Amer Med Assn 1977;238:1519–23.

9. Rogala EJ, Drummond DS, Gurr J: Scoliosis: Incidence and natural history. J Bone Joint Surg 1978;60:173–76.

10. Mottet NK: Neoplastic Sequelae. Histopatholic Spectrum of Regional Enteritis and Ulcerative Colitis. Philadelphia, WB Saunders, 1959, pp 217–35.

11. Greenstein AJ, Sachar DB, Smith H, Pucillo A, Papatestas AE, Kreel I, Geller SA, Janowitz HD, Aufses AH Jr: Cancer in universal and left-sided ulcerative colitis: Factors determining risk. Gastroenterol 1979;77:290–94.

12. Sackett DL, Whelan G: Cancer risk in ulcertative colitis: Scientific requirements for the study of prognosis. Gasteroenterology. 1980;78:1632–35.

13. Hill AB: Principles of Medical Statistics. 9th ed. London, Lancet, 1971, 309–23

14. Oral Contraceptives and Health: An Interim Report from the Oral Contraceptive Study of the Royal College of General Practitioners. London, Pitman Medical, 1974.

15. Ziel HK, Finkle WD: Increased risk of endometrial carcinoma among users of conjugated estrogens. New Engl J Med 1975;293:1167.

16. Renwick JH: Hypothesis: Anencephaly and spina bifida are usually preventable by avoidance of a specific but unidentified substance present in certain potato tubers. Brit J Prev Soc Med 1972;26:67.

17. Renwick JH: Potatoes and neural-tube defects. Lancet 1973;2:562.

18. Oliver MF et al: A cooperative trial in the primary prevention of ischaemic heart disease using clofibrate. Br Heart J 1978;40:1069–1118.

19. Miao LL: Gastric freezing: An example of the evaluation of medical therapy by randomized clinical trials. In Costs, Risks, and Benefits of Therapy, edited by JP Bunker, BA Barnes, F Mosteller. New York, Oxford University Press, 1977, pp 198–211.

20. Cobb LA, Thomas GI, Dillard DH et al: An evaluation of internal-mammary-artery ligation by a double-bind technic. N Engl J Med 1959;260:1115.

21. Foulds GA: Clinical research in psychiatry. J Ment Sci 1958;104:259–65.

22. Feinstein AR: The purpose of prognostic stratification. In Clinical Biostatistics. St Louis, Mosby, 1977, pp 385–97.

23. Hinshaw HC, Feldman WH, Pfuetze KH: Treatment of tuberculosis with streptomycin. J. Amer Med Assn 1946;132:778–82.

24. Medical Research Council: Streptomycin treatment of tuberculosis meningitis. Lancet 1948;1:582–96.

25. Yerushalmy J: On inferring causality from observed associations. In Controversy in Internal Medicine, edited by FJ Ingelfinger, AS Relman, M Finland. Philadelphia, Saunders 1966, pp 659–68.

26. Sackett DL, Gent M: Controversy in counting and attributing events in clinical trials. N Engl J Med 1979;301:1410–12.

27. Frieman JA, Chalmers TC, Smith H Jr, Kuebler RR: The importance of beta, the type II error, and sample size in the design and interpretation of the randomized control trial: Survey of 71 "negative" trials. N Engl J Med 1978;299:690–94.

28. Sackett DL: Design, measurement, and analysis in clinical trails. In Platelets, Drugs, and Thrombosis, edited by J Hirsh, JF Cade, AS Gallus, E Schonbaum. Basel: S Karger, 1975, pp 219–25.

29. Fields WS, Maslenikov V, Meyer JS et al: Joint study of extracranial arterial occulsion V: Progress report of prognosis following surgery or nonsurgical treatment for transient ischemic attacks and cervical carotid artery lesions. JAMA 1970;211:1993–2003.

30. Fletcher RW, Fletcher SW: Clinical research in general medical journals: A 30-year perspective. N Engl J Med 1979;301:180–83.

31. Neutra, R: Indications for the surgical treatment of suspected acute appendicitis: a cost-effectiveness approach. In Costs, Risks, and Benefits of Surgery, edited by JP Bunker, BA Barnes, F. Mosteller. New York: Oxford University Press, 1977, pp. 277–307.

PART IV

SOURCES OF BIOMEDICAL INFORMATION

10

THE NATIONAL LIBRARY OF MEDICINE

Martin M. Cummings

The National Library of Medicine (NLM) in Bethesda, Maryland, has served as a significant information resource in the health sciences for over 100 years. In 1956, legislation sponsored by Senators John F. Kennedy and Lister Hill transfered the library from the Department of Defense to the Department of Health, Education, and Welfare (now the Department of Health and Human Services).

HISTORY

The library traces its beginning back to 1836, when a modest collection of medical texts and journals was dignified with the name Library of the Army Surgeon General's Office. Over the years, to reflect the growing importance of the collection and the every-widening audience it served, the name was changed to Army Medical Library (1922), Armed Forces Medical Library (1952), and, finally, National Library of Medicine (1956).[1]

At the end of the Civil War, John Shaw Billings took the modest collection of medical works that existed in the surgeon general's office and, over a period of 30 years, built it into a great resource for U.S. health professionals. Under Billings's direction, the collection grew from 1,800 volumes (1865) to 117,000 books and 192,000 pamphlets at the time of his retirement in 1895.

Billings, an army surgeon, was a truly remarkable man. It was he who in 1879 developed *Index Medicus*, a guide to the world's biomedical journal literature. One of Billings's greatest achievements was the publication, beginning in 1880, of the *Index-Catalogue of the Library of the Surgeon-General's Office*. This covered all of the world's published biomedical literature—journals and monographs—in the library's collection, organized by subject and author. It was to take 15 years for the entire 16-volume catalog to be published.

To this day, descendants of the two works (the former still under its original title, the *Index-Catalogue* now superseded by the *NLM Current Catalog*) continue to be published by NLM. Whether Billings's comment on all this indexed and cataloged material—"The proportion of what is both new and true is not much greater in medicine than it is in theology"—also continues to be valid is left to the reader to decide.

William H. Welch, eminent pathologist and one of the towering figures in U.S. medicine, said:

> I have been asked on more than one occasion what have been the really great contributions of this country to medical knowledge. I have given the subject some thought and believe that four should be named: (1) the discovery of anesthesia; (2) the discovery of insect transmission of disease; (3) the development of the modern public health laboratory, in all that the term implies; (4) the Army Medical Library and its Index-Catalogue. This library and its catalogue are the most important of the four.[2]

PRESENT FACILITIES

Today, NLM occupies two handsome buildings on the gounds of the National Institutes of Health in Bethesda, Maryland. (See Figure 10.1.) The main library building, dedicated in 1961, contains the general collection and, separately, the collection of historical and rare materials. In this building are most of the functions related to ordering, cataloging, indexing, and providing public access to the literature.

The second structure, the adjacent ten-story Lister Hill Center building, was dedicated in 1980. This facility is a concrete reflection of the fact that, in the years since the main building was constructed, the library's mission has undergone considerable expansion. Housed in the new building are the Office of Computer and Communications Systems, the Extramural (grant) Program, the Toxicology Information Program, the National Medical Audiovisual Center, and the Lister Hill National Center for Biomedical Communications. These major functions have all been added to the library's responsibility since 1961.

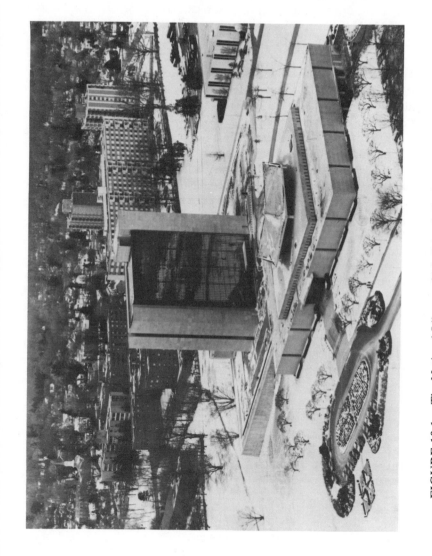

FIGURE 10.1. The National Library of Medicine in Bethesda, Maryland
Source: National Library of Medicine.

COLLECTIONS

The library's collections of over 2.5 million items may be characterized in two ways: historical and general materials, and book and nonbook materials. Table 10.1 gives statistics on the size of NLM's collections as of 1980.

Although the library houses the world's largest collection of biomedical literature, its acquisition policies are tempered by the realities of money, staff, and space. For certain core subjects (such as anatomy and surgery), NLM attempts to have a *comprehensive collection*, acquiring all scientific and scholarly literature no matter where published or in what language. There are other areas, however, in which the library exercises judgment in acquiring the literature. For certain topics (such as medical sociology and demography), NLM maintains a *research collection*, a sizable, although not comprehensive, assemblage of works relating to a subject. In peripheral areas (such as general chemistry and mathematics), the library builds a *reference collection*, a smaller number of important works carefully selected to cover the subject broadly.

Even with the library's carefully defined policies for acquiring the literature, the number of publications that arrive each year is staggering. Some 22,000 serial titles are currently received from all over the world, amounting to about 175,000 pieces annually. In addiition, 14,000

TABLE 10.1. National Library of Medicine Collections

General Collection	Number	Historical Collection (pre-1871)	Number
Book material		*Book material*	
Monographs	375,000	Monographs (pre-1871)	81,000
In process	20,000	Theses	282,000
Pamphlets	22,000	Pamphlets	150,000
Bound serial volumes	584,000	Bound serial volumes	19,000
Nonbook material		*Nonbook material*	
Microforms	76,000	Microforms	4,000
Audiovisuals	10,000	Pictures	73,000
		Manuscripts	884,000
Total	1,087,000	Total	1,493,000

Source: National Library of Medicine Programs and Services: Fiscal Year 1979, National Institutes of Health Publication no. 80-256 (Bethesda, Md.: National Library of Medicine, 1980).

monographs and 2,000 audiovisual productions are added to the collection each year.

The bulk of the collection, both historical and modern, is in closed stacks. Materials are retrieved from the stacks on request and used by patrons either in the main reading room or in the history of medicine reading room. (See Figure 10.2.) These public areas do have reference works on open shelves—bibliographies, indexes, catalogs, dictionaries, and so forth—and also some 200 frequently requested journal titles. Six carrels in the main reading room contain a wide variety of health-science audiovisual productions and playback equipment.

The library's resources for historical scholarship in the medical and related sciences are among the richest of any institution in the world. Collected over many years, they include, in addition to rarities, exhaustive materials for the support of studies in the history of human health and disease. Besides historical books, journals, and manuscripts, there is a section on prints and photographs, including portraits, pictures of institutions, caricatures, genre scenes, and fine graphic art in a variety of media illustrating social and historical aspects of medicine. Also within the history of medicine area is a collection of oral history memoirs of U.S. leaders in medicine.

ACCESS TO THE LITERATURE

Printed reference tools

The health sciences are well served by a variety of reference publications issued by commercial firms, professional organizations, and government agencies. NLM has published a number of bibliographies widely used by the health-science community around the world. Chief among these is the *Index Medicus*, used in almost 6,000 biomedical institutions.

Billings's first volume of *Index Medicus* in 1879 cited 20,169 articles.[3] These were classified into 14 major medical categories. A 1973 study showed that these same 14 categories covered only one-third of the biomedical literature cited in that year's *Index Medicus*. Today, 81 fields or disciplines are required to cover the literature. Paradoxically, this seems to be the result of both greater fragmentation or specialization in the health sciences and a broadening of the definitions of such fields as biochemistry, pharmacology, and public health. There can be no doubt, however, about the remarkable growth in the volume of the literature. Compared to the 20,169 references in 1879, *Index Medicus* cited over 230,000 in 1979.

Index Medicus today is published monthly and cumulated annually in 14 hardcover volumes. It cites, by subject and author, articles from 2,600

FIGURE 10.2. The Main Reading Room of The National Library of Medicine

Source: National Library of Medicine.

FIGURE 10.3. The National Library of Medicine's Computer Facility
Source: National Library of Medicine.

167

biomedical periodicals published in 36 languages. The library endeavors to include citations to articles published in those periodicals that are judged to be of greatest potential use to the international biomedical community. Because this is an extremely varied group, the literature coverage is broad. It includes both research and didactic literature, relating not only to the science and practice of medicine, dentistry, nursing, and public health but also to bioengineering, legal medicine, bioethics, medical economics, and other related fields.

In deciding which journals should be included in *Index Medicus*, the library has guidance from a group of nine outside experts. These consultants include distinguished health scientists, educators, editors, and librarians. NLM also solicits the suggestions and recommendations of many other subject specialists. The group of consultants, however, reviews all judgments and recommendations to assure a uniform and balanced perspective.

A smaller version of *Index Medicus*, *Abridged Index Medicus*, is available for individuals and for institutions whose users do not require the more comprehensive coverage of the *Index Medicus*. The abridged publication covers some 125 English-language journals, primarily in the clinical sciences.

Another important reference work published by the library is the *National Library of Medicine Current Catalog*. The catalog is published quarterly and cumulated annually and quinquennially. It is a permanent record of all publications cataloged at NLM, both monographic and serial.

Similar to the *Current Catalog*, but for nonprint materials, is the *National Library of Medicine Audiovisual Catalog*. This quarterly work, cumulated annually, lists by subject and title the audiovisual productions (some 2,000 each year) cataloged by the library. Each issue contains a procurement section that lists sources for purchasing the materials.

There are two general types of audiovisual productions included. The first, materials developed specifically for health-science education, are critically reviewed for accuracy and quality by non-NLM experts. The second category, which is not peer-reviewed, includes recordings of educational events—lectures, symposia, grand rounds, and so forth.

Two other types of reference publications are derived from the library's indexing of journal articles: recurring bibliographies and "literature searches." Recurring bibliographies, of which there are about two dozen, cover specialized areas of the biomedical literature. They are produced by NLM and published for sale by cooperating professional societies and other government agencies. Examples include bibliographies of varying periodicity in anesthesiology, orthopedic surgery, dermatology, neurology, dentistry, and nursing.

Literature searches are single, computer-produced bibliographies on topics of current professional interest that the library publishes and distributes without charge to some 40,000 requesters each year. Their topicality is suggested by some recent subjects covered: terrorism or civil disorders, in vitro fertilization or embryo transfer, and population control in developing countries. Literature searches usually contain between 50 and 500 references.

There is a wide array of reference works published in the biomedical sciences, in addition to those issued by NLM. To make optimum use of the literature, health professionals should become familiar with *Excerpta Medica*, *Biological Abstracts*, and *Chemical Abstracts*, which are described in Chapter 12, and *Current Contents/Life Sciences* and *Science Citation Index* which are described in Chapter 11.

Reference librarian services

An invaluable resource for any search of the biomedical literature is an experienced reference librarian. Most substantial health-science libraries have on their staff librarians and information specialists who are trained in the use of the many research tools that provide access to the literature.

NLM has a staff of 15 professional reference librarians who respond to some 50,000 requests for reference assistance each year. These requests arrive at the library by mail, telephone, and telegraph, as well as directly from readers. Their complexity ranges from simply consulting a desk-top reference aid to a comprehensive search of various published tools and computerized data bases.

Computerized access to the literature

Computers have come to play an important role in improving access to the biomedical literature. Today, there are a number of systems available, including on-line automated retrieval from data bases built from the published reference tools mentioned earlier. NLM pioneered in computerized bibliographic retrieval with its Medical Literature Analysis and Retrieval System (MEDLARS), operational since 1964 (see Figure 10.3).

MEDLARS is based on the skilled indexing and cataloging of published materials received by NLM. This labor-intensive activity has changed little in the 100 years since Billings began the *Index Medicus*. A carefully constructed thesaurus of 14,000 biomedical terms known as MeSH (Medical Subject Headings) furnishes the terms used by the indexers and catalogers to describe articles and books. Some ten to 15 subject headings are usually sufficient to characterize each article.

The principal impetus for the development of MEDLARS in the early 1960s was the growth of the biomedical journal literature and the consequent increase in size of the monthly *Index Medicus* and annual *Cumulated Index Medicus*. The first issue to be prepared by the computer and photo-composition equipment was the August 1964 *Index Medicus*. Its 13,733 references, totaling an estimated 9 million characters, took only 18 hours of computer time to collate and typeset. It was estimated to have the power of 55 Linotype operators.

MEDLARS not only achieved the automated publication of *Index Medicus* but also made possible the production of a wide variety of published recurring bibliographies and literature searches (described earlier) and the development of a retrieval service. This retrieval service allowed for searching the data base of MEDLARS references in response to an inquiry. Such individualized searches, however, were slow and required formulation by a trained search analyst before being entered into the computer. Even with a dozen search formulation centers around the country, it was never possible to respond to more than about 20,000 search requests in a year.

Spurred by increasing demands for search services and a growing backlog of requests, NLM undertook, in the late 1960s, to develop a more rapid and widely accessible system. The result, after several years of experimentation, was the implementation of MEDLARS Online (MEDLINE), a new service begun in October 1971.

THE NLM ON-LINE NETWORK

Using MEDLINE, it is possible for health professionals throughout the United States (and in several foreign countries) to have immediate access to a data base of about half a million citations to the most recent articles. These articles are from more than 3,000 different biomedical journals, including those indexed for *Index Medicus*. Access is through computer terminals that are linked to the NLM's IBM 370/168 computers by telecommunication lines. More than 1,500 hospitals, medical schools, and medical-research institutions in the United States have access to MEDLINE, and more than 2 million computer searches are made each year. In addition, several hundred foreign institutions are connected to the system.

MEDLINE is an interactive system; that is, the user identifies the journal article references needed by carrying on a dialogue with the computer by typing in successive queries on the terminal keyboard. MEDLINE recognizes some 14,000 medical subject headings, from "abattoirs" to "zymosan," that may be combined to search on a specific subject. Users may also search by an author's name, a word in the title or abstract of an article, a publication date, a language, a specific journal title, or a combination of these elements. Figure 10.4 shows a sample search of MEDLINE.

After pertinent references are located, the computer prints at the

SS 1 /C?
USER:
DEATH, SUDDEN AND HEART INJURIES
PROG:
SS (1) PSTG (3)

SS 2/C?
USER:
PRINT FULL INCLUDE AB
PROG:

```
1  AU  - Froede RC ; Lindsey D ; Steinbronn K
   TI  - Sudden unexpected death from cardiac concussion (commotio cordis)
         with unusual legal complications.
   LA  - Eng
   MH  - Adolescence ; Athletic Injuries/*pathology ; Autopsy ; Case Report
   MH  - Contusions/pathology ; Death, Sudden/*etiology ; Forensic Medicine
   MH  - Heart Injuries/*pathology ; Human ; Male ; Nomenclature
   MH  - Wounds, Nonpenetrating/*pathology
   AB  - Sudden and unexpected death may result from cardiac concussion
         following blunt force trauma to the thorax. Undiagnosed
         pathologic disease must be carefully evaluated as a possible
         contributory element. Legal complications may arise from any
         autopsy. It is recommended that a photograph be taken upon
         completion of the autopsy. This photograph and adequate records
         can be used to refute any charges against the pathologist or
         assistants for the poor condition of a body after its release.
   SO  - J Forensic Sci 1979 Oct;24(4):752-6

2  AU  - Green ED ; Simson LR Jr ; Kellerman HH ; Horowitz RN ; Sturner WQ
   TI  - Cardiac concussion following softball blow to the chest.
   LA  - Eng
   MH  - Adult ; Athletic Injuries/*complications ; Case Report
   MH  - Death, Sudden/etiology ; Heart Injuries/*etiology/mortality
   MH  - Human ; Male ; Sports ; Thoracic Injuries/*complications
   MH  - Wounds, Nonpenetrating/*complications
   AB  - We report two cases of sudden death in young men following
         softball blows to the chest. The deaths were presumed to be due
         to cardiac dysrhythmias because no significant traumatic lesions
         were found at autopsy. Cardiac concussion has rarely been
         reported to cause death. Lethal cardiac dysrhythmias may,
         however, occur following a sharp precordial blow without
         producing detectable chest wall or intrathoracic lesions.
   SO  - Ann Emerg Med 1980 Mar;9(3):155-7

3  AU  - Geppert M
   TI  - [Late death following contusio cordis]
   LA  - Ger
   MH  - Accidents, Traffic ; Adult ; Case Report ; Contusions
   MH  - Death, Sudden/*etiology ; Female ; Heart Injuries/*complications
   MH  - Human ; Thoracic Injuries/complications ; Time Factors
   SO  - Med Welt 1978 5 May;29(18):739-41
```

FIGURE 10.4. Sample MEDLINE Search. After being prompted by the query "Search statement 1 or command?," the user requests a search on the terms "death, sudden" and "heart injuries"—both terms in the controlled vocabulary of Medical Subject Headings. The number of retrieved references ("postings"—PSTG) is three. The user asks that they be printed out, including abstract. MEDLINE responds with authors (AU); title of article (TI); language (LA); main headings (MH); abstract, if available (AB); and journal source (SO).

Source: National Library of Medicine, June 1980

terminal the author, title, and journal source for each citation. English abstracts are available in about half of the citations. If a large number of references are retrieved (more than 25), they may be printed overnight at NLM and mailed to the requester the next day. The entire on-line search usually takes less than 15 minutes.

MEDLINE user aids

In most institutions, the MEDLINE search is done by a trained intermediary from information provided by the requester. Ideally, of course, users should be able to negotiate their own searches at a terminal. Experience shows, however, that most are unwilling to learn the intricacies of access protocols, command languages, search strategy formulation, and controlled vocabularies.[4] Since these elements vary widely among the many existing computerized data bases, it is not surprising that an infrequent user would be reluctant to expend the effort necessary to become proficient in searching them.

Although it is likely that trained intermediaries will always be needed to make *optimum* use of such complex retrieval systems as MEDLARS, it is possible to devise aids to enable untrained users to perform uncomplicated searches. NLM is developing several "user-cordial interfaces" to facilitate such searches by users with no special training. One of these is the Current Information Transfer in English (CITE).

The CITE interface assumes no prior knowledge of searching techniques. The searcher simply enters a question using a phrase or sentence in English. The CITE system finds documents in which the terminology in the titles and abstracts most closely matches the words in the search query. It displays the retrieved references in a ranked order, with those likely to be most relevant appearing first. Once the searcher has identified references of high relevance, the system automatically modifies the search and finds additional documents containing terminology similar to the selected relevant citations. This feature takes advantage of NLM's precise indexing without requiring the searcher to be at all familiar with the indexing vocabulary.

Other data bases on the NLM network

MEDLINE is the most important and heavily used of NLM's data bases, accounting for almost 40 percent of the 2 million on-line and off-line searches done each year. Since MEDLINE contains only recent journal article references (some 500,000 from the last two to three years of the published literature), older MEDLINE references, dating back to 1966, are put in "backfiles" and searched off-line. This means that the search query is entered at the terminal, run against the backfiles at night, and the results mailed to the requester the next day. There are some 2.5 million references in the MEDLINE backfiles.

MEDLINE can also be used to update a search periodically. The search formulation is stored in the computer, and each month, when approximately 20,000 new references are added to the data base, the search is processed automatically and the results mailed from NLM.

A number of the data bases available over the NLM on-line network are related to the broad area of pharmacology/toxicology.

Toxicology Information Online (TOXLINE) is a collection of 650,000 references from the last five years on published human and animal toxicity studies, effects of environmental chemicals and pollutants, and adverse drug reactions. Older TOXLINE material (400,000 references) is in the backfile, TOXBACK. Almost all references in TOXLINE have abstracts or indexing terms, and most chemical compounds mentioned in TOXLINE are further identified with Chemical Abstracts Service (CAS) registry numbers. The references are from five, major, published secondary sources and five special-literature collections maintained by other organizations.

Chemical Dictionary Online (CHEMLINE) is a file of 900,000 names for chemical substances, representing 450,000 unique compounds. CHEMLINE, created by NLM in collaboration with CAS, contains such information as CAS registry numbers, molecular formulas, preferred chemical nomenclature, and generic and trivial names. The file may be searched by any of these elements and also by nomenclature fragments and ring-structure information, making chemical structure searches possible.

The Registry of Toxic Effects of Chemical Substances (RTECS), is an annual compilation prepared by the National Institute for Occupational Safety and Health. RTECS contains acute toxicity data for approximately 36,000 substances. For some compounds, there are also threshold limit values, recommended standards in air, and aquatic toxicity data.

The Toxicology Data Bank (TDB) contains chemical, pharmacological, and toxicological information and data on approximately 1,500 substances. Information on an additional 1,000 substances is being prepared. Data for TDB are extracted from handbooks and textbooks and reviewed by a peer-review group of subject specialists.

Several of the data bases are used predominantly by librarians for obtaining cataloging information and for locating specific journal titles.

Catalog Online (CATLINE) contains about 200,000 references to books and serials cataloged at NLM since 1965. CATLINE gives medical libraries in the network immediate access to authoritative cataloging information, thus reducing the need for these libraries to do their own original cataloging. Libraries also find this data base a useful source of information for ordering books and journals and for providing reference and interlibrary loan services.

Serials Online (SERLINE) contains bibliographic information for about 34,000 serial titles, including all journals that are on order or cataloged for the NLM collection. For 20 percent of these, SERLINE has locator information for the user to determine which U.S. medical libraries own a particular journal. SERLINE is used by librarians to obtain information needed to order journals and to refer interlibrary loan requests.

Finally, there is a series of on-line data bases covering nonprint materials and specialized subjects. These are Audiovisuals Online (AVLINE), containing citations to 8,000 audiovisual teaching productions used in the health sciences; three cancer-related data bases sponsored by the National Cancer Institute; *Health Planning and Administration*, containing about 130,000 references to literature on health planning, organization, financing, and so forth; and certain highly specialized data bases, such as History of Medicine Online (HISTLINE), BIOETHICSLINE, and EPILEPSYLINE.

All institutional members of NLM's on-line network have access to these data bases 18 hours a day (3:00 A.M. to 9:00 P.M., eastern time), Monday through Friday. A backup computer is maintained at the State University of New York (SUNY) in Albany to ensure that the system is always available during these hours. Users have a choice of connecting either to NLM's computers in Bethesda, Maryland, or SUNY's computers in Albany. NLM levies a modest charge for each hour a user is connected to the computers and a charge for each page of off-line printout.

DOCUMENT DELIVERY

The ability to search the biomedical literature rapidly and identify needed journal articles and books is of little advantage if the user cannot then conveniently obtain the original document, or a copy of it. A health practitioner, for example, wishing to review a recent article pertinent to a clinical problem currently being faced, requires not only rapid retrieval of a reference but expeditious delivery of the actual document. Unfortunately, the long-term trend of an increasing number of journals, combined with the recent phenomenon of decreasing library budgets, makes it unlikely that a health professional will be able to locate in a single library all the journal articles identified in a thorough search of MEDLINE (or a printed reference work). To ensure that health professionals have access to their literature, NLM, in the late 1960s, instituted a formal regional medical library (RML) network in the United States.

The network is hierarchical. At its base are more than 3,000 local institutions, usually hospitals, with modest collections (100 to 200 current journal titles) and a well-defined group of health professionals for whom reader and reference services are provided. The next level in the hierarchy, and the level that local libraries first turn to for help, is the resource library. There are about 120 resource libraries in the United States, most connected with medical schools, that have substantial collections with some 2,000 to 3,000 journal titles available.

The RML is the next level in the network. There are 11 RMLs at major health-science libraries associated with leading medical schools and medical societies. (See Table 10.2.) They have large collections (3,000 to 5,000 journal titles) and provide document delivery services for materials otherwise unavailable in their geographic regions. RMLs also assist in coordinating on-line services within their regions, provide consultation and training opportunities for local health-science librarians, and serve as a regional resource for reference services. NLM assists in funding RMLs through contracts.

The backup for the entire network is NLM. NLM provides document delivery service from its collection of some 2.5 million items, including 22,000 serial titles. NLM provides about 250,000 interlibrary loans each year and supports another 750,000 loans through the RML network. Together, these represent about 50 percent of all interlibrary loan activity in the health sciences in the United States.

One trend of increasing importance within the network is that of consortium development. Health-science libraries, faced with a rapidly growing corpus of biomedical literature that is increasingly expensive, are finding it advantageous to join together with others in their area to form a consortium to plan, develop, and operate cooperative programs of resource development and sharing.

Beginning in 1977, NLM has emphasized the awarding of grants to fund consortia of health-science libraries in the United States. By 1980, the library had provided almost 3 million dollars to about 100 consortia, representing some 600 institutions. These formal cooperative arrangements at the local level constitute a vital component of the national biomedical communications network in the United States, and they have resulted in improved library service to the user community.

FUTURE SYSTEMS

Computerized, on-line bibliographic systems are but the first phase in the development of individualized information-retrieval services. Future advances will require that the various information requirements of patient care, research, and health-science education be integrated into a general network of compatible, computerized subsystems.

The broad field of "health computing" can be divided into four areas: scientific computing, health information systems, educational computing,

TABLE 10.2. Regional Medical Libraries

Region	Library
I	New England Regional Medical Library Service (Connecticut, Massachusetts, Maine, New Hampshire, Rhode Island, and Vermont) Francis A. Countway Library of Medicine Harvard University 10 Shattuck St, Boston, MA 02115
II	New York and New Jersey Regional Medical Library New York Academy of Medicine Library 2 E 103 St, New York, NY 10029
III	Mideastern Regional Medical Library Service (Delaware and Pennsylvania) Library of the College of Physicians 19 S 22 St, Philadelphia, PA 19103
IV	Mid-Atlantic Regional Medical Library (District of Columbia, Maryland, North Carolina, Virginia, and West Virginia) National Library of Medicine 8600 Rockville Pike, Bethesda, MD 20209
V	Kentucky-Ohio-Michigan Regional Medical Library Program Wayne State University Shiffman Medical Library 4325 Brush St, Detroit, MI 48201
VI	Southeastern Regional Medical Library Program (Alabama, Florida, Georgia, Mississippi, South Carolina, Tennessee, and Puerto Rico) AW Calhoun Medical Library Emory University, Atlanta, GA 30322
VII	Midwest Regional Medical Library (Illinois, Indiana, Iowa, Minnesota, North Dakota, Wisconsin) Library of the Health Sciences University of Illinois at the Medical Center 1750 West Polk St, Chicago, IL 60612
VIII	Midcontinental Regional Medical Library Program (Colorado, Kansas, Missouri, Nebraska, South Dakota, Utah, and Wyoming) Library of Medicine University of Nebraska Medical Center Omaha, NB 68105

IX	South Central Regional Medical Library Program (Arkansas, Louisiana, New Mexico, Oklahoma, and Texas) University of Texas Health Science Center 5323 Harry Hines Blvd, Dallas, TX 75235
X	Pacific Northwest Regional Health Science Library (Alaska, Idaho, Montana, Oregon, and Washington) University of Washington Health Sciences Library Seattle, WA 98195
XI	Pacific Southwest Regional Medical Library Service (Arizona, California, Hawaii, and Nevada) Biomedical Library Center for the Health Sciences University of California at Los Angeles Los Angeles, CA 90024

and management. Each area has its own specialized requirements in terms of the kind of trained professionals needed to develop and operate the systems. One reason that computer technology is underutilized by the health-care community is the lack of professionals who are equally and intimately familiar with both the problems of biomedicine and the potential applications of computer technology.

Training

As one step in remedying this problem, NLM began a unique training program in 1972. The objective is to promote the complete and effective integration of computer technology into all phases of clinical medicine—teaching, practice, and research. It was decided at that time that the most practical projects to be supported (by grants) would be those designed to train teachers or potential faculty members in the health sciences. NLM is supporting such training programs in ten academic institutions in the United States.

Some concentrate on postdoctoral training for those with a professional health degree, an academic degree in one of the health sciences, or an advanced degree in computing science. Other programs accommodate those who do not possess an advanced degree and provide training both in computer technology and the health sciences. It is expected that graduates of the program will advance to positions of leadership in their disciplines.

Almost 200 individuals have been trained under this grant-supported activity.

In 1979, the library announced two new grant programs to foster the careers of investigators who are working in the health-related information sciences. The first, the New Investigator Award, provides funds for researchers who are, for the first time, seeking support for research projects of their own design. This program is intended to bridge the transition from predoctoral and postdoctoral training status to that of an independent and productive research scientist.

The second, the Research Career Development Award, is a full-time salary grant for a single support period of five years. The purpose of this program is to enhance, at an early stage, the careers of individuals who have demonstrated outstanding potential for research contributions to the health-related information sciences.

MEDLARS III

A third-generation computer-based system, MEDLARS III, is now under development at NLM. The original MEDLARS, operational in 1964, was primarily a means of producing *Index Medicus* and other bibliographies rapidly and efficiently. Several years later, a query-response system was installed to allow the processing of individual searches in a "batch" mode. MEDLARS II made possible direct on-line access to the store of MEDLARS references, beginning in 1971. MEDLARS III will apply computerized techniques to controlling the internal library processes of indexing, cataloging, acquisitions, serial processing, inventory control, and document delivery and the integration of all these processes through a single, authoritative master bibliographic record.

There are four basic network services that would be of great value to the health-science community and that will be incorporated as major components in MEDLARS III. These are standardized bibliographic control and support for centralized record creation and maintenance, bibliographic retrieval, centralized national locator information with automated linkages to a national document delivery system, and the document delivery system itself. Only two of these network services exist at present—bibliographic retrieval, which is already highly automated, and document delivery, essentially a manual interlibrary loan operation dependent on the postal service.

The problem of improving the document delivery system is the subject of several developmental efforts now going on at the library. The first of these employs a digital facsimile network called International Electronic Post (INTELPOST) to send black-and-white text material via satellite between the British Lending Library and NLM. Although the initial demonstration was successful, there are still unanswered questions regarding costs and standards of quality for transmitting photographs (for example, X rays), complex drawings, and fine print.

The second research effort is to develop a system that will store large quantities of information from printed documents on optical discs and allow rapid retrieval and transmission of the information. The contents of up to 108,000 pages can be stored on both sides of one optical disc, and NLM is now exploring the possibility of a system capable of storing 1,000 such discs with on-line access time of a few seconds. Such a system, if implemented, would occupy less than 100 square feet of floor space and contain a collection equivalent to several million journal issues. The ability to store tens of millions of pages of text and graphics, combined with a system that would provide access to and display this information at terminals in medical libraries around the country, would be a true revolution in handling medical information.

"Knowledge bases" for practitioners

Practitioners engaged in health-care delivery are required to have at their command a vast amount of disparate information if they are to provide high-quality care for their patients. Biomedical research is constantly uncovering new procedures, drugs, and methods of treatment, and it is an impossible task for conscientious practitioners to keep abreast of all they need to know about the many illnesses and disabilities encountered in their practice. To help with this problem, new methods are being developed to bring to health-care professionals the current and reliable information they need, when they need it, and in a form that can be readily understood and used.[5]

NLM, in a departure from its traditional involvement in bibliographic work, is engaged in building a series of computerized "knowledge bases." Knowledge bases may be described as computer-based, condensed representations of published information, organized in several levels of detail, including citations to the original articles upon which the synthesis is based. The information is entered into a minicomputer and accessible by keyboard terminals. A prototype has been developed and is being tested on a first such knowledge base—on hepatitis.[6] The content of the knowledge base has been selected and is continually updated by a group of experts, and it is being field-tested at their institutions by physicians, medical students, librarians, and other health professionals.

The computerized hepatitis knowledge base contains 2 million characters (corresponding to approximately 400 printed pages) and is organized hierarchically by topic. For each topic heading, there is an accompanying synthesis statement that represents the state of current knowledge. Each heading and synthesis is followed by supporting elements derived from published source documents. Updating of the hepatitis knowledge base is facilitated by use of a computer conferencing network that serves as the principal medium of communication linking the geographically dispersed experts with the NLM.

Two additional knowledge bases, on peptic ulcer and human genetics, are in early stages of development. Also under investigation is the important question of how to make these knowledge bases conveniently accessible to health practitioners.

All of the services and resources described in this chapter are available to health professionals—students, educators, scientists, and practitioners. Access is provided through local or regional medical libraries or by direct inquiry to NLM. Scholars will find the materials in the History of Medicine Division well organized and readily accessible. Scientists will find the scope and coverage of the journal collection broad and comprehensive. Students and teachers will find the texts and reference works useful for most educational and scientific endeavors.

Through its extramural grants program, NLM supports research in information handling, training of librarians and information scientists, library resource development, studies in the history of the life sciences, and the publication of specialized indexes, abstracts, atlases, monographs, and recurring bibliographies. It also supported the construction of 11 new medical libraries. Since the passage of the Medical Library Assistance Act in 1965, NLM has awarded more than $100 million to individuals and institutions concerned with the creation, management, and distribution of biomedical information.

The literature of biomedicine, vast as it is, is presently well served by a variety of printed and computerized tools that permit rapid bibliographic access. [7] The challenge for the future is to devise new ways to bring not just references but the actual information contained in documents, and even authoritative syntheses, to those working in laboratories, classrooms, and patient-care settings.

The communications technology to do this exists. The successful development of communications satellites has provided new mechanisms for reliable, inexpensive, and rapid information transfer internationally. New glass-based communications cables with wide-band width are cheaper than copper and provide opportunities for telefacsimile and other types of communications. These advances, coupled with the marked reduction in cost for computer memories and the introduction of new storage devices (such as the optical disc), offer remarkable opportunities for new and improved biomedical communications systems.

Communications systems, however, are only as good as the information they transmit. Whether based on modern technology or on Billings's painstaking methods of 1879, the heart of the biomedical communications enterprise is the human intellect.

In summary, NLM was created to acquire, organize, and distribute the world's biomedical literature. Its services are made available to individuals in the health professions through a network of local and regional medical libraries. In addition to publishing *Index Medicus* and *Current Catalog*, NLM produces a wide array of specialized recurring bibliographies that are made available through professional societies or medical organizations. It provides computer-based reference and bibliographic services upon demand and is involved in the development and application of new computer technologies to improve access to and transfer of medical information.

REFERENCES

1. An excellent recounting of the library's history is in Schullian DM, Rogers FB: The National Library of Medicine. Libr Quart 1958 Jan;28:1–17; Apr;28:95–121.
2. Hume EE: Victories of Army Medicine. Philadelphia, Lippincott, 1943, pp 45–46.
3. Corning ME, Cummings MM: Biomedical communications. In Advances in American Medicine: Essays at the Bicentennial, Vol 2. Edited by JZ Bowers, EF Purcell. New York, Josiah Macy, Jr. Foundation, 1976, p 730.
4. Doszkocs TE, Rapp BA, Schoolman HM: Automated information retrieval in science and technology. Science 1980 Apr 4;208:25–30.
5. Schoolman HM, Bernstein LM: Computer use in diagnosis, prognosis, and therapy. Science 1978 May 26;200:926–31.
6. Bernstein LM, Siegel ER, Goldstein CM: The hepatitis knowledge base: A prototype information transfer system. Ann Intern Med 93:169–81, 1980.
7. One of the best brief guides to the literature is Beatty WK: Searching the literature and computerized services in medicine: Guides and methods for the clinician. Ann Intern Med 1979; 91:326–32.

11

THE INSTITUTE FOR SCIENTIFIC INFORMATION

Eugene Garfield

The biomedical information and knowledge industry is a vast, pluralistic enterprise. Governmental organizations, such as the National Library of Medicine (see Chapter 10); private organizations such as the Institute for Scientific Information; and professional societies, such as the American Medical Association, all play an important role. In one way or another, they help professionals in the daily information-gathering process.

The various publications and services provided by these and other institutions serve two basic functions. First, they help professionals "keep up" or maintain current awareness, whether in research or in clinical practice. Second, they help professionals locate information on specific problems as the need arises.

As Arnold Relman points out (see Chapter 5), the average physician can keep up by the judicious selection of a small number of journals. Clinicians who want to get an even broader view of the current literature can use the excellent abstracting services found in such journals as the *Journal of the American Medical Association (JAMA)*. Those who want a more systematic approach to their specialities or special interests can rely on a variety of mechanisms described here. It is important to note, however, that browsing through contents pages or abstracts cannot replace the regular perusal of journals. Using secondary information services is undoubtedly efficient and stimulating, but it is necessary to keep in touch with the original journals, whether by using them in libraries or by personally subscribing. Indeed, in my experience, the heaviest users of current-awareness services regularly peruse six to 12 journals.

Most biomedical and clinical research scientists and clinicians today supplement their primary journal usage with *Current Contents (CC)*. Indeed, scanning *CC* often leads them to articles in the journals they receive. More often, though, it leads to journals available in local libraries.

While *CC* comes in seven discipline-oriented editions, biomedical researchers usually use *Current Contents/Life Science (CC/LS)*, which covers over 1,000 basic research journals, the most important clinical journals, and about 500 multiauthored books per year. Clinicians may prefer *Current Contents/Clinical Practice (CC/CP)*, which covers approximately 750 clinical journals and 500 new books. There is some overlap between *CC/LS* and *CC/CP* in the coverage of the most important clinical journals. These journals have been identified by extensive citation analysis and include such titles as *New England Journal of Medicine, Lancet, British Medical Journal*, and *Annals of Internal Medicine*. These journals have also proven to be those most widely read by clinicians.

CC includes facsimile reproductions of the contents pages of the latest issues of journals. Each weekly issue includes all weekly journals, such as *JAMA* and *Nature*, as well as whichever monthly or quarterly journals are processed that week. At the Institute for Scientific Information (ISI) in Philadelphia, where *CC* and a number of other information services are produced, each journal issue is rapidly processed so that entries can be included as soon as possible after the journal is published. (See Figure 11.1.)

In addition to the names of authors and article titles, *CC* entries include the journal title and publisher, volume and issue number, and date of publication. *CC* also indicates the language in which the journal articles and abstracts are published.

Most readers of *CC* either thumb through the entire issue or one of the main categories, such as oncology, pharmacology, or clinical medicine. Others limit their scanning to selected contents pages by using the journal or subject indexes.

With *CC*, as with any other secondary information service, there is always the question of how to gain access to journals or articles that are not available locally. Interlibrary loan services (see Chapter 12) are available at most medical libraries, and ISI offers Original Article Tear Sheet (OATS) service, which provides articles cut from journals at a small fee. But most *CC* readers use the author index and address directory in each issue to request reprints. Of course, personal reprint collections can be built up by a variety of mechanisms, but it is always a special compliment to the author when you request a reprint after reading the paper.

Scientists and physicians who lack the time for browsing use the indexes in each *CC* issue to quickly pinpoint just those articles of interest to them.

FIGURE 11.1. Sample Contents Page from *Current Contents*. From *Current Contents/Life Sciences* 23(28):125, 14 July 1980.

For example, if there is a particular journal you would like to see, you can check the journal index at the front of *CC* to see if it appears in that issue. To follow the work of a particular author, use the Author Index and Address Directory. To locate material on a specific subject, use the Weekly Subject Index (WSI). Every significant word, in every article title, is included in this

CC Pg   J Pg

DIABETES-MELLI
TUS
85   355
104   258
164   1267

FIGURE 11.2. Entry from *Current Contents Weekly Subject Index* Source: *Current Contents/Life Sciences* 23(28):87, 14 July 1980.

subject index. For example, to find articles on diabetes mellitus, check this term in WSI. (See Figure 11.2.)

Besides the weekly indexes, physicians and scientists interested in the recent literature can use the *Quarterly Index to Current Contents/Life Sciences (QUICC/LS)* to retrospectively search the last 13 weeks of *CC/LS*. Each issue of *QUICC/LS* indexes a journal index, an author index (including coauthors), and a title-word index covering every item that appeared in *CC* during the 13 weeks covered. Each entry gives the exact *CC* issue and page number on which the relevant item may be found.

Other more modern and personalized mechanisms for finding out about new articles on a specific subject are available. These "selective dissemination of information" (SDI) systems are often used by researchers as "awareness insurance"—to insure that they do not miss anything important.

This insurance is especially valuable when you do not have time to scan journals or such current-awareness tools as *CC* regularly or when your subject is highly interdisciplinary. For example, ASCA (Automatic Subject Citation Alert) and ASCATOPICS, ISI's SDI services, select articles from over 5,000 journals in the sciences and social sciences.

All SDI services have several characteristics in common. They require the formulation of a subject profile—a list of words, word stems, authors, and so forth—that delineates the subject on which the user wishes to retrieve information. They require that the profile be matched against information from recent publications. This can be done by computer, as in ASCA or ASCATOPICS services, or manually by using the indexes in *CC, Excerpta Medica*, or *Index Medicus*. The user receives a weekly and monthly list of bibliographic descriptions of the recent publications that "matched" at least one of the profile terms.

SDI services are run commercially and by some libraries in government, industry, and academia, but the most personalized (and probably the most valuable) of these services have been underused. This is because a truly personalized service requires that scientists or physicians help create their own subject profiles. Some do not want to take the time. Others find it difficult to formulate the profile terms. At ISI, specialists help create ASCA profiles from lists of profile terms provided by subscribers. They consult with users on profile construction and "fine tune" the profile after the service has begun. In any event, the construction of the profile does take some effort on the part of the subscriber—an effort that many people do not wish to make. Sometimes this may be due to the vagueness and/or complexity of the subjects involved.

For those who want the benefits of SDI without the hassles, there are "standardized" profile SDI services. The profiles for these services are created by subject specialists rather than the subscribers. Clients simply indicate the "prepackaged" subject they want to be informed about. At ISI, we have constructed hundreds of ASCATOPICS profiles. These standardized profiles are more general than those used in the personalized service. They must satisfy the needs of many users. Typical prepackaged profiles cover diseases, such as sickle-cell anemia and alcoholism, and subjects, such as pediatric psychiatry, forensic medicine, and so forth.

Such organizations as ISI, the National Library of Medicine, and Chemical Abstracts Service make their computer tapes available to many foreign and domestic organizations so that they can provide SDI services. Large-scale services are provided in Canada, Israel, Scandinavia, Germany, and elsewhere.

Whereas SDI services and *CC* are generally used as current-awareness tools, printed and computerized indexes are used for retrospective literature searching—for finding out what has already been written about a topic. Since scientists build on the work of others, searching the literature in your field is an important part of the research process. Searching the literature can also give you more thorough answers to questions that arise in daily practice than you would get through merely asking colleagues.

Suppose you are asked by a patient or colleague about vitamin B15. You can look it up in a medical dictionary, such as *Dorland's*, and find out that it is pangamic acid, "an amino derivative of glycuronic acid . . . a water-soluble substance originally discovered in the kernel of the apricot; tentatively assigned to the fifteenth position in the list of vitamins in the B complex."[1] This is not very enlightening. What you really need is a good recent article (preferably a review) on this subject. If you want to find a book, you use a library catalog. If you want to find an article, you use an index to the scientific literature. These are provided by information services, such as

Index Medicus, Science Citation Index (SCT), Index to Scientific Reviews (ISR), Chemical Abstracts, Excerpta Medica, and *Biological Abstracts.* You can also turn to on-line (computerized) sources, including Medical Literature Analysis and Retrieval System Online (MEDLINE), SCISEARCH, CA Search, BIOSIS Previews, and *Excerpta Medica* on-line.

The type of information offered by information services varies. For example, *Chemical Abstracts, Excerpta Medica,* and *Biological Abstracts* are best described as abstracting services. *Index Medicus, SCI,* and *ISR,* on the other hand, are indexing services. They do not include abstracts or summaries.

While *SCI* and *ISR* index articles according to their subject matter, they are best known as comprehensive "citation indexes." *SCI,* begun in 1961, is published bimonthly and is cumulated annually and every five years. *SCI* covers every *significant* journal and every branch of science and medicine. Much of this selection is based on citation analysis.

The principle behind citation indexing is simple. Almost all papers, notes, reviews, and so forth, contain citations or references. These refer to publications that support, illustrate, elaborate, or provide precedent for what the author is saying. In short, there is a subject relationship between cited works and the articles that cite or reference them.

For example, if you have read an article and want more information on the same topic, you would probably scan the list of publications cited by the author. You would do this because you know that articles and books cited by the article are most likely to be on the same subject as the article itself. Conversely, if you wanted more recent articles on the subject, you would turn to *SCI* and look for articles that cited the paper you had read or any of the papers you had selected from the footnotes. A scientist entering a new field of research or trying to gather more information on a familiar subject can build up a comprehensive bibliography of articles by beginning a search with a single paper or chapter and tracing other articles related to it through citations.

SCI annually covers materials from nearly 3,000 journals and over 35,000 chapters a year from nearly 1,200 multiauthored books. You can use this index to find out whether an article has been cited during a specific time period, whether the methods described in a paper have been updated, or if any recent articles have been published on a topic of interest.

ISR is similar to *SCI.* However, rather than covering all articles published during a given period, it indexes only the review articles. *SCI* covers over 600,000 items per year, while *ISR* covers about 30,000. Review articles are valuable to the scientist approaching a new field of research because they synthesize previously published information. In addition, they often include comprehensive bibliographies. For this reason, *ISR* is a good starting point when you are approaching a new or unfamiliar research topic.

Each issue and cumulation of *SCI* and *ISR* is actually a group of indexes that cover the same body of scientific literature in different ways. These are the *Source Index*, the *Citation Index*, and the *Permuterm Subject Index (PSI)*.

If you already know of an important author, article, or book relevant to the subject being researched, you will begin your search with the *Citation Index*. This index lists every document referenced (or cited) in the articles indexed. For example, if your research subject is pharmaceutical applications of vitamin B15 and you know W. N. French has written an important paper in this field, you will turn to his name in the *Citation Index*. If French has been cited during the period covered, his name and bibliographic information on the articles cited will appear in the *Citation Index*. Underneath each article will appear the names of authors and journals that have cited the article in a paper. To get complete bibliographic information on these newer papers, you will turn to the *Source Index*. Special sections of the *Citation Index* list anonymously authored items and patents cited in articles.

An excellent starting place for researchers entering a new field is *PSI*. This is a title-word index. It is sometimes called a natural language index. Every significant word in every title covered by *SCI* or *ISR* is listed in this index. Each word is also permuted—that is, paired—with every other significant word in the title. You conduct a search through *PSI* by looking up a primary, or often-used, word or phrase from the field being researched. You then check the coterms listed under this word until you find another word that more specifically identifies the area being researched. Beside each of these coterms are found the names of all authors who used the primary word and coterm in the title of their articles. (See Figure 11.3.) Once you have these authors' names, you can look them up in the *Source Index* for a full bibliographic description of their articles. Since you generally conduct your search through *PSI* using words you encounter in the titles of papers, there is no need to consult a thesaurus. For example, if you wish to locate articles on pangamic acid, you can find papers with these words in their titles.

The *Source Index* can be used to follow the work of a specific author or organization. However, you will probably find that it is most often used in conjunction with the *Citation Index* or *PSI*. The *Source Index* is actually an author index to all papers and other editorial items indexed during the time period covered by *SCI* or *ISR*. It is organized alphabetically by first authors, and coauthors are cross-referenced to the first author entry.

Each entry in the *Source Index* begins with the name of the first author. This is followed by the names of all other authors, information on the language in which the paper is published, and all other standard bibliographic information. Also included are the number of references in the article and the full mailing address of the first author.

VITAMIN-B15

```
                         ♦BULLEID JN
                         ♦DARNTONH.I
                         ♦HOWELLS G
ACID     · · · · · · ♦FEKETE S
         · · · · · · ♦HERBERT V
ACTIVITY · · · ·   FEKETE S
BROILERS · · · ·        "
FEED-UTILL · ·          "
INFLUENCE · · ·         "
INOZIT · · · · · ·      "
PANGAMIC · · ·          "
             · ·   HERBERT V
SERUM-GOT · ·      FEKETE S
WEIGHT-GAIN ·          "
```

FIGURE 11.3. Entry from *SCI Permuterm Subject Index*. From *Science Citation Index, 1979 Annual. Permuterm Subject Index* Philadelphia: ISI Press, 1979. Vol. 13, Column 62547.

The *Source Index* also includes a Corporate Index, which is used to locate authors by their geographic location and corporate affiliation, and an index to anonymously authored items.

Suppose you have asked a colleague about vitamin B15 and he or she refers you to a 1966 article by W.N. French and L. Levi, entitled "Pangamic Acid (Vitamine B15 Pangametin Sopangamine)—Its Composition and Determination in Pharmaceutical Dosage Forms" (*Canadian Medical Association Journal* 94:1185–7, 1966). After reviewing this article, you may decide that you would like to find out what has happened since this paper was published. You may want to know if the information provided by these researchers has been confirmed or denied or if new applications for the vitamin have been found. You should now use the index that was specifically designed to answer these questions—*SCI*.

Your first step in this search will be to turn to the most recent volume of *SCI* in your library. The best way to find articles along the same lines as the French and Levi article is to look under the name of the first author, W. N. French, in the *Citation Index*. Here you will find the names of authors who have cited the 1966 article in the papers they have published during the indexing period. For example, V. Herbert's name appears in the 1979 *Citation Index* listing for the 1966 French and Levi article. As shown on Figure 11.4, Herbert's name is followed by the name, volume, page number, and year of the journal in which has article appeared. To find full biblio-

```
FRENCH WN ................................................................
  65 J PHARMACEUTICAL SCI   54 1133
     MASSE J          J THERM ANA              14    299    78
  66 CAN MED ASSOC J    94  1185
     HERBERT V        AM J CLIN N              32   1534    79
  73 J CHROMATOGRAPHY    86    211
     KIRCHNER JG      BK #07437          R     14      3    78
  74 J CHROMATOGRAPHY    97    223
     PLUYM A          J PHARM SCI        N     68   1050    79
     THOMAS JP        ANALUSIS                  7    221    79
        ''            J CHROMAT               172    107    79
  75 J PHARMACEUTICAL SCI    64 125
     VANKERCH C       J PHARM BEL              34     13    79
```

FIGURE 11.4. Entry from *SCI Citation Index*. From *Science Citation Index, 1979 Annual. Citation Index* Philadelphia: ISI Press, 1979. Vol. 2, Column 16622.

graphic information on the article, you should turn to the 1979 *Source Index* listing for V. Herbert. This listing, presented as Figure 11.5, includes bibliographic information on every article V. Herbert published in 1979, including the article citing French.

At this point, you can either obtain the Herbert article from the library and use it as an update on vitamin B15 or go back through earlier issues of *SCI* to find additional articles that cite the French article. You may wish to examine the 44 references cited in the Herbert article for more information.

The information provided in *SCI, Index Medicus, Excerpta Medica, Chemical Abstracts*, and *Biological Abstracts* is also available on-line. On-line services use computers to search the literature. The data bases from which the indexes are derived are stored in a central computer. Subscribers gain access to the computer by tying their terminals into the computer by a phone call. In an on-line service, users are in direct contact with the computer, which can retrieve information they request in a matter of minutes, once they are connected.

On-line searching has several advantages. It is very fast; a search can be completed and the results printed out in only a few minutes. On-line services, which are updated weekly or monthly, also provide access to more current information than do the print indexes. These services also permit you to specify the type of items you wish to retrieve—only items from certain years, for instance. Finally, the services permit very complex, multiterm searches that would be difficult, if not impossible, to do in the print indexes.

In most cases you, the end-user, will not do the search yourself. A trained search analyst will do the actual searching. This means you will have

HERBERT V

NUTRITIONALLY AND METABOLICALLY DESTRUCTIVE
NUTRITIONAL AND METABOLIC ANTI-NEOPLASTIC DIET OF
LAETRILE PROPONENTS
    AM J CLIN N   32(1):96-98   *79*   *34R*
      VET ADM HOSP,HEMATOL & NUTR LAB, BRONX, NY   10468
GARDNER A COLMAN N—EVIDENCE FOR POSSIBLE LACK
OF SAFETY FOR HUMAN CONSUMPTION OF
DICHLOROACETATE, A SISTER COMPOUND AND FREQUENT
INGREDIENT OF THE NON-VITAMIN B-15 (PANGAMATE)♦
MEETING
    AM J CLIN N   32(4):952   *79*   *3R*
      VET ADM HOSP, BRONX, NY   10468, USA
LAETRILE - CULT OF CYANIDE PROMOTING POISON FOR
PROFIT ♦ REVIEW
    AM J CLIN N   32(5):1121-1158   *79*   *190R*
      VET ADM MED CTR,HEMATOL & NUTR LAB, BRONX, NY

PANGAMIC ACID (VITAMIN-B15)
    AM J CLIN N   32(7):1534-1540   *79*   *44R*
      VET ADM HOSP,HEMATOL & NUTR LAB, BRONX, NY   10468

MANUSSEL C DAS KC—EVIDENCE FOR RECIPROCITY OF THE
DENOVO AND SALVAGE PATHWAYS TO DNA-SYNTHESIS -
DU SUPPRESSION TESTS AND THYMIDINE SUPPRESSION
TESTS OF DNA-SYNTHESIS IN HUMAN-BONE MARROW-CELLS
AND PHA-STIMULATED LYMPHOCYTES ♦ MEETING
    CLIN RES   27(2):A510   *79*   *NO R*
      VET ADM HOSP, BRONX, NY   10468, USA
GARDNER A COLMAN N—EVIDENCE FOR POSSIBLE LACK
OF SAFETY FOR HUMAN CONSUMPTION OF
DICHLOROACETATE, A SISTER COMPOUND AND FREQUENT
INGRE DIENT OF THE NON-VITAMIN B-15 (PANGAMATE)♦
MEETING
    CLIN RES   27(2):A551   *79*   *3R*
      VET ADM HOSP, BRONX, NY   10468, USA
ASCORBIC-ACID AND VITAMIN-B12 ♦ LETTER
    J AM MED A   242(21):2285   *79*   *3R*
      SUNY DOWNSTATE MED CTR, BROOKLYN, NY   11203, USA
GARDNER A COLMAN N—DICHLOROACETATE A MUTAGEN♦
LETTER
    N ENG J MED   300(11):625   *79*   *2R*
      VET ADM HOSP, BRONX, NY   10468, USA

see	BACKER RC	J AM MED A	241	1891	79
see	COLMAN N	BK # 07496	4	525	79
see	"	CLIN RES	27	A291	79
see	"	"	27	A460	79
see	COOPER B	CLIN CHEM	25	1136	79
see	MASSARRA.S	BK # 06476	1978	32	78

FIGURE 11.5. Entry from *SCI Source Index*. From *Science Citation Index, 1979 Annual. Source Index* Philadelphia: ISI Press, 1979. Vol. 8, Column 7467.

to discuss or write out your search needs before the analyst can begin. The more information you can provide, the more relevant the search results will be. As do the personalized SDI services discussed earlier, on-line searching—to be efficient—requires a certain amount of thoughtfulness and time from you.

One of the most important things you should bring to your meeting with the search specialist is five to ten very specific words that describe the topic you want searched. These should be words apt to appear in the titles of papers you would want to locate. If you have a problem identifying these key words, bring a few important papers or books from your field to the meeting. The search specialist should be able to identify key words from these. The names of people and organizations that are currently doing work in the field should also be brought to the interview. When using *SCISEARCH*, the *SCI* on-line system, the search specialist will also want to see references for landmark papers and established authors in your field.

You should also be aware that you may have to pay for an on-line search. Subscribing organizations are charged by the retrieval services for the computer time they use, and your library may pass some or all of this cost along to you. You should ask about the costs before you ask for a search.

Despite potential costs, on-line searches can sometimes be the most efficient way to retrieve information. It is important to be aware of the special advantages the on-line files afford, such as a savings in the time necessary to conduct a literature search, access to information not found in the printed indexes, and information that is more up-to-date than that in the printed indexes.

As is its printed counterpart, *SCI*, *SCISEARCH* is valuable for searches on interdisciplinary subjects. It covers over 3,000 journals from the full range of scientific disciplines—plus over 800 clinical, agricultural, and engineering journals not indexed in *SCI*.

The *SCISEARCH* file, like *SCI*, may be searched by citations, title words, and authors. But *SCISEARCH* offers you several ways to narrow your search. For example, using *SCISEARCH*, the search specialist can find you all English-language articles published on a specific subject in four particular journals in 1979. You can specify the items that should be retrieved according to the year written, the subject matter, the authors' names, the documents they cite, the authors' affiliations, the journal and language in which the articles are published, or the type of document.

ISI is now experimenting with new on-line and printed search tools to meet the needs of the physician, biomedical researcher, and student. The first of these, *ISI/BIOMED SEARCH*, is an on-line system that can be used by anyone who has access to a computer terminal. It provides the inexperienced searcher with a bibliography of the most important, recent articles in about

1,700 different research specialties. *ISI/BIOMED SEARCH* is currently being tested at several institutions.

The second service, our *Atlas of Science* series, is actually a print collection of condensed literature reviews. These brief summaries of active research specialties are supplemented by bibliographies of both the core, and the most recent, literature in the field, and by a map illustrating the relationship between the papers comprising the core literature.

Both *ISI/BIOMED SEARCH* and the *Atlas of Science* series let you quickly review the literature and determine how deeply your research on a subject must go. You can use them for a fast answer to your question or for an in-depth research project. These services deliver highly targeted information on specialty areas because they have been designed to reflect the specialty structure of science.

The intellectual structure of biomedical research can be defined as a network of research front specialties: discrete, but interacting, and sometimes overlapping, areas of intense research activity and rapid advance. The focus of these specialties and the pattern of interaction between them comprises a map of the cutting edge of biomedical research. ISI has developed a way, employing citation analysis, of producing this map and using it to index the biomedical literature.

The description of the atlas and on-line system will be more meaningful if I first explain how they are compiled. Research front specialties are defined through a process called "cocitation clustering." Each cluster is a group of highly cited, closely related papers—the core literature of a given specialty. Each cluster represents the most significant work in a particular research area.

Our first step in assembling these clusters is to identify articles cited a given number of times—say, 15—by the source articles in the *SCI*. This gives us a group of about 25,000 articles that are considered most important by the world's publishing research scientists. Our next step is to identify the articles that are cited together, or cocited. By a single link clustering route we cluster a smaller group of highly cocited documents or authors that are linked to one another a posteriori by current research investigators. Many of these highly cocited works appear in the various lists of most-cited papers published in *CC*, for example, in our study of the opiate receptor field.[2]

In citation analysis, we assume that highly cited articles represent the significant concepts or methods in a field. On the basis of our research, we have also found that cocitation relationships between papers reveal related concepts or methods.

A cluster program, which I have described elsewhere,[3,4] is run against our data base yearly. Clusters usually reform at this time because of the advancing nature of scientific research. The literature that is cited changes from year to year, so the clusters also change to reflect the evolving nature of biomedical research. Since the articles that belong to the cluster are highly cited in the most recent literature, we believe they represent areas of very active and important research. These clusters form the underlying structure of the two services being described here.

With *ISI/BIOMED SEARCH*, our experimental on-line service, any physician or researcher with a computer terminal can gain direct access to a bibliography of documents that cites cluster articles. As mentioned before, each cluster, and those articles that cite it, represent the most up-to-date information on a field. For this reason, we refer to a search through this system as a research front specialty search. The bibliography displayed during a search represents the leading edge of a research specialty.

ISI/BIOMED SEARCH currently consists of articles from nearly 1,300 biomedical journals from 1979 to the present. In the future, the file will cover the previous two years plus the current year, giving the searcher up to 36 months of information. This data base is updated monthly, with more than 230,000 new articles to be added each year. However, only a fraction of these will be pertinent to the clusters we identify. This is a kind of quality filter.

Designed primarily for the biomedical researcher, *ISI/BIOMED SEARCH* offers several advantages over existing on-line systems. The most obvious is that you need not be a search specialist to use it. Through the use of clusters and advanced computer technology, we have been able to eliminate many of the steps usually required in an on-line search. At first, physicians and researchers who use *ISI/BIOMED SEARCH* will have to access it through their library's computer terminal. However, I am convinced that most professionals will have terminals in their offices in the near future.

Another advantage of *ISI/BIOMED SEARCH* is that it allows you to take advantage of citation indexing without requiring that you begin with a particular author or paper. Instead, you begin with a research front specialty name.

Each subscriber to this service is given a guide or index to the more than 1,700 research front specialties emphasized in this data base. This index is used to determine if your area of interest is represented by a research front. Each significant word appearing in a research front name is alphabetically arranged in this index, followed by a list of the research front names in which it appears. Next to each name is the number of that specialty.

Once you have found the appropriate research front name, you simply key its research front specialty number into the terminal. Bibliographic citations of articles that cite members of the cluster are then displayed, or printed out if you wish. They can be displayed in a number of ways. For example, the most current papers can be listed first. When doing a search, you can also request that the articles that cite the most members of the cluster be the first displayed. This insures that you see the most germane articles first. You can further specify the type of articles you want according to the author's name or institution, journal title, language, and document type.

ISI/BIOMED SEARCH will provide you with a highly focused bibliography. However, our *Atlas of Science* series also brings together the ideas from a specialty bibliography in a condensed literature review. This is a printed service designed to provide students, physicians, and researchers with short, comprehensive overviews of specialty areas. Each of these specialties is identified through cluster data. We may also include these minireviews in our on-line system.

The first of this series is the *Atlas of Biochemistry* a collection of minireviews of biochemical specialties as defined by our 1978 cluster data. Each chapter in the atlas has four sections: an essay, a specialty map, a list of the cited core documents, and a list of the citing source documents. The essay provides an historical summary of the specialty, describes what scientific papers have played an important role in the specialty, and summarizes ongoing research. This essay is supplemented by bibliographies of both the core, and the most recent, literature on a field. A map illustrating the relationships between the papers comprising the core literature is also included.

In a sense, this *Atlas of Science* series picks up where a medical encyclopedia leaves off. It might be properly called a current atlas encyclopedia of research fronts! It provides current information and tells you where to go for additionl information. A physician or researcher would probably use the atlas to update or to become familiar with a specialty, or to get the answer to a question. If one of the essays does not answer your question completely, the core or citing literature most likely will.

It is apparent that both printed and on-line indexes offer an efficient means of gaining access to the biomedical literature. Since so much information is now available, it is important that researchers or clinicians be able to limit themselves to the most relevant material possible. A familiarity with the printed indexes and a knowledge of how to take advantage of the computerized systems can save you a great deal of time and effort in both your current-awareness and research activities.

While some of the printed and on-line services duplicate their coverage in one way or another, you will find that generally they complement one another admirably. For example, you may do a quick search using *Index Medicus*. Perhaps you have located a particularly interesting and relevant paper published in 1977. You might then immediately turn to *SCI* to determine if this paper has been cited in recent literature. Having found a comprehensive 1980 paper in *Nature, Science,* or the *New England Journal of Medicine*, you would examine this paper and decide which, if any, of the papers cited warrant further investigation in the library. If the subject you have chosen is very new or hot, you may want to start a search with the currently fashionable term either in *QUICC/LS* or *SCI's PSI*. If you want to do an on-line search, you can use almost any of the existing data bases to search by title words. These search strategies should be learned in order to get maximum advantage out of the time spent in tracking down pertinent literature. Using the right strategies can make using the literature an enjoyable challenge rather than necessary drudgery.

There has been a tendency in recent years to overemphasize the large size of the biomedical literature. This tends to create a sense of hopelessness among new professionals that is unwarranted. The fact is that thousands of professionals do manage to cope with the literature. Indeed, one can rightfully say that they control the literature before it overwhelms them. Depending upon your specific interests, from time to time you may feel that the literature is getting out of hand. However, by knowing how to be selective and how to read selectively, you can indeed maintain a proper balance.

There is no single prescription that solves the literature ills of every biomedical professional. Those with a high degree of curiosity will need access to a variety of media. Others, who simply want to be sure they are maintaining professional competence, will be satisfied with a few, well-chosen journals and one or two abstracting or SDI services. Others will simply want to review the newsmagazines of medicine and keep up by attendance at postgraduate courses and society meetings. If you choose to ignore the vast wealth of information that is now accessible, it should not be because you feel it cannot be done but rather because it is not worth your effort. It may be that you need to delegate some of this effort to others. However, in the long run, the professional is the person who is truly in control of all available information resources.

REFERENCES

1. *Dorland's Illustrated Medical Dictionary, 24th Edition.* Philadelphia: W.B. Saunders Company, 1965. p. 23
2. Garfield E. Controversies over opiate receptor research typify problems facing awards committees. *Current Contents* (20):5–19, 14 May 1979.
3. _____. ABCs of cluster mapping. Part 1. Most active fields in the life sciences in 1978. *Current Contents* (40):5–12, 6 October 1980.
4. _____. ABCs of cluster mapping. Part 2. Most active fields in the physical sciences in 1978. *Current Contents* (41):5–12, 13 October 1980.

SUGGESTED READINGS

Aaronson S. The footnotes of science. *Mosaic* 6(2):22–7, March/April 1975.
Anderson J and Begon F, eds. (whole issue). *Med. Inform.* 3(3), September 1978.

Beatty W K. Searching the literature and computerized services in medicine. *Ann. Intern. Med.* 91(2): 326–32, August 1979.

Conger LD. Multiple system searching: A searcher's guide to making use of the real differences between systems. *Online* 4(2): 10–21, April 1980.

Garfield E. *Citation indexing*. New York: Wiley, 1979.

Garfield E. The citation index as a subject index. *Current Contents* (18): 5–7, 1 May 1974. (Reprinted in Garfield E. *Essays of an information scientist*. 3 vols. Philadelphia: ISI Press, 1980.)

Powell J R. Excerpta Medica (EMBASE) online—A reacquaintance. *Online* 4(1): 36–41, January 1980.

Ross J C. Searching the chemical literature via three on-line vendors: A comparison. *J. Amer. Soc. Inform. Sci.* 30(2): 103–6, March 1979.

12

LIBRARIES AND HOW TO USE THEM

William K. Beatty

Libraries need not be mysteries. If you feel that you have stepped into a strange land when you cross a library's threshold, you need help and should ask for it. You can provide part of this help for yourself by going directly to the reference desk. This is usually front and center, and it often has a sign on it: reference, information, or readers' service. Ask there for a guide to the library and for information about tours and classes that the library may give. If you would like help for a current question or problem with the literature, ask one of the reference librarians in specific terms. You usually try to solve a clinical or research mystery by setting out the clues, piecing them together to make a whole, and seeing if they lead you to the solution. If you then need more help, you ask one of the specialists in that type of detective work, for example, in the library, one of the reference librarians.

Medical libraries today are practical combinations of people and materials designed to make your task—the effective and efficient use of the literature—as simple and painless as possible. Find out about the intellectual and physical tools you need to solve your problem, and then get to work.

Libraries not only provide information and materials on site, but they can also (by using telephones, computers, and interlibrary loans) locate information and materials in other libraries and institutions. Each time you leave a library, you should either have the answer to your question or be aware of the positive steps that the library staff will take to find the answer.

Much of the section on searching the literature is a modified and updated version of a paper that originally appeared in the *Annals of Internal Medicine* 1979 Aug; 91(2):326–332.

TYPES OF LIBRARIES

You will usually have access to at least one medical library as a part of your institution. This may be the library of a medical school, a hospital, medical center, research institute, or a society. Each of these types tends to have different levels and sizes of staffs, collections, and services and to have different regulations for the use of the collections and the facilities.

The medical-school library will usually have a staff that includes several reference librarians, some of whom may have backgrounds in the biological sciences and some capability with one or more foreign languages. This type of library will usually have at least one computer terminal with access to the major National Library of Medicine (NLM) data banks and possibly others as well. The typical medical-school library is in an upper echelon of the regional medical library system for your area (it may even be a "regional library"), and it usually has a substantial collection of currently received journals, backfiles of journals, and various types of books. Most medical-school libraries now have an audiovisual department either within the library or elsewhere in the school. The more progressive medical-school libraries also have browsing collections of nonmedical books, magazines, and news-papers, so that students, faculty members, and research investigators can keep up with the world around them and also ground their medical knowledge and practice in the broader context of the humanities.

The hospital library is the most common medical type. Many of these are small and may have only one professional staff member (or, more likely, a person with little or no formal training in librarianship) and possibly a full- or part-time clerical assistant. Thanks, however, to the workshops sponsored by various associations and by various regional library programs, the quality of the staff in hospital libraries is much higher now than it was back in the 1950s. A wide variety of consortia and other cooperative programs among hospital libraries is also improving local staff, programs, and services. The typical hospital library may consist of only one or two rooms and a small number of journals and books, but you, as a potential user, will often find out—especially if you make a point of asking the librarian—that the hospital library is not a cul-de-sac but rather an open-ended station in an active and efficient network of information.

The typical medical-center library may be an enlarged hospital library or a combination of a medical-school and a hospital library. Some of the larger medical-center libraries may also serve additional schools, such as those of nursing, dentistry, pharmacy, and allied health. Here you will find some of the most innovative medical-library activities, for example, the remarkably effective clinical library program, which attaches a specially qualified librarian to the medical team as it goes on its rounds.

Research medical libraries run the gamut from the highly specialized, small collections devoted to narrow topics, to collections of considerable size associated with a broad disease category, such as cancer. These libraries will often have one or more librarians with strong backgrounds in the subjects related to the major area of the institute.

Society libraries range from the few shelves found in a county medical society to the massive collections available at such institutions as the New York Academy of Medicine and the College of Physicians of Philadelphia.

The important thing to remember is that none of these libraries exists in a vacuum. Each one is a part of at least one formal or informal network. In other words, whenever you, as a legitimate user of a library, take a question to a member of that library's staff, you should always come away with an answer or the assurance that steps will be taken to provide you with the answer.

Medicine is no longer a neatly compartmentalized subject. You may have to consult nonmedical as well as medical libraries. Your quest may take you to a university or college library, to a public library (some of these rank among the top research collections in an area), or to a high specialized library devoted to a narrow subfield in biology, chemistry, or some other discipline even less closely related to medicine. If such an additional trip becomes necessary, see if your librarian will call or write ahead so that the staff of the distant library will be expecting you and will have some idea of the nature of your request. Bear in mind that you will be a guest in that library and act accordingly. We can all recall how upset we became when "outsiders" messed around in "our" library.

A final type of medical library is the personal collection. You usually do not become aware of the fact that you have a personal library until you prepare to move either your office or your home or until you begin to realize that the increasing traffic of your colleagues and students is not the result solely of your magnetic personality. There are several methods, or non-methods, for building up a personal library: by membership in organizations, purchase, inheritance, book reviewing, or even "borrowing" from unsuspecting colleagues.[1] Your personal collection can become an effective arm in your daily work and continuing education as well as a broadening agent in your understanding of the growth and development of your profession.

MATERIALS

The journal is the basic unit in the medical literature. A current estimate puts the number of biomedical journals throughout the world at 20,000.[2] Some of these, it is true, are newsletters and other ephemeral items, but many are substantive. Therefore, keep this number in mind the next time a colleague tells you that he has made a comprehensive search of the literature.

Authors use journals as vehicles for their reports of recent clinical and research activities. More and more journals are starting sections for brief reports, clinical notes, and other short papers, as a means of speeding up the printing (and, therefore, the availability) of information. Many journals contain letters that provide useful information, for example, a correction of an error in an article in an earlier issue, an extension of a point touched on by the author of an article, a succinct report of personal experience with a current topic discussed in earlier articles or letters, or a call for medical or scientific action. Editors draw the attention of their readers to important new hypotheses and proposals, to new information that should be widely and immediately known, and to major organizational or political problems. Keep in mind that practically all current journals have table-of-contents pages and that bound volumes usually have cumulated author and subject indexes. These are good places to look first if you are interested in specific topics or authors.

Books come in many forms, from the massive treatise (such as the classic *System of Ophthalmology* in 15 volumes by Stewart Duke-Elder) to the information-packed, specialized monograph, to the pamphlet that may be of great value, for example, for a particular public-health problem (the World Health Organization produces many of these). Books are good places to start in your search for a broad picture of the basic, reasonably current knowledge in a field. Encyclopedias, handbooks, and similar reference tools are the most suitable places for finding specific facts.

Reports from federal, state, and municipal governmental bodies and research institutes can be fruitful sources for highly specialized subjects and are often more up-to-date than formally published books.

If history is one of your interests, you will soon find yourself in the rare-book area of some library. Here you will see an intriguing mixture of the medical classics (for example, Harvey, Vesalius, Bright) and the clinical guides your professional ancestors used 100 or more years ago. A knowledge of medical history can enlarge your own outlook and can often help to drive a point home to a colleague or a student.

More and more medical libraries are establishing archives, often in the same area as the historical books. In the archives, you will find the papers (correspondence, drafts and revisions of articles and books, and a broad variety of diaries, record books, and related materials) of your predecessors in that institution or of individuals who had practiced in that region. Archival materials often provide insight into the life and work of individuals and into treatments used during a particular period or in a particular area.

Audiovisual is the word librarians customarily use for slides, films, photographs, tapes (sound and video), and all of the other "nonprint" materials. The various types of audiovisual items are used primarily for formal or informal education. If you do not see such materials in your library, be sure to ask a reference librarian where they are.

You may assist your librarian in improving the collection by recommending journals, books, and other items for addition. You may also wish to present some items as gifts. Most librarians welcome such help, although each recommendation will (for one or several cogent reasons) not necessarily be obtained, nor will each gift necessarily be retained.

ACCESS

With all of these materials potentially at your fingertips, how do you go about actually getting your hands on the items you need? You will probably find either a card catalog or a computerized catalog in your institutional library. In this country, most of the card catalogs are either of two types: the dictionary or the divided. Practically all of these use the three-by-five-inch card we all know so well and dislike so heartily. The dictionary catalog combines the possibilities of approaching a specific book by its author, major subject, and title. The cards for these three approaches are interfiled alphabetically into a single arrangement. In other words, books by John Blankenship, on the subject of blindness, and with titles like *Blood Cells and Plasma Proteins* will appear near each other in a dictionary catalog. If, however, the title is not helpful in identifying a book, you will probably not find a card for it in the catalog. If, on the other hand, your library's card catalog is divided, you will usually find all the authors and titles in one arrangement and subjects in the other.

Be sure to find out which type of card catalog your library (or the one you are planning to use) has before you start searching through it. Another basic question to which you will need an answer before you seek access to a collection through a card catalog is whether or not the library has two catalogs separated by date. For example, if a library added a large new area around 1960, or took on another school to serve in 1970, or began to use a new classification system in 1972, you may find that the library has two catalogs, with the newer one begun in the year mentioned.

More and more libraries, especially the larger ones, are turning to computerized catalogs. These require that you consult one or more terminals or microform readers for access to the various sections of the catalogs you may need. Computerized catalogs are still in the experimental stage, and the reactions of users and librarians have been mixed.

In addition to the card or computerized catalogs, libraries will often have various lists, records, and guides that may be helpful. Be sure you are aware of these time- and energy-saving items. The lists run from a single sheet stuck on the end of a range of stacks telling you where the major subject classification areas are located to long computer printouts of journal holdings housed in pullout drawers throughout the stacks.

Two examples of records will illustrate the possibilities afforded by this type of access. The shelf-list, card-file surrogate to the books and journals as they are placed on the shelves, may be helpful in verifying information or pinning down the exact location of hard-to-find items. The second example of a useful record illustrates another transitional element in librarianship. This, the serials check-in record, shows exactly what issues of each journal the library has received and often when the item arrived. Additional information concerning the scheduling for binding, temporary locations, and even more esoteric problems may also be found here. Access to this record (especially important to the user eager to consult a specific issue) is usually through a staff member. Some libraries have these records in a visible card file or similar system, while others have a wide variety of computerized programs for this purpose.

Guides to the library can take one of two major forms: either a mimeographed or printed description and listing of the library's layout, schedule, staff members, and services or more or less sophisticated signs. The guides are usually quite informative and practical. You might find it helpful to have one in your office or laboratory. Some libraries have diagrams posted throughout the library showing the arrangement of the collection and staff offices, and at least one library has a set of these diagrams thoughtfully placed in each elevator. Many libraries produce mimeographed or printed acquisition lists, newsletters, or bulletins. Find out if your library provides such a service, and, if so, ask to be placed on the mailing list.

PEOPLE

Libraries contain not only journals, books, and audiovisual items but also a broad variety of people. These fall conveniently into two groups: the professionally trained (including subject specialists) and the nonprofessional or clerical. Generally speaking, the individual you will work with most often will be a reference librarian. These individuals are often, when seated, at a desk near the entrance or in an office near the computer terminal or the card catalog. A reference librarian can help you make efficient use of the collection and can also help you sort out and organize your search programs (for example, by determining whether you should perform the search with printed sources or a computer terminal). The earlier you get to know your reference librarian, the more profitable will be your experience in the library.

The individual who handles the computerized searches available in your library may also be a reference librarian, although this is not necessarily the case. This individual will help you design your approach to the computerized searches and will usually serve as your agent in performing the search. As these searchers are often kept busy, you may find it helpful to call ahead and make an appointment. Keep in mind that the subsidized computer search, like the free lunch, is becoming rarer each day. Computer searches will probably cost you (or your department or grant) some money. Do not begrudge this expense, because with it you are buying information and time, two valuable commodities.

Another useful member of the library staff (either professional or clerical) is the individual who takes care of interlibrary loans. If the journal or book you need is not in your institutional library, the appropriate staff member will probably be able to obtain it for you from another library. The interlibrary loan process was the first major cooperative effort most libraries engaged in, and it is still one of the most productive. You should, however, keep several points in mind to help this system function efficiently and pleasantly. First of all, when you submit a request for an interlibrary loan, be sure to include as much identifying information—and make it as accurate—as possible. This will speed up the process. Two vital elements in this information are the source of your citation and a statement as to whether you will pay any charges involved. The first item is important because your library has to provide this source before the lending library will process your request. Second, as costs increase, more libraries are having to make such cooperative activities at least partly self-supporting. The final item to watch carefully is the date on or before which your interlibrary loan librarian wants you to return the borrowed book or journal. Be sure to honor this date since in the interlibrary loan process both you and your library have received a service, not a right.

The serials librarian is usually the individual you will consult to find out where that issue is that should have been on the shelf. This individual can often give you helpful factual information and useful suggestions for alternative locations.

You will probably seldom see one of the most valuable members of the library staff, the cataloger. This is the individual who deals with the intellectual content of the books in the collection, describes them, and arranges them by subject. Without the cataloger, you could not have the subject and descriptive dimensions in the catalog or the subject classification of the books on the shelves.

SERVICES

Medical libraries offer many services, not all of which will be found in all libraries. Reference and searching services, interlibrary loans, serials, and cataloging have already been briefly described. If you need a literature search and do not have the time to do it yourself, you may be able to find a staff member who will undertake this for pay outside the regular workday. There are also commercial services that regularly undertake searches and other library activities on a fee-for-service basis. You may also find either of these methods helpful if you need an article translated from, or into, a foreign language.

Most libraries now have a photocopier (or several of them), and these machines can be most helpful in copying pages from indexing journals, so that you may search for these citations later, or for copying needed information or pages from a large or noncirculating journal or book. Whenever you photocopy something, be sure to put the full reference on the first page so that you will later be able to identify the source. Pay attention to the copyright regulations that will probably be posted by the photocopying machine.

Many libraries provide carrels, study rooms, or, occasionally, small offices for users who wish to work in more secluded surroundings or who are engaged in writing a review article or a book. If you do not see such facilities, ask if they are available.

SEARCHING THE LITERATURE

The searching of the literature for information for clinical or research purposes is probably the major intellectual exercise you will engage in in a library. This does not have to be a difficult or unpleasant task. If you acquaint yourself with the basic printed guides, computerized services, and searching procedures, you will find that you have acquired two valuable commodities: information and time.

Current Literature

The searcher for information in this vast outpouring of medical literature needs all available assistance. If you are planning a trip, the first thing you need is a road map. If you are planning to search the literature, you will need a similar guide. The basic road map for a search of the medical literature through the services of NLM is a publication called *Medical Subject Headings* (widely known as *MeSH*), which appears each year as Part 2 of the January issue of *Index Medicus*. *MeSH* will serve you efficiently as a road map for subject headings. It will tell you if the highway you plan to take is open or, if not, what alternative routes you can travel. It will give you

WISSLER'S SYNDROME

C5.550.114.843.823   C5.799.825.823
C17.257.823   C20.543.928

65

X   SUBSEPSIS ALLERGICA
X   SUBSEPSIS HYPERERGICA
X   WISSLER–FANCONI SYNDROME

WIT AND HUMOR

K1.517.946

X   HUMOR

WITHDRAWAL SYMPTOMS see DRUG WITHDRAWAL SYMPTOMS

WITTENBORN SCALES see under PSYCHIATRIC STATUS RATING SCALES

WOLFF–PARKINSON–WHITE SYNDROME

C14.280.67.558.865

FIGURE 12.1. Section from Alphabetical List of *MeSH* Showing Valid Subject Heading, Wolff-Parkinson-White Syndrome, and Its Code Number for the Tree Structures (From *Medical Subject Headings* 1980, p. 419).

useful route numbers, and it will even tell you what the inhabitants now call that little widening in the road everyone used to refer to as Four Corners.

As one of the products of the NLM's Medical Literature Analysis and Retrieval System (MEDLARS), *MeSH* contains two major lists. The first alphabetizes all the subject headings and cross-references the indexers use in putting together the issues of *Index Medicus*. You should take to this alphabetical list the most specific term you can apply to your topic. For example, you may be interested in cardiac arrhythmias and, more specifically, in the Wolff-Parkinson-White syndrome. Looking at the appropriate place in the alphabetical list (Figure 12.1), you will find this term given in large capital letters. Your *MeSH* road map has told you that this road is open, that the indexers use this heading.

Two recent changes in the MEDLARS program are also apparent in Figure 12.1. The "65" under Wissler's syndrome tells you that this heading has been used in *Index Medicus* since 1965 and, therefore, that the searcher for information on this subject may safely use this heading back through the 1965 *Cumulated Index Medicus*. At that point, you would look in the new terms list to find the proper heading (rheumatism) for 1964. The cross-reference just above Wolff-Parkinson-White syndrome, "Wittenborn Scales, see under Psychiatric Status Rating Scales," conveys two items of information. It tells you that you will probably find the subject heading Psychiatric Status Rating Scales in *Index Medicus*. However, because of recent changes in producing *MeSH*, you should look up Psychiatric Status Rating Scales in the alphabetical list to make sure that it is a used heading and not another cross-reference. The second item of information is that, although you will not find the heading Wittenborn Scales in *Index Medicus*, you will be able to search this term in the program MEDLARS Online (MEDLINE), the computerized search program.

The next searcher might be investigating blood groups, more specifically the Kidd blood-group system. The alphabetical list has this term also, but it is in small capital letters. The *MeSH* road map has informed this searcher that the planned road is not passable and that he must seek an alternate route. As a useful map should, it gives this alternate route and tells the searcher that he should look under a broader term, *blood groups*.

A third searcher may be seeking information on bacterial endocarditis. When he turns to the B part of the *MeSH* alphabetical list, he does not find bacterial endocarditis. However, a little readjusting of terms will suggest an alternative heading—endocarditis, bacterial—and this turns out to be the key.

A search starts off, therefore, when you first ascertain the most specific term for your subject and then match it to the alphabetical list in *MeSH*. If you find a subject heading matching yours, you are well on the way. If you find a cross-reference, look at the referred-to heading to make sure that it is a valid one. If you find nothing, you than have three choices: inverting your term; taking the term up to the next, more general level; or, finally, seeking help from the reference librarian in your local medical library.

One further step in *MeSH* may be helpful before you move on to the *Index Medicus* itself. To return to the Wolff-Parkinson-White syndrome, you will see (Figure 12.1) a code number, C14.280.67.558.865, that will take you to the second of the two major lists in *MeSH*. This, the tree structures, shows the relations among all the terms used in a broad area. (See Figure 12.2.) For example, Category C14 is entitled "Diseases—Cardiovascular." By scanning the four pages under C14 you will see all the subject headings the indexers have used in this area, and you may find one or more (that you had not thought of before) that will be helpful additions in your

C14 – DISEASES–CARDIOVASCULAR

CARDIOVASCULAR DISEASES

CARDIOVASCULAR DISEASES	C14
HEART DISEASES	C14.280
ARRHYTHMIA	C14.280.67
ARRHYTHMIA, SINUS	C14.280.67.93
ASYSTOLE ·	C14.280.67.146
AURICULAR FIBRILLATION	C14.280.67.198
AURICULAR FLUTTER	C14.280.67.248
BRADYCARDIA	C14.280.67.319
EXTRASYSTOLE	C14.280.67.470
HEART BLOCK	C14.280.67.558
ADAMS–STOKES SYNDROME	C14.280.67.558.137
BUNDLE–BRANCH BLOCK	C14.280.67.558.323
SINOATRIAL BLOCK ·	C14.280.67.558.750
WOLFF–PARKINSON–WHITE SYNDROME	C14.280.67.558.865
SICK SINUS SYNDROME	C14.280.67.829
TACHYCARDIA	C14.280.67.845
TACHYCARDIA, PAROXYSMAL	C14.280.67.845.695
VENTRICULAR FIBRILLATION	C14.280.67.932
CARCINOID HEART DISEASE ·	C14.280.129

FIGURE 12.2. Section from Tree Structures of *MeSH* Showing How Subject Heading Wolff-Parkinson-White Syndrome Fits into Listing for Cardiovascular Diseases (From *Medical Subject Headings* 1980, p. 524.)

present search. The asterisks in Figure 12.2 after the terms *asystole*, *sinoatrial block*, and *carcinoid heart disease* indicate that these headings can not be searched in *Index Medicus* but can be searched in MEDLINE.

Medical terminology is continually changing by addition, division, and subtraction. Just as the old familiar Four Corners may have become Jones City since you last drove through it, the subject term you have used successfully in the past may have been changed to match more closely current information and hypotheses. For example, if you had in the past searched through the list under amino acids while seeking references on amino acids, branched-chain, you will now find your more specific interest matched by the indexer's new term. Two lists near the beginning of each annual *MeSH* enable you to move back and forth between the new and old terms that have recently been changed. A third list, designed for the prospective searcher, shows him which heading to change to if his earlier term is no longer being used.

Index Medicus

Armed with the right subject headings from your *MeSH* road map, you can now go efficiently to the current issue of the *Index Medicus*. Subject searches are generally best made in reverse chronologic order, enabling you to find the current material first. If you are lucky, you will find a good, recent review that may save you considerable time and effort.

The *Index Medicus* has two major sections and several smaller, but also valuable, parts. The subject section lists references under general headings and more specific subheadings. By carefully using these subheadings, you will be able to save much effort. The second major section, name, lists authors and the personal subjects of biographic articles and obituaries. The valuable small parts at the front include the subject index to reviews. Each reference gives the number of citations listed by the review's author as well as full bibliographic information for the review. The front matter of each issue also contains lists of the regional medical libraries, foreign MEDLARS/ MEDLINE centers, and some recent literature searches made at NLM. This last list can be especially useful if a search has recently been made in one of your areas of interest. All you have to do then is write to the address given, ask for a copy of that list by number, and it will be sent to you free.

Your reverse-chronologic search of *Index Medicus* will eventually bring you back through the January issue of the current year. The next step is to the bound *Cumulated Index Medicus*. Each annual set (the one for 1979 contains 14 volumes or "books") combines the information from the 12 monthly issues, so that each subject heading or author entry will list a complete index-year of references in that one place.

Under each subject heading, whether in the individual monthly issues or in the cumulated annual set, you will find general articles listed first, for example, under escherichia coli infections. (See Figure 12.3.) More specialized articles are often listed under subheadings, for example, under cerebrospinal fluid, complications, and drug therapy. The articles in English are given first and are listed alphabetically by the title of the journal. An article on escherichia coli infections—drug therapy in *Infection* will appear ahead of one in *Kidney International*. Articles in foreign languages follow those in English and have their references contained within square brackets. These references are listed alphabetically by language. An article in Polish precedes one in Spanish on the same subject. Within each language group, the references are again alphabetized by title of the journal.

Knowing these arrangements can save you much time, effort, and frustration if you want to limit your search to specific journals that are immediately accessible to you or to those languages you can read with productive, even if not graceful, results. If an article in a foreign language contains an English abstract or summary, this fact is noted in the *Index*

ESCHERICHIA COLI INFECTIONS

Suppurative pyephlebitis and multiple hepatic abscesses with silent colonic diverticulitis. Waxman BP, et al.
Med J Aust 1979 Oct 6;2(7):376-8

CEREBROSPINAL FLUID

Alterations in cerebrospinal fluid outflow resistance in experimental bacterial meningitis. Dacey RG, et al.
Trans Am Neurol Assoc 1978;103:142-6

COMPLICATIONS

[Unsuccessful heparin treatment of intravascular dissemination coagulation in infants with E. coli septicemia] Wytrychowski M, et al. **Pol Tyg Lek** 1979 Nov 5; 34(45):1755-7 (Eng. Abstr.) **(Pol)**
[Pleural empyema caused by E coli, in a child. An immunodeficient subject?] Pinto LF, et al.
Rev Chil Pediatr 1978 Jan-Dec;49(1-6):190-5 (Eng. Abstr.) **(Spa)**

DRUG THERAPY

Comparative in vivo activity of bacampicillin and amoxycillin. Ekström B, et al. **Infection** 1979;7 Suppl 5:S438-42
Efficacy of bacampicillin and ampicillin in experimental pyelonephritis in the rat. Ritzerfeld W. **Infection** 1979;7 Suppl 5:S443-5
Pharmacokinetics of gentamicin in the treatment of renal infection: a therapeutic anomaly explained. Miller T, et al.
Kidney Int 1979 Feb;15(2):160-6
[Urinary tract infections. Therapeutic failures and course monitoring (author's transl)] Abdou MA. **MMW** 1979 Oct 19;121(42):1371-4 (Eng. Abstr.) **(Ger)**

FIGURE 12.3. Section from Subject Index of *Index Medicus* Showing Heading Escherichia Coli Infections and Subheadings (From *Index Medicus* 1980 Apr; 21[4]:304.)

Medicus reference. This means that you might profit from an examination of that article even though you do not read the original language. If the English version of the article's title was translated by the author, this is also noted. (See Figure 12.3.)

The first book of the *Cumulated Index Medicus* contains the *MeSH* for that year. The 12 monthly sections of medical reviews are cumulated in the second book. The 2,700 journals indexed in *Index Medicus* are listed in the second book by abbreviation and full title. The list by abbreviation is helpful if you are trying to expand a confusing reference. The list by full title gives you access to the proper abbreviations to use for the references you will be citing in your own paper. A separately issued publication, *List of Journals Indexed in Index Medicus*, lists these journals also by subject and country of publication.

In addition to the journals, the *Index Medicus* has for several years indexed a few multiauthored monographs (most of which are proceedings of meetings). These are listed in the front of each issue and cumulated set. The references for these are given under the various headings and subheadings as though they were in journals whose titles begin with the letter *i*, because each monographic title is preceded by the word *in*.

Abridged Index Medicus

If you want to obtain references from only those journals that are in English and are available in most areas—if not in most libraries—you should use the *Abridged Index Medicus*, which covers about 120 journals (primarily clinical) from the United States, Canada, the United Kingdom, and several other countries. This helpful monthly index also has an annual cumulation.

MEDLARS

NLM has pioneered in computerized control of the medical literature. Modern machine methods were first applied to the production of the *Index Medicus* in the mid-1960s. Production with the aid of computers led to the capability of searching the literature with computers. The original MEDLARS program has gone through several changes, and the current system is accessible through terminals in more than 800 institutions. Call your local or regional medical library to find out if such a terminal is available and to which data bases your terminal provides access. You will be able to search these data bases either directly or with the aid of a member of your library staff who has been trained by NLM. Charges for searches vary in different institutions.

The major advantages or disadvantages of a computerized search in relation to the manual search vary from topic to topic. The advantages generally include access to more recent materials; use of more subject headings; availability of age, sex, geographic, and other subheadings that are not found in the printed index; and increased speed, especially for topics that combine subject headings in a way that the manual search could not easily duplicate.

Before you can have a computerized search run through the NLM programs, you will have to engage in some planning with the operator of the terminal. The two of you will work out the appropriate subject headings (just as you did with *MeSH* for your manual search) and the pertinent combinations of these terms by using *and*, *or*, and *not*, the vital three little words of contemporary information processing.

Many data bases are accessible through the NLM. (See Table 12.1.) These include MEDLINE (a computerized approach to some of the journals in *Index Medicus*), TOXLINE (which makes available references to human and animal toxicity studies and related material), CANCERLIT, and several other disease-oriented data bases, and MEDLEARN (a computer-assisted instruction program that demonstrates how to use MEDLINE).

Computerized programs are valuable for making you quickly aware of the contents of the relatively current medical literature, but there are also nonmachine techniques and printed guides you can use to keep yourself up-to-date.

After completing a current search, look over your references and note the journals that provide most of them. You have thus identified several journals that regularly publish articles of interest to you. Next, go to the current journal shelves of your local library and look through the issues of those journals that have been printed since the last issue of each journal appeared in the *Index Medicus*.

Current Contents

Current Contents, one of several valuable publications from the Institute for Scientific Information, will also help you keep current. This weekly journal, which appears in seven editions (including *Life Sciences*, *Clinical Practice*, and *Social & Behavioral Sciences*), reproduces the tables of contents of hundreds of journals. Each issue has a subject index and an author index, which not only refers you to an article by that author but also gives the author's address, so that you can immediately request a reprint. By skimming over the tables of contents of the pertinent journals in one or two

TABLE 12.1. Selected Searchable Data Bases at the National Library of Medicine

Data Base	Total Records	Dates Covered
1. AVLINE[a]	8,641	Through 1980
2. BIOETHICS[a]	9,597	Jan 73–Oct 79
3. CANCERLIT[a]	202,653	Jan 63–Mar 80
4. CANCERPROJ[a]	16,984	1976–80
5. CATLINE[a]	197,600	1965–80
6. CHEMLINE	439,817	n.a.[b]
7. CLINPROT[a]	1,669	n.a.
8. EPILEPSY[a]	25,635	1945–Present
9. HEALTH[a]	142,700	Jan 75–May 80
10. HISTLINE[a]	40,160	n.a.
11. MEDLINE	468,899	Jan 78–May 80
12. MED77[c]	253,234	Jan 77–Dec 77
13. MED75[c]	642,953	Jan 75–Dec 76
14. MED72[c]	669,106	Jan 72–Dec 74
15. MED69[c]	668,258	Jan 69–Dec 71
16. MED66[c]	501,802	Jan 66–Dec 68
17. RTECS	36,851	1978
18. SDILINE	18,140	May 80
19. SERLINE[a]	34,359	1979
20. TOXLINE	692,394	n.a.
CBAC	360,958	1974, Vol. 31 4,5
TOXBIB	135,268	1974–Apr 80
IPA	37,717	1974. Vol. 16 23
HEEP	80,243	1974–Feb 80
PESTAB	18,243	1974–Jan 80
EMIC	27,701	1960–Dec 79
ETIC	16,497	1950–Aug 79
RPROJ	14,417	Jan 79–May 80
21. TOXBACK	379,299	n.a.
CBAC	167,668	1965–73
TOXBIB	127,104	1968–73
IPA	19,188	1970–73
HEEP	24,680	1971–73
HAPAB	12,816	1966–73
HAYES	10,043	1940–66
TMIC	4,552	1971–75
TERA	13,248	1960–74

[a]Files available only through the National Library of Medicine.

[b]Not applicable.

[c]MEDLINE backfiles (MED77-66) and TOXBACK are available only through offsearch

editions of *Current Contents* each week, you will be able to keep an eye on what many journals are printing. The Institute for Scientific Information offers a variety of manual and computerized services that also might be helpful to you. Its address is given, along with those of other services, in Table 12.2.

Meetings

Many papers are first given at meetings, and frequently these do not appear in a proceedings volume or in the regular journal literature for months or even years. Nevertheless, you can often locate references and information concerning these papers by consulting guides to meetings, such as *Directory of Published Proceedings* (*InterDok*) and the Institute for Scientific Information's *Index to Scientific & Technical Proceedings*. Another guide for meetings, *Conference Papers Index*, published monthly with detailed quarterly indexes, carries you one step farther by indexing many papers from the final programs of meetings or from volumes of abstracts issued before the meetings are held.

Many other useful indexes exist, and a consultation with your local medical reference librarian will probably result in the suggestion of some additional pertinent items. These may range from the *Hospital Literature Index* to annual listings of research projects and investigators, such as the *General Embryological Information Service*. Your librarian may decide that a computerized service is the most suitable for your needs. An example is the Smithsonian Institution's Scientific Information Exchange, which contains information about researchers and their work in the medical and biological sciences. (See Table 12.2.)

---

at the National Library of Medicine and the State University of New York.

Note: No. 5 contains cataloging information for books recently cataloged and some location information for libraries other than NLM. No. 6 is an on-line chemical dictionary. No. 7 is part of the cancer data base. No. 9 is basically the data base for the *Hospital Literature Index.* No. 10 is for the history of medicine. Nos. 12–16 are earlier files of MEDLINE material. No. 17 is the Registry of Toxic Effects of Chemical Substances. No. 19 is roughly the serials equivalent of No. 5. Nos. 20 and 21 are collections of data bases dealing with toxic effects. CBAC = Chemical-Biological Activities. IPA = International Pharmaceutical Abstracts. HEEP = Abstracts on Health Effects of Environmental Pollutants. PESTAB = Pesticides Abstracts. EMIC = Environmental Mutagen Information Center File. ETIC = Teratology Information Center File. RPROJ = Toxicology/Epidemiology Research Projects. HAYES = Bibliographic collection on pesticides formed by W. J. Hayes, Jr. TMIC = Toxic Materials Information Center File. TERA = Teratology File.

Source: Adapted from *NLM Technical Bulletin*, 1980 April, 132:2.

TABLE 12.2. Computerized Services for Literature Search

BioSciences Information Service (BIOSIS), 2100 Arch Street, Philadelphia, PA 19103 (215-568-4016)

BIOSIS will perform individually designed searches of its files back through 1959. An estimate of the cost will be made after the requester has filled out and sent in the appropriate form. The printout can include citations or abstracts. Current-awareness searches on one of 28 topics can be done on the current file once or three times a month.

Chemical Abstracts Service (CAS), P. O. Box 3012, Columbus, OH 43210 (614-421-6940)

CAS does not perform searches directly. Write or call for a list of the organizations that have been licensed to use its computer-readable files.

Excerpta Medica, 3131 Princeton Pike, Lawrenceville, NJ 08648 (609-896-9450)

The Excerpta Medica data base (EMBASE) is available on-line through the Lockheed DIALOG system, which is accessible with any standard terminal. Searches on this data base, which runs from April 1975, through the present, can produce citations or abstracts.

Institute for Scientific Information, 3501 Market Street, University City Science Center, Philadelphia, PA 19104 (800-523-1850)

The search service performs retrospective searches and the Automatic Subject Citation Alert (ASCA) provides weekly reports. SCISEARCH, which covers the data from several years of the *Science Citation Index* and *Current Contents*, is available on-line through the Lockheed DIALOG system.

Psychological Abstracts Information Service, American Psychological Association, 1200 Seventeenth Street, N.W., Washington, DC 20036 (202-833-7600)

The data base includes material published in *Psychological Abstracts* from 1967 through the present. Retrospective searches will produce lists of citations.

Smithsonian Science Information Exchange (SSIE), Inc., Room 300, 1730 M Street, N.W., Washington, DC 20036 (202-381-4211)

SSIE will search its active file for notices of research projects. The exchange also performs selective dissemination of information searches either monthly or quarterly. Historical searches cover the five years prior to the active file. The SSIE data base is also available on-line to users who have access to a computer terminal.

Toxicology Information Response Center (TIRC), Information Center Complex, P. O. Box X, Oak Ridge, TN 37830 (615-576-1743)

TIRC performs retrospective searches on a wide variety of data bases. Continuing searches for current material can also be arranged.

Source: Compiled by the author.

Excerpta Medica

Abstracting journals give more information than indexing journals, although they generally pay for this increased material by needing a longer time for the editorial and printing facets of publication. A good abstracting journal will offer you three basic approaches to the literature. You can use it for keeping up, searching, and for overcoming the barriers of language.

Excerpta Medica is divided into 43 subject sections (Table 12.3), each of which appears ten to 12 times a year. There is a section for each basic and clinical science, and other sections deal with specific diseases, a group of diseases, or with general areas. For example, if you want to keep up with much of the important work on supraventricular and nodal arrhythmia being

TABLE 12.3. Subject Sections in *Excerpta Medica*

Anatomy, Anthropology, Embryology, and Histology	Human Genetics
Anesthesiology	Immunology, Serology, and Transplantation
Arthritis and Rheumatism	Internal Medicine
Biophysics, Bioengineering, and Medical Instrumentation	Leprosy and Related Subjects
Cancer	Microbiology: Bacteriology, Mycology, and Parasitology
Cardiovascular Diseases and Cardiovascular Surgery	Neurology and Neurosurgery
Chest Diseases, Thoracic Surgery, and Tuberculosis	Nuclear Medicine
Clinical Biochemistry	Obstetrics and Gynecology
Dermatology and Venereology	Occupational Health and Industrial Medicine
Developmental Biology and Teratology	Ophthalmology
Drug Dependence	Orthopedic Surgery
Endocrinology	Oto-, Rhino-, Laryngology
Environmental Health and Pollution Control	Pediatrics and Pediatric Surgery
Epilepsy	Pharmacology and Toxicology
Forensic Science	Physiology
Gastroenterology	Plastic Surgery
General Pathology and Pathological Anatomy	Psychiatry
Gerontology and Geriatrics	Public Health, Social Medicine, and Hygiene
Health Economics and Hospital Management	Radiology
Hematology	Rehabilitation and Physical Medicine
	Surgery
	Urology and Nephrology
	Virology

Source: Compiled by the author.

reported in medical journals throughout the world, select the appropriate subject section, cardiovascular diseases and cardiovascular surgery, and examine the table of contents on the inside of the front cover. You will find that the subheading supraventricular and nodal arrhythmia has the code number 11.2 and that abstracts of articles on that subject appear on the pages listed next to that code number. This means that if you take a few minutes to look at each issue of that subject section as it appears, and read the abstracts in Part 11.2, you will find pertinent material selected from thousands of journals.

You can search individual issues of *Excerpta Medica*, or the annual bound volumes, by using the subject and author indexes in each. The language problem becomes less of a hurdle, because all of the abstracts are in English even though many of the original articles are in foreign languages.

Excerpta Medica also produces four express monthly publications that make abstracts available a month or so after the original articles have appeared. These valuable journals, entitled *Core Journals in...*, cover the major journals in the fields of clinical neurology, obstetrics/gynecology, ophthalmology, and pediatrics.

The Excerpta Medica Company has a broad computerized program that can be used in several ways. Write to them at the address listed in Table 12.2 for additional information and charges.

Abstracting and Indexing Services

Medicine is no longer the neatly circumscribed field it was when a Benjamin Rush or a Daniel Drake was a medical student or an apprentice taking care of his master's office and horses and preparing some of the medicines. The current searcher for medical information must be acquainted with such printed publications as *Chemical Abstracts*, *Biological Abstracts*, *BioResearch Index* (now: *Biological Abstracts/RRM*—reports, reviews, meetings), and *Psychological Abstracts* and with their manifold computerized services.

Chemical Abstracts includes a vast amount of material, a portion of which is related to clinical medicine. It began publication in 1907 and now appears weekly with two alternating issues. The first deals with biochemistry and organic chemistry, whereas the second covers macromolecular and applied chemistry, chemical engineering, and physical and analytical chemistry. *Chemical Abstracts* covers thousands of journals and many books, reports, and patents. It will substantially increase your coverage of the medical and related literature. Each issue has keyword, numerical patent, and author indexes and a patent concordance that relates new patents to those already abstracted. A series of cumulated indexes saves the searcher great amounts of time. The first five cover ten years each, and the next four (beginning with the sixth, 1957–61) cover five years each.

Biological Abstracts also covers material of clinical medical interest. It includes thousands of journals, book reviews, letters, and notes. Begun in 1926, *Biological Abstracts* is now produced on a semimonthly basis. Each issue has author and subject indexes, biosystematic index (by phylum, class, order, and family), a generic index (by genus and species), and a concept index (for relating broad subject areas). Although *Biological Abstracts* has no large cumulated indexes, each volume has its own indexes.

Biological Abstracts/RRM (the former *BioResearch Index*), a complementary publication to *Biological Abstracts*, includes a substantial amount of material pertinent to clinical medicine. Now a monthly publication, *Biological Abstracts/RRM* has appeared since 1967. It covers many journals, annual reports, bibliographies, books and chapters, and several other types of publications. Each issue and volume have the same indexes as those found in *Biological Abstracts*.

Psychological Abstracts covers much material of clinical medical interest. Begun in 1927, it is now a monthly publication that includes many journals, technical reports, monographs, and other types of literature. It has two major cumulated indexes, each one having a series of supplements. The author index covers the *Psychological Index* (1894–1935) and *Psychological Abstracts* (1927–58). There are supplements for 1959–63, 1964–68, 1969–71, and 1972–74. The subject index covers 1927–60, with supplements for 1961–65, 1966–68, 1969–71, and 1972–74.

When you first examine any indexing or abstracting journal that is new to you, be sure to read introductions or prefaces carefully, examine the types of indexes these journals have (subject, author, biosystematic, and so forth), and look around the neighboring shelves for any cumulated indexes that conveniently combine five, ten, or some other number of years of material.

Books and Audiovisuals

Books and audiovisual materials can also be useful. Two basic publications provide helpful information: the *National Library of Medicine Current Catalog* and Bowker's *Medical Books and Serials in Print*. The *Current Catalog*, issued quarterly with an annual cumulation, indexes recently published books by subject and author and, until 1978, also included much helpful information on films, cassettes, and other audiovisual items. Beginning in 1978, a separate publication, *National Library of Medicine Audiovisuals Catalog*, has dealt solely with audiovisual materials. The Bowker publication, an annual listing of books in English by subject, author, and title, increased its coverage of the medical literature in 1978 by listing serials as well. This guide gives full bibliographic information and cost for books and serials and, for the latter, sometimes gives circulation figures and the titles of indexing and abstracting journals covering that serial.

Older Literature

If you need to go back into the literature before 1960 (when the current series of the *Index Medicus* began), you will consult the *Current List of Medical Literature* (for 1952–59), *Quarterly Cumulative Index Medicus* (1927–56), *Quarterly Cumulative Index to Current Medical Literature* (1916–26), and the first three series of *Index Medicus* (1879–99, 1903–20, 1921–27). You should also look at the 61-volume set entitled *Index-Catalogue of the Library of the Surgeon-General's Office*. This army publication came from the predecessor of the current NLM. The *Index-Catalogue*, in its five series, provides the searcher with access by author and subject to books and by subject to journal articles for millions of pieces of the medical literature. This is a gold mine with which any serious searcher of the medical literature should become thoroughly familiar.

If you are interested in the historical development of a medical subject, you will find valuable *A Medical Bibliography (Garrison and Morton)*, edited by Leslie T. Morton. The third edition (1970) is available from J. B. Lippincott Company. This reference work lists chronologically under each subject the books and articles that are important in the growth of that subject. Many of the entries are annotated. *Garrison and Morton* is the volume for a searcher who wants to know the important persons in a field, in what publications major events are reported, and how to locate these vital contributions bibliographically.

Perhaps you have a partially remembered quotation in mind or want to find a quotation that will sum up or underline your point or thesis. In these frustrating cases, you should consult *Familiar Medical Quotations*, edited by Maurice B. Strauss and published by Little, Brown, and Company in 1968. For example, if you want to identify and quote correctly, "Attempt the end, and never stand to doubt;/Nothing's so hard, but search will find it out," you will find in *Familiar Medical Quotations*[3] that Robert Herrick, the seventeenth-century English poet, wrote this two-line poem, which is in his collection *Hesperides*.

Science Citation Index

Throughout this section, we have been either searching back into the older literature or attempting to keep up with the current literature. A major publication, *Science Citation Index*, produced by the Institute for Scientific Information, offers you the opportunity of seeing how ideas, methods, and hypotheses have fared after they have been described in the literature. The *Science Citation Index*, which goes back to 1961, shows who is citing whom. (See Figure 12.4.) It lists by author all the references cited in some 3,300 journals and more than 1,000 new books annually (there is a separate subject index). This arrangement means, for example, that if you have found a particular article of help in your work, all you have to do to see how later authors have added to the material in that article, modified it, or even contradicted it is to look up the author's name in the current bimonthly or annual issue of *Science Citation Index* and examine the listed articles that have recently cited the original article of interest to you. Two, five-year cumulations, 1965–69 and 1970–74, will help you save time. The *Science Citation Index* opens many useful paths for investigating the literature.

In 1969, the institute started the *Social Sciences Citation Index* and, in 1977, the *Arts and Humanities Citation Index*. Either or both of these may also be helpful in your searching.

Translation

If you need information from an article in a foreign language, you may be able to obtain it from an English abstract located in one of the printed or computerized services. However, if this does not provide you with the necessary information, you will have to take another step. Obtain the help of a competent individual and go over the paper together orally. This will cost money, but it may either give you the required information or pinpoint sections to be translated in writing. This process is justifiably expensive, since, if the article in question is, for example, from a Japanese ophthalmological journal, your translator must be competent in Japanese, English, and ophthalmology.

PERSONAL FILES

None of the materials or data you have obtained in your searches will be of the slightest use to you unless you can locate the item you need when you need it. A personal file system is a necessity for the effective and efficient handling of information. In evaluating your present system, or developing a new one, two questions are of the utmost importance. First, will this system handle your needs five years from now? Second, do the processing and materials used in this system match—or at least not run counter to—your personality and the available clerical help?

Personal files can range from a simple pack of cards listing citations to articles and books to a file drawer of folders arranged by subject to more exotic varieties involving optical coincidence cards or computerized systems.

WARREN KS ....
60 J LAB CLINICAL MED 56 687
  LOCKWOOD AH   BRAIN RES   181   259 80
61 AM J TROP MED HYG 10 870
  JONES LG   Z PARASITEN   60   185 79
62 NATURE 195 47
  BERGMANN SR   CIRCULATION   61   34 80
  BREIMAN A   J GEN MICRO   116   201 80
64 J LAB CLINICAL MED 64 442
  WOODBURY DM BK# 11263   R   27   249 80
65 ANNALS INTERNAL MED 62 1113
  DATTA DV   I J MED RES   70   825 79
67 AM J PATHOLOGY 51 735
  AMSDEN AF   INFEC IMMUN   27   75 80
  HELMYKHA.S   TROPENMED P   30   426 79
  KAURBEDI AJ   INT J PARAS   9   401 79
  KAYES SG   EXP PARASIT   49   47 80
  KURITA N   MYCOPATHOLO   68   9 79

FIGURE 12.4. Section from Citation Index Portion of *Science Citation Index* Showing References to Six Papers by K. S. Warren. The sixth entry shows that Warren's paper published in the *American Journal of Pathology*, 1967, vol. 51, pp.735– , was recently cited by A. F. Amsden in an article in *Infection and Immunity*, vol. 27, pp. 75– , 1980, and by four other authors. (From *Science Citation Index.*, Jan/Feb 1980, col. 10534.)

The choice and use of such a file is a highly personal matter. Whatever the file system you design or adapt, you will need criteria for addition and weeding and a definite program for maintaining its currency. You must avoid either becoming bogged down with processing or succumbing to the seductive idea that now that you have a personal file system you will never have to go out again to search the literature.

The following reading list cites specific articles describing various personal file systems and general articles reviewing major types of systems and the reasons for selecting specific types.

Basic Indexes

Dralle, Dorothy. How to Hang on to It! *Resident Physician* 1969 June; 15(6):119–20, 122.

Silk, Arthur D. Where Did I See It? How Can I Find It? *Physician's Management* 1973 Feb; 13(2):37D.

Based on own subject headings:

Reece, Richard L. Fast Way to File and Find Journal Articles. *Hospital Physician* 1967 Sept; 3(9):59–61.

Reishus, Allan D. Try This Filing System for Retrieving Medical Pearls. *Medical Economics* 1979 July 9; 56(13):137–8.

Based on textbook table of contents and index:

Gaeke, Richard F., and Gaeke, Mary Ellen B. Filing Medical Literature: A Textbook-Integrated System. *Annals of Internal Medicine* 1973 June; 78(6):985–7.

Fuller, Ellis A. A System for Filing Medical Literature, Based on a Method Developed by Dr. Maxwell M. Wintrobe. *Annals of Internal Medicine* 1968 Mar; 68(3):684–93.

Singer, Karl. Where Did I See That Article? *JAMA* 1979 Apr 6; 241(14): 1492–3.

Based on printed classification:

Parker, Virginia. Organizing a Reprint File. *Bulletin of the Medical Library Association* 1972 Jan; 60(1):149–51.

Fawcett, Patrick J. Personal Filing Systems Revisited. *Ear, Nose and Throat Journal* 1978 Sept; 57(9):410–3.

Levenson, Steve. A Simple Scheme for Filing Articles. *New Physician* 1975 May; 24(5):34–5.

Inverted File

Hellmers, Henry. A Simple and Efficient File System for Reprints. *BioScience* 1964 Feb; 14(2):25.

de Alarcon, Richard. A Personal Medical Reference Index. *Lancet* 1969 Feb 8; 1(7589):301–5.

Holmes, Thomas F., and Gentry, Castelle G. A Foolproof Personal Filing System. *Audiovisual Instruction* 1979 May; 24(5):40–2.

Specialized Cards

Sheplan, L. An Inexpensive Simple Method of Data Retrieval. *Southern Medical Journal* 1969 Apr; 62(4):418–20.

de Alarcon, Richard. A Personal Medical Reference Index. *Lancet* 1969 Feb 8; 1(7589):301–5.

Computerized

Calvin, William H. A Computer-Assisted Personal Literature Reference System. *Computer Programs in Biomedicine* 1972 Nov; 2(4):291–6.

Garfield, Eugene. Introducing PRIMATE: Personal Retrieval of Information by Microcomputer And Terminal Ensemble. *Current Contents* 1978 July 17; (19):5–9.

Reviews

McClelland, R. M. A. Information Retrieval. In Recent Advances in Surgery, 7th ed., edited by Selwyn Taylor, pp. 622–52. Boston, Little, Brown, 1969.

Bartlett, Lloyd C. Filed AND Found: A Personal Information Storage and Retrieval System. *JAMA* 1967 Mar 27; 199(13):adv. 244–5, 250, 264.

Shultz, Suzanne M. Filing System Lends Order to Chaotic Office. *Pennsylvania Medicine* 1979 Jan; 82(1):27, 30.

Fawcett, Patrick J. Personal Filing Systems Revisited. *Ear, Nose, and Throat Journal* 1978 Sept; 57(9):410–3. The article by Fawcett is an excellent place to start your reading.

CONCLUSION

Coping with the biomedical literatures requires basic information about the use of libraries and their contents. The more you know about the various types of medical and nonmedical libraries, and the varieties of access to their contents, the more efficiently you will be able to draw upon them for aid. The different types of materials in these libraries can help you answer different types of questions. Each member of the library staff will be able to guide you in a particular facet of your work with the literature. The searching of the literature is not necessarily a complicated activity once you know the basic printed and computerized tools and some search methods. A pertinent and comfortable system for your personal file of information will enable you to control large amounts of material and retrieve a specific item when you need it. When you have put all of these elements together, you will find that the thought of coping with the literature conjures up, not frustrating desperation, but satisfying productivity.

REFERENCES

1. Marshall, Mary Louise. The Physician's Own Library—Its Development, Care, and Use. Springfield, Ill., Thomas, 1957.
2. National Library of Medicine. Introduction. In Index of NLM Serial Titles. Bethesda, Md., National Library of Medicine, 1972. (DHEW Publication No. [NIH] 73-314).
3. Strauss, Maurice B., ed. Familiar Medical Quotations. Boston, Little, Brown, 1968, p. 498a.

INDEX